"Dr. Hugh Marr has given us a masterpiece of power of story across the spectrum of psychotherapy, major expansion of narrative theory. From the role of story in the theories of Sigmund Freud, Carl Jung, Michael White, and other innovators to the more recent 21st century developers of new ideas in psychotherapy, this book has it all. Dr. Marr provides us with a fine-grained analysis of the elements of a complete story, such as the witness, roles, themes, and plots, and gives each of these a chapter of its own, including an explanation of how changes in each element change the patient's life. There is much more. The book concludes with guides for therapists to increase the efficacy of their own work through the explicit recognition of the power of story in psychotherapeutic healing. Outstanding!"

—**Jay Noricks**, PhD, psychotherapist and author of *Healing Amelia* and *Parts Psychology*

"Dr. Marr's book is remarkable. He shows us that although we cannot literally change the failures and afflictions of the past, we can change the way we think about them. In fact, we can see how they have helped create the person we have become and can help us attain what C. G. Jung called *amor fate*—namely, to love who we have become."

—**Julie Bondanza**, PhD, Jungian analyst and former Training Director of Analytic Training for the New York C. G. Jung Institute

"*A Clinician's Guide to Foundational Story Psychotherapy* is a breakthrough guide, combining a comprehensive understanding of narrative and its importance in human life with strategies for utilizing this knowledge in finding the client's overarching and subtheme stories, and, when necessary, reframing them to support a richer and more fulfilling life. Dr. Marr's book is certain to become one of the classics in psychotherapy."

—**Carol Pearson**, PhD, author of *Persephone Rising: Awakening the Hero Within*; coauthor with Dr. Marr of the PMAI assessment and *What Story Are You Living?*; past Provost and President of Pacifica Graduate Institute

"The field of psychotherapy needs a comprehensive book like this that includes both theory and practical applications. I have yet to find a book that offers such a clear and foundational overview in its approach to narrative psychotherapy and includes so many creative tools and techniques. I think clinicians will use the book to become acquainted with the narrative approach to psychotherapy, enhance their existing understanding, and learn new techniques for applying narrative in clinical practice. I look forward to further enhancing my existing clinical skills and story-based writing exercises."

—**Kim Schneiderman**, LCSW, psychotherapist and author of *Step Out of Your Story: Writing Exercises to Reframe and Transform Your Life*

"Master clinician and trauma teacher Dr. Hugh Marr has created a gem that will be a treasure to all healers. It is about life stories that may limit or empower us. Like authoring a coherent book, we each need to make explicit, clarify, edit, and complete the story of our lives to find meaning, order, perspective, healing, and happiness. Marr explains how to do this with wisdom, warmth, wit, and many clear, practical explanations. This is a brilliant and fascinating read, one that I'll keep and reread."
—**Glenn R. Schiraldi**, PhD, Lt. Colonel (Ret.), University of Maryland School of Public Health (Ret.); author of *The Post Traumatic Stress Disorder Sourcebook*, *The Resilience Workbook*, and *The Self-Esteem Workbook*

A Clinician's Guide to Foundational Story Psychotherapy

A Clinician's Guide to Foundational Story Psychotherapy draws together a range of theories and models to examine the use of narrative psychotherapy in clinical practice.

Illustrated with case examples and biographical vignettes, the book outlines the importance of foundational and life stories in treatment and delineates new techniques for co-assessing and changing stories. A wealth of concrete tools is included, such as the Foundational Story Interview and Family of Origin Map, as well as diagram templates and questionnaires for use during clinical sessions.

Integrating theory and practical applications, *A Clinician's Guide to Foundational Story Psychotherapy* introduces a range of therapeutic options rooted in a narrative context and is a valuable resource for practicing and student psychotherapists.

Hugh K. Marr, PhD, is a clinical psychologist in private practice in Alexandria, Virginia. He has worked in all phases of community mental health, culminating in running a partial hospital program for clients with the co-occurring disorders of substance use and major mental illness. He is the coauthor of the books *What Story Are You Living?* and *Introduction to Archetypes*.

A Clinician's Guide to Foundational Story Psychotherapy

Co-Changing Narratives, Co-Changing Lives

Hugh K. Marr

NEW YORK AND LONDON

First published 2020
by Routledge
52 Vanderbilt Avenue, New York, NY 10017

and by Routledge
2 Park Square, Milton Park, Abingdon, Oxon, OX14 4RN

Routledge is an imprint of the Taylor & Francis Group, an informa business

© 2020 Hugh K. Marr

The right of Hugh K. Marr to be identified as author of this work has been asserted by him in accordance with sections 77 and 78 of the Copyright, Designs and Patents Act 1988.

All rights reserved. No part of this book may be reprinted or reproduced or utilised in any form or by any electronic, mechanical, or other means, now known or hereafter invented, including photocopying and recording, or in any information storage or retrieval system, without permission in writing from the publishers.

Trademark notice: Product or corporate names may be trademarks or registered trademarks and are used only for identification and explanation without intent to infringe.

Library of Congress Cataloging-in-Publication Data
Names: Marr, Hugh K., 1949– author.
Title: A clinician's guide to foundational story psychotherapy : co-changing narratives, co-changing lives / Hugh K. Marr.
Description: New York, NY : Routledge, 2020. | Includes bibliographical references and index.
Identifiers: LCCN 2019036202 (print) | LCCN 2019036203 (ebook) | ISBN 9781138542099 (hbk) | ISBN 9781138542105 (pbk) | ISBN 9780429506291 (ebk)
Subjects: LCSH: Narrative therapy. | Psychotherapy.
Classification: LCC RC489.S74 M37 2020 (print) | LCC RC489.S74 (ebook) | DDC 616.89/165—dc23
LC record available at https://lccn.loc.gov/2019036202
LC ebook record available at https://lccn.loc.gov/2019036203

ISBN: 978-1-138-54209-9 (hbk)
ISBN: 978-1-138-54210-5 (pbk)
ISBN: 978-0-429-50629-1 (ebk)

Typeset in Bembo
by Apex CoVantage, LLC

 Printed in the United Kingdom by Henry Ling Limited

For Granddaddy Overman, who first told me stories
and
For Paula, who shares my own.

Contents

List of Figures	xii
List of Tables	xiii
Acknowledgements: A Professional Journey Story	xiv
Preface	xvii
Introduction	1

PART 1
The Shoulders of Giants — 7

1 Major Background Theorists — 9

PART 2
The Aspects of Story and the Foundational Story Model — 27

2 The Aspects of Story — 29

3 The Foundational Story Model — 42

4 Foundational Stories: Russian Dolls and Magic Mirrors — 49

PART 3
Life and Foundational Story Assessment — 63

5 Gathering Stories — 65

6 Understanding Foundational Stories — 72

Contents

7 Assessing the Impact of History and Context: The Foundational Story Interview and Family of Origin Mapping — 85

8 The Seminal Importance of Roles — 96

9 Assessing the Life Story Plot and Characters: Plot Diagramming and Character (or Ego State) Mapping — 103

PART 4
Changing Foundational and Life Stories — 113

10 Introduction and Sources of Change — 115

11 Changing Context: Story Receiving and Storytelling — 126

12 Helping Transform Characters — 133

13 Changing Plot — 148

14 Thematic Change — 156

15 Transforming the Moral and the Whole Story I — 163

16 Transforming the Moral and the Whole Story II: Foundational Storyboarding — 173

PART 5
Trauma and the Life Story — 181

17 From Fat Farm to Child Abuse — 183

18 The Trauma Story: Holes, Shards, and Morals — 188

19 A Trauma Treatment Primer: Phases of Trauma Treatment — 193

PART 6
Listening to Your Own Story — 209

20 Working With Yourself — 211

21 Growing as a Therapist — 216

PART 7
Conclusion: Weaving It Together   219

22 Without and Beyond Story   221

23 Integrating a Storied View With Your Own Theory   226

Appendices   233
   Appendix I: The Foundational Story Interview Template   235
   Appendix II: Foundational Story Diagram Form   239
   Appendix III: Family of Origin Mapping (FOOM) Procedure   240
   Appendix IV: Trauma List   246
Index   248

Figures

6.1	Example Foundational Story Diagram	81
7.1	Example Family of Origin Map (FOOM)	88
9.1	Example Plot Map	105
9.2	Example Character Map	108
10.1	Relationship of Therapeutic Relationship and Severity of Problems	116
16.1–16.8	Foundational Storyboarding Example	175
23.1	Type of Change in Different Therapies	227
III.1–III.9	Family of Origin Mapping Diagram	240

Tables

13.1	Foundational Story CCRT Example	150
14.1	Life Story Themes Derived from Jeffrey Young's Schema Therapy	158
15.1	Life Story Chapter Outline	168
15.2	Relationship Between Stories in Theories with Two Stories	171
III.1	Example Family Roles	243
III.2	Example Family Values	244

Acknowledgements: A Professional Journey Story

First and foremost, I must thank the hundreds of clients who over the years have allowed me to be part of their story. It is an honor that I hope I have treated with the respect it deserves. I have learned something about psychotherapy and about myself from each of you. For most of you, I regret that I couldn't know what I know now. I might have been more helpful.

Writing a book involves a cast of thousands, and, at the same time, is an intensely lonely process. I cannot begin to mention all the mentors and supervisors and colleagues and friends who have been an integral part of my professional development, and thus of a culminating book like this. Know that I thank you. I will mention only a very few, most of whom happened into the turning points in my professional life.

I suppose I should start with the late Gatey Workman, chair of the Davidson College psychology department. It was while sitting in on your group psychotherapy sessions with the seriously mentally ill at Broughton State Hospital that I knew I had to be a clinician. You probably knew it earlier; or at least knew I wouldn't be a researcher when I named my rat (Burrhus, for B. F. Skinner), then begged you to not euthanize him, but let me take him home that summer. What I didn't tell you was that in the Trailways bus on the way home, Burrhus gnawed through my gym bag and escaped, causing a bit of an uproar among my fellow passengers. He and I were unceremoniously dumped by the side of some rural highway.

After four years of working in what at the time was the exciting frontier of community mental health and of alcohol rehab, I knew I needed more training and a graduate degree. Jean Nidorf was my clinical supervisor in that first foray into grad school. Jean, I don't think you know that you started me on this narrative journey when you said, "If you want to be a psychotherapist, read novels. Therapy is about story."

Returning to the East Coast, I got a job in community mental health in Montgomery County, Maryland with a fantastic group of colleagues, all of us young and curious and eager. Re-joining you in a peer supervision group some 20 years later felt like coming home.

In the first of those 20 years after leaving Montgomery County, I was Director of Emergency Services for a Washington, D.C. mental health center—only the way it operated, there weren't many emergencies. What there was were training agreements with Georgetown University Department of Psychiatry and St. Elizabeth's Hospital. I was in simultaneous supervision with two different psychoanalysts and with a teacher for Murray Bowen's family therapy program at Georgetown. Thank you, Steve Quint, for selecting and finding some potential in my younger self.

Around this time, I entered a five-year Jungian analysis with Jerome Bernstein. Jerry, thank you for helping me assume authorship of my own story.

After D.C. mental health, I became rehab director for a non-profit, and ran day programs for developmentally disabled and chronically mentally ill clients. I left there to begin a 14-year stint as director of a partial hospital for Fairfax County, Virginia, serving clients dually diagnosed with substance abuse and serious mental illness. I was blessed to have a boss who is an evolved and decent human being. Davey Zellmer, I don't think I ever thanked you enough.

It was during this period that I returned to graduate school for my doctorate in psychology, yes, while working full time. Those years are a bit of a blur, and I would not have made it had it not been for two advisors. The late Tom Magoon, who kept me focused by reminding me that "Father Time is picking your pocket," and, later, Jan Birk.

By the time I left Fairfax County, I had completed my PhD. My three children had asked to come to my dissertation defense. Rachael and Lauren were nine and Chris was 13. They made the point that they were part of my doctorate, and so should see me defend. I had to agree. I made them promise to be quiet, and they were. Now in the next year Lauren will be defending her own dissertation. I will be there. I promise to be quiet.

My dissertation was the beginning of what is now a 23-year collaboration with Carol Pearson (can you believe it, Carol?!). I worked with Carol first to develop an instrument to help people learn which of 12 archetypes are prominent in their current life and how to capitalize on the resources; it has come to be the Pearson-Marr Archetype Indicator, and has been used by thousands. Carol and I then wrote *What Story Are You Living* about the archetypal stories that inspire people's lives. It has been such an honor to co-write with you.

I left Fairfax to go at last into private practice; I can't believe I have been in practice for longer than I was director of partial hospitalization. I joined a semi-structured, loosely organized group of ex-pats from area community mental health centers. Thank you all for your wisdom and for providing a place where I can admit that most of the time I don't know what the hell I'm doing.

Throughout all of the years since returning from San Diego, Paula and I have had two dear friends: Linda Gantt and Lou Tinnin. Two or three long weekends each year we would join them and a few other therapist friends at their lake house in West Virginia. Lou and Linda ran a trauma clinic in Morgantown, West Virginia long before trauma was a thing. Lou was intensely curious, and he and Linda were passionate about trauma being at the heart of most mental health issues. But *I* didn't take it to heart; and it didn't occur to me that every one of the substance-abusing, seriously mentally ill partial hospital clients I worked with was a trauma survivor. It wasn't until I went into private practice that I listened. Lou's phases of trauma response holds up today, and I have been inspired by and incorporated Linda's graphic narrative into the storyboarding that I do. Lou has since passed, but Linda continues to teach and consult. Thank you for your insight and your friendship.

In the early 2000s, just as I was beginning to formulate my own ideas about ego states and imagery, I took a workshop at the Washington School of Psychiatry with Mark Lawrence, MD. I joined one of his consultation groups, and for six or more years studied the intricacies of imagery and ego states. Mark had just begun his own book when he was tragically killed. I learned much about therapy from Mark, but mostly I gained permission to not restrain my own work. Even all these years after the loss of Mark, the Ego State Consultation Group continues.

When I went into private practice, I knew I would need a case consultant. I chose Julie Bondanza, a Jungian analyst who was Director of Training for the Jung Analytic Institute in New York, but who lives in D.C. Julie has such a gift of wisdom and intuition. Julie, you have been such a help over the years. You've also read drafts, helped me practice story interviewing, and continued to encourage me to write this book. Again, I've finally listened. Thank you.

Thanks, too, to first Nina Guttapalle, then Anna Moore, Ellie Duncan, and the editorial staff at Routledge/Taylor and Francis. I had steeled myself to shop this manuscript numerous times. I figured I would start at the top, and you got back in a day. I so appreciate that you share my vision.

And then there is Paula Howie. Wife and best friend and companion for 41 years, you have given me encouragement and supported me in taking the time to write. A dynamically trained art therapist, past President of the American Art Therapy Association, and editor of two books herself, I have been able to discuss cases and hash out theory with her. In so many ways this book, and the story I live, is a collaboration with Paula. Thank you.

Preface

First, a note about some of the conventions I have adopted. To add an extra layer of anonymity to case stories, I have called every male client "Nathan" and every female client "Harriet." The second client mentioned in Chapter 3 would thus be called "Nathan 3.2;" the first female client referenced in Chapter 8 would be "Harriet 8.1." Where clients have named internal characters, I have changed the names but tried as best as possible to preserve any linguistic connection.

I have alternated the gender of pronouns in an unsystematic manner, sometimes using "he" to refer to a generic client or therapist, and sometimes "she."

For brevity and clarity's sake, I have focused upon the simpler process of the individual therapy of adult clients. The overall story metaphor and many of the techniques apply equally well in group, family, and couples modalities. These formats give an additional potential level of intervention. In these settings the group itself has or forms a story, the changing of which can modify the life narrative of the clients involved. The therapist can focus upon the individual stories of the clients, or upon the group story; or the therapist can shift back and forth between the two as needed.

In the therapy of young children, the story is enacted along with or instead of the told story. Learning that additional language of enaction, of play, is not only enormously gratifying to the young internal characters of the therapist—having that ability also enhances her work with adults.

One of my own specialties is that of co-occurring disorder treatment. Although I have used some examples and insights from the field of substance abuse therapy, it was the wise counsel of colleagues who convinced me that the addition of a section on co-occurring disorder treatment would unnecessarily lengthen the book while giving but short shrift to a broad and complex topic. It may instead better become the subject of another book.

Introduction

On the face of it, it was a very odd and unappealing tour. My daughter was living in Chicago at the time, and she insisted that my wife and I accompany her. We boarded a badly re-painted school bus that periodically enveloped following vehicles in a smelly cloud of black smoke. The seats were hard, and patches of white cotton showed through the worn vinyl seat backs. Besides doing occasional u-turns in four-lane streets, the bus stopped at vacant overgrown lots and narrow darkened alleyways and the occasional once-opulent building now fallen into decay. Objectively it was a waste of time and money, this visit to the seamier parts of Chicago quite unlike the beautiful skyscrapers on the architectural river tour. We paid money to spend much of a day this way; and we enjoyed it immensely.

You see, this was a ghost tour. It was not about the objectively overgrown sites, nor about the comfort in getting there. It was about the stories. And the tour guide was a wonderful storyteller.

Our species, *homo sapiens*, was one of five or six hominids, and arguably not even the most successful if we measure success by the length of time on the planet. *Homo erectus* has that distinction hands down, having survived for some two million years, ten times longer than we have so far (or six times as long, if new research in Western Morocco holds up; this places the earliest humans at 300,000 to 350,000 years ago). We like to distinguish ourselves from other creatures on the planet, believing that the gods have chosen us or even made us in His image (the Plains Indians believed that the Great Spirit caused all other animals to stand in one spot, and humans in another. Soon a chasm appeared between the two groups, growing ever wider by the moment, separating humans from the other creatures for all time. Finally, at the very last moment, the Dog jumped across).

And we do have a distinction, although it is not what we typically believe. Typically, we think it is our language that sets us apart; and, it is true that language is a foundation of our different-ness. But it is not what sets us apart. Many, if not most, creatures (think of bees or ants) communicate. Elephants communicate with one another through sounds. And chimpanzees can warn one another that there is a lion at a certain spot by the river.

Even more remarkable, in laboratory experiments it can be shown that they can lie (Harari, 2014). But their language is forever confined to the world of objects.

This was arguably the human leap. Some 70,000 years ago we humans began what has been called the cognitive revolution. We began to enter the realm of meaning and imagination. Ever since that time we have straddled two equally real worlds simultaneously: the world of objects, and the world of meaning.

The two worlds interact and influence each other. But they are not the same. We are forever cursed and forever blessed to simultaneously span the two. An undoubtedly early way of coping with the straddling was to deny one world by defining it in terms of the other. Because both worlds are equally real and impactful, and cannot be reduced to each other, such attempts are always incomplete and unsatisfactory. Nonetheless, this primitive means of coping has persisted and is evident in the history of most disciplines.

In my own discipline of psychology, for example, we have had our positivist strain—think of the early behaviorists who cared nothing for the "black box" between the ears, hoping to predict output solely on the basis of input. And our meaning strain: think of the existentialists where the lone man (and, of course, it usually was a man) must choose his reaction at every step or face an inauthentic life. Even today the ignoring and reduction continues with the blossoming of research on the brain. We try to define mind in terms of brain, thereby reducing the experience of a mountain scene or a field of flowers to a neural pathway, and depression to a dearth of neurotransmitters.

But with the cognitive revolution of 70,000 years ago, when humans first entered the twin universes of the concrete and the imaginative, they also crafted a tool to help them walk a path between the two and adapt to an ever-changing world: *stories*.

Stories allow us to harness the imagined future and to recreate the remembered past. They are the primary way that we communicate. They are the template of our memory and the structure of our thoughts. They determine with whom we relate and how we organize our time. We humans swim in a sea of story.

Stories, then, allow us to make and organize meaning, and to interact with the physical and the social world. They define the beliefs that shape our world and the lens through which we view the world of objects. In short, they comprise what we regard as "real," no matter how fantastical that reality may seem from outside. Thus "reality" may be the giant turtle on whose back our world sits; or the formation of the world and all its creatures by an all-powerful entity some 4,000 years ago; or the idea that all we perceive as "solid" is in fact mostly empty space, and that there exists in the center of each galaxy an infinitely collapsing rabbit hole down which none of the familiar and basic ways of operating apply. As Joseph Campbell famously said, "Mythology may, in a real sense, be defined as other people's religion" (Campbell, 2013, p. 8). Arguably, even our basic sense of selfhood is as the protagonist in an unfolding story.

By the age of three, when we tell our first story, we have already heard thousands of stories in the conversations of our siblings, our parents, on television, and in the books we have been read and the lullabies we have been sung.

And because of the millions of stories we have heard, we only need to hear a very small vignette, or see an image, or sometimes hear even one of the parts of a story to grasp the potential whole story. We are so steeped in stories that a single image or a chance comment conjures a complete story.

At first our stories are disorganized and loose. Nursery rhymes appropriately mimic this. Think:

> Hey Diddle, the Cat and the Fiddle;
> The Cow jumped over the moon.
> The Little Dog laughed to see such sport;
> And the Dish ran away with the Spoon!
> (Crane, 2012)

Folk songs, too, mimic this disorganized style, but for different reasons. A good example is that of a famous American folk song, "Green Rocky Road." Although the music and words were copyrighted—and sung—by Len Chandler and Robert Kaufman, it was a signature song of Dave Van Ronk in 1963 (the real life inspiration for the title character in the movie *Llewyn Davis*), and covered by hundreds of musicians, including Emmylou Harris and Peter, Paul, and Mary. It has roots in an Alabama Black folk song (Kimpel, 2014), and a children's game before that.

The lyrics ramble from returning to Baltimore where the singer has no carpet to asking the audience to follow him—not to Baltimore, but to Galilee down the green rocky road. After a brief sojourn to talk about a crow that does not walk, only flies, the song then proceeds to ask who you love, and whether your mother chews tobacco.

Folk songs become this way as each performer makes subtle changes that over time collectively make the lyrics unrecognizable. Think of the children's game of "telephone" where the first child is whispered a message which s/he then whispers to the next child, and so on. When the last child repeats the message, it is nothing like the original. What a happy synchronicity that folk songs are frequently sung around small children, mimicking the style of story they tell. We shall see later that this has an important analogy in the dynamics of how memory operates.

Broadly speaking, we each have at least two stories composed by and starring ourselves. The first is the sequence of tales about ourselves, or our life story. That selection of tales is but a small sample of the millions of events both mundane and epic that have occurred in our lives. Those particular tales are not chosen randomly to represent our life story; rather, they are selected by a template for choosing the important feeling tone, setting, plotline, and theme. That template I call the "implicit life story."

Early stories become essential in defining one's implicit life story. Early vignettes form the foundations of one's view of self, others, and the world; that is why I have termed these early stories "foundational stories." Right from the beginning, with the disorganization of plot, the feeling tone is of primary importance. This early feeling tone becomes the feeling that pervades a person's sense of the world, often for life.

As stories become increasingly organized, they begin to carry a theme and a moral. The moral of early foundational stories is frequently retained as the moral of one's implicit life story. After the initial disorganization, the plotline of children's stories becomes increasingly organized. These foundational plots are frequently formed to support the feeling and moral previously internalized.

These early life feeling tones and relational themes, extended and specified by story morals created in young childhood—with a young child's ways of understanding—form the template for a lifelong implicit story about oneself. That evolving story determines how we perceive ourselves, with whom and how we relate, and what sort of environs we seek for work and for home. It defines our potential, and places a governor on our sense of happiness and well-being. It is the lens through which we live the world; it is our implicit life story.

That story may limit us; or it may empower us. It may be sad or upbeat. It may be tragic, or it may be comic in the ancient Greek conception of comedy—not as a funny story, but rather a story with a happy ending.

Some aspects of that implicit life story we are aware of telling ourselves via the voices in our minds and through our reflections on self. But much of the story remains enacted rather than told, for it is so ubiquitous, so much a definer of our waking moments and our dreams, that we are not aware of it. For awareness comes of reflection, which requires a perspective from outside (from the Latin *reflectere*, to bend back). We cannot bend back upon something which engulfs us.

Our implicit life story is at the core of our self. In a very real sense, it is who we are. Understanding and changing one's life story is the function of psychotherapy. Thus, *psychotherapy is the art and science of understanding and co-changing implicit life stories*. And changing life stories most effectively and efficiently involves changing the associated foundational stories. It is this perspective to which you will be introduced in the chapters to follow. In the course of those pages you will become acquainted with numerous examples and techniques—some completely new, others drawn from a variety of modalities. Ultimately, it is not the technique or even the modality that is important to this work, but the perspective—a view of therapy as co-changing and co-creating implicit life stories. With story as the scaffolding, you will see how disparate theories actually relate. Whatever your own persuasion, be it attachment or third wave CBT, Jungian or narrative or constructivist, I hope you will discover both ideas from other modalities and an appreciation for how all of our approaches are of a piece. As my grandmother—a lifelong member of a conservative evangelical church and veteran of revivals and tent meetings—surprisingly told me many, many years ago, "All doors lead home."

In the pages that follow, there is a blend of theory and story, including case story, as an application of how we learn best (i.e. via story). Part 1, *The Shoulders of Giants*, discusses major background theorists to a storied understanding of psychotherapy. In Part 2, *The Aspects of Story and the Foundational Story Model*, we will examine some overall characteristics of life stories and their context, including the cultural and the archetypal. We shall see the synergism between foundational stories and life stories, noting how foundational stories encapsulate one's implicit life story; and, in turn, how one's implicit life story impacts both the choosing and the telling of foundational stories. Next we will discuss the developmental progression of how children understand story, and why this is so crucial, even in adult psychotherapy. We will then look more closely at the aspects that make up all stories through the example of an old ballad (one of the "Child Ballads," named for Francis James Child, who collected them in the 19th century) from the British Isles. Into the delineation of story components we will note how different therapeutic approaches emphasize different story elements, a subject we will return to in more depth in the section on treatment.

Part 3, *Life and Foundational Story Assessment*, is a how-to for gathering and assessing foundational stories. Along the way, I will introduce the Foundational Story Interview, as well as a new way of mapping family influences (Family of Origin Mapping, or FOOM). Complete templates for both techniques are available in the appendices. We will also explore a particular technique for mapping character and plot in foundational story, with a clinical example that forged the prototype.

Part 4, *Changing Foundational and Life Stories*, is about co-creating life story change with the client. It begins with an understanding of the mechanisms of change, then shows how to apply them to transforming foundational stories and their elements. Because of the synergism between foundational and implicit life story, a change in a foundational story alters one's implicit life story. Methods for helping to integrate changes into a person's life are delineated. Example applications from numerous psychotherapy approaches are included.

We now know that virtually all mental and emotional disorders are either caused by, exacerbated by, or lead to trauma. Beginning with a seminal study that showed the large-scale impact of trauma, Part 5, *Trauma and the Life*

Story, shows the particular impact of trauma on one's implicit life story, and how to assess the impact in a manner that allows you to use the information to promote healing. The traumatic incident frequently becomes a disjointed foundational story, and as such, impacts one's implicit life story. Thus, any effective treatment for trauma must both heal the disjointed foundational trauma story, and ameliorate the impact upon one's larger life story.

Part 6, *Listening to Your Own Story*, helps clinicians apply some of the techniques previously described to themselves, and understand how their own story interfaces with that of their clients. This lends some practical paths to handling challenging client situations. Recommendations for further professional growth are suggested.

Part 7, *Conclusion: Weaving It Together* speaks first to instances of the absence of a life story. It then discusses integrating a storied view with one's own therapeutic approach. The section is designed to give an overall integration to a theory that you will likely find both unspokenly familiar and excitingly new. Hopefully it will answer some of the questions that you will have posed in earlier chapters.

Part 7 is followed by appendices that give you specific forms and procedures described in the book, including the Foundational Story Interview and Foundational Story Diagram, the Trauma List Questionnaire, and the Family of Origin Mapping Procedure. A bibliography follows each chapter.

My goal in presenting this work is not only to help further the importance and use of foundational and life story, both explicit and implicit, and to provide clinicians with ideas and techniques from a lifetime of clinical work, but also to write the clinical book that I would most want to read. I sincerely hope that it is very close to the work that you have always wanted to read as well.

Hugh K. Marr, May 2019

References

Campbell, J. (Kennedy, E., ed.). (2013). *Thou Art That: Transforming Religious Metaphor*. New York, NY: New World Library.

Crane, W. (2012). *Mother Goose's Nursery Rhymes: A Collection of Alphabets, Rhymes, Tales, and Jingles*. Urbana, IL: Project Gutenberg. Retrieved June 7, 2019 from: www.gutenberg.org [EBook #39784], p. 175.

Harari, Y. (2014). *Sapiens: A Brief History of Humankind*. New York, NY: Random House.

Kimpel, D. (2014, February 12). Len Chandler: True tales from the gaslight. *Music Connection Magazine*. Retrieved from: www.musicconnection.com.

Part I

The Shoulders of Giants

> If I have seen further than others, it is by standing upon the shoulders of giants.
>
> —Sir Isaac Newton (1643–1727); from letter to Robert Hooke, 1675 (Historical Society of Pennsylvania, Simon Gratz Autograph Collection, Box 12/11, Folder 37)

Chapter 1
Major Background Theorists

The realization that stories are seminal in people's lives, and that psychotherapy involves understanding and helping people to change their stories is an often unstated undercurrent in how many if not most psychotherapists operate. Many seminal clinicians and thinkers have contributed either knowingly or unknowingly to this view. In this section, I shall highlight a few whose impact on psychotherapy and story has been essential.

This chapter explores the understanding and contributions by major theorists to the centrality of story in making meaning in psychotherapy. The techniques and theories of a myriad of other clinicians will be integrated especially into Part Two, but also throughout the rest of the book. The major theorists and their contributions to a storied understanding in Chapter 1 include Sigmund Freud, Carl Jung, Alfred Adler, Eric Berne, Michael White, and Dan McAdams. Let us begin with Freud.

Sigmund Freud (1856–1939)

No history of psychotherapy contributions would be complete without mentioning Sigmund Freud. Freud had a profound effect on the establishment and course of psychotherapy, and he set in motion many trends, some of which inform our work today, and from some of which we are still recovering.

Freud began his medical career in Vienna as a neurologist. From early on, he had visions of a grand theoretical synthesis that explained both the mundane and the pathological. In those early years he held the view—not unlike so many professionals today—that the unifying theory would be biological in nature. You may remember from the introduction that humankind is destined to live in two equally real and overlapping worlds—the world of objects and the world of imagination—and that neither can be reduced to the other. In his early career, Freud believed neurophysiology could explain everything (the world of objects). He very quickly ran up against the limits of the tools available in the Victorian era. When Freud graduated from medical school in 1882, bleeding had fallen out of favor as a treatment for many diseases, but blistering (raising blisters on the skin by applying red hot implements or caustic chemicals) was still a common treatment for many maladies, including psychiatric disorders like hysteria and hypochondriasis; neurological tools such as the ƒMRI were a century away. Indeed, X-rays would not be discovered for another 13 years.

Despairing of then-current neurology, Freud began a journey to the other pole, the use of fantasy as both cause and cure of mental disorder. But he never relinquished the hope that neurobiology would eventually explain all emotional problems.

The Victorian era was replete with strange neurological/emotional illnesses, the likes of which we seldom see in modern first world countries. There were cases of paralysis and of blindness and of fainting for which no biomedical cause could be determined. Even with the neuroanatomical knowledge of the late 19th century, it was clear to Freud and his colleagues that some of these illnesses involved separate bodily systems that were unlikely to be simultaneously affected. Thus, these illnesses were likely psychogenic in origin; they were termed "hysteria."

Freud's friend Josef Breuer got Freud interested in a promising treatment for hysteria called "hypnosis," and the two of them traveled to Paris to study under the eminent hypnotherapist, Jean-Martin Charcot (Sandhu, 2015).

After returning to Vienna, Freud became disenchanted with hypnosis, and developed another "talking cure:" that of having a patient lie on a fainting couch (the fact that these small couches were called "fainting couches" speaks to how ubiquitous hysteria had become) and say whatever came to her mind. The analyst would sit behind the patient and note not only where the associations led, but when the patient hesitated or otherwise blocked herself from immediately revealing her associations.

As Freud worked with more and more young women with hysteria, he heard more and more tales of childhood sexual abuse. He wrote a paper ("The Aetiology of Hysteria") in 1896 (Freud, 1896/1962) describing how child abuse was at the root of hysteria. Indeed, Judith Herman, in her seminal 1997 book *Trauma and Recovery*, talked of hysteria as trauma-related symptoms that were caused by child abuse, and which formed one of the three traumatic scourges of humankind through the ages (the other two were war and domestic abuse).

Unfortunately for the treatment of trauma, Freud recanted his position on childhood sexual abuse and hysteria. This likely set the understanding of the ubiquity of child abuse and the need for trauma treatment back almost one hundred years. It is understandable for Freud, and we should not judge him harshly. After all, he had already proposed radical theories beginning with the idea that children were *not* just little adults, which was the prevalent theory at the time (and, of course, that prevalent view is a short step from justifying child labor and child sexual abuse). Then he talked of the importance and ubiquity of sexual drives even though he was writing in a Victorian age. Finally, Freud was a Jewish doctor in a time when the medical establishment was overwhelmingly Gentile. Had he also (rightly, it turns out) accused male family members of sexually abusing their female children, we may never have heard of Freud. It likely would be a bridge too far, and he may have been silenced as just another crackpot.

The way that Freud changed his views on childhood abuse was to say that women's stories of abuse did not occur in *reality*. Rather, it was their *fantasy* of abuse that drove their symptoms. Thus, he completely switched poles from neurobiology (the world of objects) to the treatment of mental fantasy and its debilitations (the world of imagination). The fantasy *story* of abuse had to be changed. And the way to change that story was by helping the patient gain the insight that she was reliving that story in the consulting room by placing on the analyst the characteristics of important figures from the past, and placing on her relationship with the analyst the template of her relationship with those figures.

While Freud missed the use of story to connect objects and imagination to the detriment both of understanding trauma, and potentially to the detriment of his patients feeling trusted and accepted, he did see that reliving the same anachronistic story plotline is at the root of many psychological symptoms (what Freud called the "repetition compulsion"). And Freud himself was a great storyteller. He was the fourth recipient of the Goethe prize in literature (Storr, 1998), and in 1936 he was nominated for the Nobel prize *in literature*. His case studies read like a whodunit mystery story, with the solution appearing at the end from putting together the overlooked pieces of evidence along the way.

Freud was seminal to the use of story in psychotherapy in yet another way as well. He was one of the first to understand that early human development proceeds through phases. Since his was a bodily psychology (given his predilection for physiology and neurology), he thought of each early phase as oriented toward a particular bodily system, with one exception. Thus, the oral phase was named for the infant's focus on the mouth and the oral cavity in suckling. The anal phase was named for the body system involved in toilet training; and the phallic phase was named for the emphasis on the penis (or lack thereof). Psychological problems were metaphorically and literally related to these phases. Thus, a problem with dependency was connected to the oral phase; and because the oral phase precedes other phases, such problems were thought to be more primitive. So far there is a certain consistency, if illogic, to the theory. The consistency is in relating a class of problems to the bodily system to which they metaphorically relate. The illogic is in confusing the metaphorical with the literal. Thus, a person's dependency in relationships and emphasis upon eating (or smoking cigars!) is metaphorically related to a time in life of dependency and suckling; *therefore*, that person's problems must relate to that literal infancy time in his/her life.

The one inconsistent period in these stages is that of the Oedipal. The Oedipal period was hypothesized to be the period of origin of the majority of neurotic problems Freud encountered, including hysteria. And that phase is the one not named for a bodily system but, instead, for a mythical *story*. More to the point, it is related to a partial story, not even the whole story.

Most of us are generally familiar with the broad outline of Sophocles' (reprint 1991) play *Oedipus Rex* (Oedipus the King). In it our protagonist, Oedipus, like so many mythical heroes, is raised as an orphan. For Oedipus, the orphaning occurs because of the prophecy that he would one day kill his father. When his father, the king, received this prediction, he sent the infant Oedipus into the woods with a forester who was to murder him. Instead, the forester takes pity on the baby and gives it away to be raised in secrecy. When, as a young man, Oedipus consults the oracle at Delphi, he is informed that his fate is to kill his father; and, even more, that he is to marry his mother. Not recognizing his parents (nor they him), since he did not grow up with them nor had he seen them on Facebook, Oedipus encounters his father, they duel, and he kills the older man. He then marries a beautiful older widow. This is where the story ends for Freud (but not for Sophocles; see Sophocles, reprint 1991).

Freud saw this as a template for wishes of the young (pre-operational) child—that he secretly wishes to eliminate his father so as to have his mother all to himself (this involves quite a bit of license, as the wish to possess Jocasta was not what motivated the duel for Oedipus with his father; and Oedipus *was* more powerful than the king). The successful ending for Freud was in identifying with the more powerful father ("identification with the aggressor") and, in being like him, ultimately finding a mate who in important ways was similar to his mother ("sublimation"). The successful ending for Sophocles finds Oedipus, distraught over what he had done, blinding himself and wandering in the dessert. He finally emerges to claim the throne and rules with great insight. Freud seems to skip over the role of fate in the tragic part of the story—that precisely by trying to avoid one's tragic fate, one manages to fulfill it. It is this fulfilling fate by trying to avoid it that links Oedipus with his father, not Oedipus' personal identification with the father.

Why this large inconsistency in Freud's theory? Why that particular story? And why only one story, when each of the proposed childhood (and later life phases) could easily be related to their own mythical narrative examples? I don't know.[1] But expanding the story template for numerous stories that inform both a person's life as well as her/his difficulties awaited the genius of our next contributor—Carl Jung.

Thus Freud's contributions to narrative psychotherapy include the importance of listening carefully to the patient's life stories (even if Freud listened through speakers pre-tuned to the psycho-sexual); seeing story as a template for emotional problems; and understanding that in psychological disorders the same plotline recurs over and over. The importance of the Oedipal period for Freud (roughly Piaget's pre-operational period), as we will see in Chapter 4, is precisely the period that is important for the formation of foundational stories. The mechanisms which Freud noted work to protect the dreamer from threatening wishes in dreams—condensation, displacement, symbolization, secondary elaboration (Freud, 2010)—accurately describe the manner in which a young, pre-operational child thinks. In all of these ways, plus for the initiation of the broad acceptance of psychotherapy, narrative therapists in particular and the entire field of psychotherapy in general owe Freud appreciation.

Carl Gustav Jung (1875–1961)

The early 1900s was a time of incredible excitement in psychology, a bubbling cauldron of ideas and approaches. Wilhelm Wundt in Germany was one of the founders of the psychology of perception; at Cornell, Edward Tichener, student of Wundt, developed a structural theory of consciousness by having people introspect and meticulously record their perceptions, images, and feelings. Tichener is known as the founder of experimental psychology. Contrasting to Tichener's inward journey was the behaviorist John Watson, who brashly challenged anyone to send him a child who he could then turn into a doctor or lawyer through behavioral principles (no one sent him a child). More balanced and with a broad prescient and philosophical curiosity that ranged from social psychology to religious experiences was another American, William James. On the continent was the founder of intelligence testing, Alfred Binet, and the controversial theorist Sigmund Freud and his emerging protégée Carl Jung. Also on the continent were the psychoanalyst Sandor Ferenzi, and two men who would later become Freud biographers—A. A. Brill and Ernest Jones. It was the genius of the eminent psychologist (and first president of the American Psychological Association) G. Stanley Hall to invite most of them to speak or attend a colloquium at Clark University (Evans, 1985), where Hall served as president. Unfortunately, Binet died before the conference. Wundt declined to attend (possibly to attend the 500th anniversary of the University of Leipzig instead of the 20th anniversary of Clark University).

This 1909 conference would be Freud's only trip to America. He and Jung traveled by steamship, a weeklong journey, and they filled their time just as you might expect—by interpreting each other's dreams. None of Freud's dreams survive. Freud was intensely private, and Jung refused to reveal the older man's confidences even after Freud died. We do have one of Jung's dreams, as recorded in his autobiography *Memories, Dreams, and Reflections* (Jung, 1961/1989, p. 158). In the dream, Jung finds himself in the upper story of a "two storey (*sic*)" house, which he realizes is his own. It is a salon with fine furnishings and valuable paintings. But Jung is curious about the lower stories, and so descends first through a Medieval section, then into a cellar from Roman times where he finds a ring set into the stone floor. He pulls on the ring to reveal a narrow stairway which he descends into a small cave filled with pottery shards like the remains of a primitive culture. There he sees two old and desiccated skulls.

As Jung states in the first line, the dream of this house—and its interpretation—contains two stories ("storeys"). One story is that of Freud, who, seeking the aspects of the dream potentially revealing of the personal (Freudian) unconscious, asked Jung to associate to the two skulls. Freud argued the skulls were the relevant aspect of the dream, and represented for Jung a death wish toward his parents.

Here we see the contrast between the two. Freud was reductionistic and used a repetitive template to view psychic phenomena. For him, a part of one universal story (that of *Oedipus Rex*) would suffice.

The other story ("storey") is that of Jung, who saw in this dream a model of the unconscious as multilayered and hierarchical. In Jung's *Collected Works* he mentions the word "story" but once. Yet Jung was a mythologist and religious scholar fascinated by the universal symbols in myth which form all the layers of his dream house but the first story. Within this house (psyche) were layers which transcended the personal. For Jung, the deepest layers unite that which is human, and undergird the cultural and personal differences among people. Jung, in contrast to Freud, was expansive. He explored how his patients' individual stories were informed by symbols from hundreds of myths, including those they had never directly encountered. This one dream forms a pithy summary of Jung's theory; and, at the same time, presages his emancipation from Freud. For Jung, it is neither the psychosexual nor the ubiquity of conflict that is central; rather it is the universal and transpersonal aspects of being human above which is layered the personal.

As with most scholars, Jung did not come by his theory all at once, like Athena springing from the head of Zeus; rather, it evolved from very practical and experimental beginnings. A few late nights of insomnia may lead one in the desperation of the wee hours to old movie depictions of psychological evaluations where the psychologist presents one word at a time for the patient's association ("walk"—"run"; "dinner"—"food"). The so-called Word Association Test, no longer commonly used in psychological evaluations, was extended and quantified by Jung. Indeed, the second volume (*Experimental Researches*) of his collected works is dedicated almost entirely to studies of the Word Association Test. Jung quantified and systematized the test, coming up with a standard list of 100 words. Not only would he note the subject's response to each cue word, but he would measure the response time, surmising in part that longer response times reflected a rejection of the initial response, then creating a more "acceptable" response which was actually delivered to the examiner.

In reviewing hundreds of test results, Jung noted that our minds seemed to be organized in clusters of associative networks, each with a core feeling. Jung coined the term "complex" to describe the phenomena, a term which both Freud ("Oedipus Complex") and Adler ("Inferiority Complex") borrowed.

Jung began to note that some complexes were universal. The recognition of this struck Jung in the course of working with a psychotic patient at the famous Saltpetre Hospital under the tutelage of Eugene Bleuler, a famous psychiatrist of the time, and the first to catalogue the symptoms and course of what was later to be known as "schizophrenia." Jung's patient was an uneducated young man who, like many in the hospitals of the time, had already spent years of his life on the ward. The young man drew an image of a sun with a penis. At the time this was dismissed as a sort of visual psychotic ranting, the equivalent of verbal "word salad." Jung thought otherwise, recognizing the painting as the same symbolic depiction that played a central role in a small Mithraic religion. The young man was uneducated, and had spent his entire life in the town in which he grew up or in the hospital. There was virtually no way he could have encountered this symbol; and, yet, there it was.

Jung realized that certain symbols and complexes are universal, even if unconscious. These he called "archetypes." Taken together they form the collective unconscious, that universal, shared, deep knowledge that formed the lower levels of the house in the dream he revealed to Freud.

These archetypes frequently occur in myth and folktales. Thus, certain narratives have universal symbols and themes. Rather than beginning with the narrative, Jung begins with the archetypal and sees it reflected in story, each story becoming a facet that reflects one of many expressions and aspects of the archetypal. Rather than one universal myth (Freud) Jung saw a multitude of universal myths, some reflecting differing aspects of the same archetype. Like an individual, a mythic story has its particular personal aspects, but it has echoes that root it in the universal experience beneath all cultures and all times.

Psychotherapy for Jung was especially pertinent in the second half of life (another contrast with Freud, who stressed the importance of analysis in early adulthood) when one has more or less dealt with the outer world and is prepared to look inward. That inward view involves not just coming to terms with one's own personal conflicts, but connecting with the larger Self which is conversant with the symbols and myths from all societies and all time. This allows one to become more uniquely oneself, neither cut off from the universal nor possessed by it—a process Jung referred to as "individuation."

Jung's writings influenced a host of scholars from many disciplines, including sinologists like Alan Watts; mythologists like Joseph Campbell; and anthropologists like Claude Levi-Strauss. In psychotherapy, his legacy not only includes Jungian analysts and Jungian-oriented therapists, but personal mythologists like Stanley Krippner et al. (2007); David Feinstein and Stanley Krippner (1988, 2006); and Sam Keen and Valley-Fox (1989).

Thus, with Jung we see narrative understanding expand to the myriad of universal stories and myths.

Alfred Adler (1870–1937)

Whereas Freud had begun his medical career as a neurologist, Alfred Adler began as an ophthalmologist. In 1902 Freud invited him to join the Wednesday discussion group at his home, which would eventually become the Viennese Psychoanalytic Society. Adler came to serve as president of the group, but, like Jung, parted company over theoretical differences with Freud.

Adler founded his own school of therapy which he called "Individual Psychology." Like Jung, Adler rejected both Freud's drive theory (sexuality and aggression as the prime motivators of humans) and Freud's emphasis on the monomyth of Oedipus. Instead, Adler believed that underlying neurosis were feelings of inferiority that led to a compensatory striving for superiority. Much has been made of the influence of Adler's own early life, for as a child he suffered from the crippling bone disease of rickets (a vitamin deficiency disease). He overcame its debilitating effects and was inspired to pursue a medical career. In fairness, all theories bear the stamp of their makers' stories.

His therapy involves understanding what he called a person's "lifestyle," which was their characteristic manner of moving through the world in pursuit of a personal and often implicit goal. In other words, Adler sought to understand a person's life story. He stated:

> There are no "chance memories": out of the incalculable number of impressions which meet an individual, he chooses to remember only those which he feels, however darkly, to have a bearing on his situation. Thus his memories represent his "Story of My Life;" a story he repeats to himself to warn him, to comfort him, to keep him concentrated on his goal, and to prepare him by means of past experiences, so that he will meet the future with an already tested style of action."
> (Alfred Adler, in Ansbacher, 1956, p. 351)

Adler presaged much modern understanding. For example, he believed that a person's movement through life resulted from a combination of inheritance and childhood environment. That childhood environment included one's position in the birth order. It also included what he called "guiding lines," or what it meant to be a woman (or man) in one's family culture—in other words, the story template that one is to follow, given one's gender. His understanding was not that the individual is a passive result of environment and inheritance; rather, the individual takes an active organizing role in determining and following one's life goal given his/her genetic and environmental resources. Often people justify their situation and pursuits with what

Adler called "private logic," which is very similar to the errors in thinking which the cognitive behaviorists identified many years later.

If Freud was especially interested in how one (mythical) story played out in people's lives; and Jung was intrigued by the multitude of universal stories that inform one's path, then Adler was all about a person's individual life story ("lifestyle"). One of Adler's major approaches to learning about one's lifestyle was that of asking for what he called "early recollections," by which he meant early foundational stories. He would ask a person to recall their first memory, then their second, and so on for three to five stories. He insisted it be in story form—not the more general "I remember that when I was little my family would go to the beach in the summers." Adler wanted a particular story episode.

Adler and his followers became quite adept at interpreting how these vignettes were a condensed version of one's life story. At the end of treatment Adler would again ask for early recollections. Often it would no longer be the same recollections as previously recalled; and even when it was, the story would have changed to reflect the changes in therapy to the client's life story. When a person's life story changes, their memories change as well. The notion of memory as contextual was at least 60 years prescient.

Eric Berne (1910–1970)

Eric Berne (*ne* Bernstein) was a Canadian psychiatrist who came to study and live in the United States. He had hoped to become a psychoanalyst and entered two analytic institutes, one before his World War II service and one after. Although he studied with and was analyzed by two very famous analysts, Paul Federn and Erik Erikson, his candidacy to become a psychoanalyst was denied. In his disappointment, Berne decided to develop an alternative psychotherapy.

While the roots of his theory very clearly tap Freud, Federn, and Erikson, he was one of the first theorists to emphasize the interpersonal patterns in problems, and, later, one of the first to directly classify and work to change life stories. Berne was determined that the language in his theory would be accessible, in contrast to the obtuse and technical jargon of psychoanalysis. His initial idea was that there are two, then added a third, universal ego states: Parent, Adult, and Child.[2] From there Berne made the interpersonal leap that virtually no one else had at the time. If person one is at the moment in their Parent ego state when they are interacting with person two, person two may be in their own Parent, Adult, or Child and the interaction will be different accordingly. When Person Two responds out of one of their ego states, the resulting communication may be complementary (in which case all is well and both are satisfied); or crossed (in which case there is dissatisfaction or conflict).

Berne's followers saw that identifying these three primary ego states was helpful, but not sufficient. Accordingly, they divided the Parent and Child ego states into types of parents and children (e.g., Critical Parent, Nurturing Parent, Adapted Child, Free Child). In fact, as we will see in Chapter 14 on the treatment of characters, any artificial limit on the number of ego states limits the therapy's ability to be individualized. However, being aware of common ego states can help the therapist become attuned to a client's current presenting or recurring character.

Having identified universal ego states (read characters) that everyone inhabits at different times, and then applied this to interpersonal interaction, Berne went on to identify common repetitive patterns of communication which he colloquially called "games." His book to enable therapists to identify and treat games became an international mass market bestseller: *Games People Play* (Berne, 1964). Berne identified over 100 games, and their pithy names have become common parlance—names like "Ain't It Awful," "Let's You and Him Fight," "Wooden Leg," and "NIGYSOB" ("Now I've Got You, You Son of a Bitch").

Each game was a repetitive mini story with its own plotline and thesis that solidified the person's worldview. For example, in Wooden Leg, the thesis was "what can you expect of a person with a wooden leg (poor childhood, lower back pain, depression, etc.)?" The payoff in Wooden Leg is the avoidance of responsibility (the secondary gain in Freudian terms); and playing the game reinforces the person's self-image as broken.

After writing *Games People Play*, Berne began piecemeal to develop his concept of "script," or life plan. His colleague and protégé Claude Steiner extended and systematized the concept in his book *Games Alcoholics Play* (1984), which remains an extremely helpful understanding of the stories that alcoholics live. After *Games Alcoholics Play* came out, Berne collected his own thoughts on the subject in the book *What Do You Say After You Say Hello?* Unfortunately, the book is long and rambling, as Berne died of a heart attack before having the opportunity to edit and proof it.

The script was essentially a predetermined life story that encompassed one or more repetitively played games and led to an ultimate conclusion. In fact, Berne wrote early on of scripts, "they follow the Aristotelian principles of dramaturgy with remarkable fidelity: there is prologue, climax, and catastrophe, with real or symbolic pathos and despair giving rise to real threnody" (Berne, 1976, p. 126). Minimally, a script consists of a covert injunction from a parent in the form of "Don't" ("don't feel satisfied;" "don't feel anything;" "don't think;" and, especially harmful, "don't exist"); and the child's resulting decision about him/herself and others, expressed in the form of "I'm OK/not OK; you're OK/not OK." Berne classified scripts as those making for either a winner, a loser, or a non-winner. The loser scripts were those of a tragic life story, and are frequent among psychotherapy clients. Berne further classified these tragic scripts according to prepositional or adverbial phrases: *Until; After; Never; Always; Over and Over;* and *Open-ended*. Each of these types was exemplified by a Greek myth. Thus, for example, a person with an *Until* script cannot be happy *until* some accomplishment or event (the children are grown, the house is perfectly clean, you find the right partner, etc.). This mirrors the story of Hercules, who could not become a god until he had spent 12 years as a slave.

The *Open-ended* script is of particular interest. That is the "non-winner" situation of life after the script is finished. Often this arrives later in life: the person who has organized her life around work, and now retires; the mother whose children have grown and left, etc. Berne characterizes this as the time between the end of the script and death. In Chapter 24 we will meet both positive and negative situations of having no life story.

The *Counterscript* is one of the most perceptive and innovative aspects of Steiner and Berne's work. The counterscript is essentially a second life story that contrasts with the script story. Tragic life stories do not plod along in a linear fashion, becoming increasingly consequential until some ultimate tragic ending. Rather, the programmed problematic life story (or script) is interspersed with periods of relative calm and happiness. This has its counterpart in Aristotle's view of how both tragedies and comedies have reversals of fortune. Thus, the alcoholic has multiple periods of sobriety, and the depressive has times when he can get out of bed or meet with friends or accomplish tasks at work in relative peace. For Steiner, these interludes are from shifting into the alternate life story of the counterscript. The counterscript is the result of verbalized injunctions and well wishes on the part of the parents: "Be successful!" or "Be happy," for example. These verbalized positive wishes are not as powerful as the non-verbal example of the opposite-gender parent or the indirect admonitions ("he's the spitting image of his Uncle Pete"—who was a successful and very unhappy businessman, and veteran of three marriages). Ultimately the negative script reasserts itself and the person resumes drinking, or has a minor loss that precipitates another depressive episode.

Berne's determination to make the language of his theory colloquial succeeded in making his ideas accessible, in contrast to the removed and obscure language of the psychoanalysts with whom he wished to contrast. Unfortunately, as with any opposition, it suffered from the same deeper theme or problem as that of the analysts.[3] Terminology such as "game," "racket," etc. has the effect of minimizing both the anguish and the unintended, unconscious nature of people's suffering (as if one could just responsibly choose to not play a harmful "game"). One's life story in important ways is who they are, not a problematic mantle they have adopted.

Another difficulty related to the period in which Berne lived was the implied blame of parents. It was the injunction, or negative message, given the child by the opposite-sex parent together with the same-sex parent's example that is absorbed as the child's life script (e.g., the boy whose mother gives the implied message "Don't think!" together with the father's example of alcoholism becomes "Don't think (and here's how you do it)—drink!").

This fails to take into account the synergistic aspect. It is not just the messages one receives, but what one takes from them and how one organizes the result that has the impact. This is true just as in trauma, where two people can each experience a very similar car crash; one goes on with her life, or even uses the experience to effect societal change by joining MADD, whereas the other becomes completely debilitated.

Despite the seeming failure of empathy for those living in tragedy; the over-crediting of parental impact; and the limiting of the number and type of characters (ego states) people live, Berne was a pioneer in many areas. He moved beyond a theory of the individual to characterize common social and interactional patterns, a focus unheard of in the psychoanalysis of the era, and he extended Freud's concept of the repetition compulsion and the myth of Oedipus to the larger fated life story (script) characterized by one of several myths containing recurring elements.

Michael White (1948–2008)

White was an Australian family therapist who, by himself and with the collaboration of David Epston, developed a narrative approach to therapy. Although he is usually thought of as a family therapist, his approach was often applied to individuals, organizations, and communities. When working with an individual, the family aspect was often in bringing in the client's circle of family and/or friends to validate and celebrate changes made. He applied his approach to a wide range of problems from ADHD and bedwetting to schizophrenia, eating disorders, and the impact of dislocation on Aboriginal people.

White was as much philosopher as clinician, and the inspiration for his ideas was derived more from philosophy than from psychology. He likened therapy to playing jazz, and noted that improvisation derives from intense practice. White would record and often meticulously transcribe his client interviews, then review them to find a more fruitful line of questioning.

Like virtually all of the theorists reviewed in this section, from Freud on, his theory was a work in progress. He and Epston had made plans to meet to completely re-envision their work when White died suddenly of a massive heart attack during dinner after the first day of a training conference in San Diego. White was only 59 (Epston, 2016).

The role of the therapist in narrative therapy is that of a collaborative co-author. For White, clients' problems arise from an oppressive and dominating story that does not fit with the person's lived experience (Carr, 1998). The therapy is about finding and then helping a client live an alternative story. Through creative questioning the therapist joins the client, then helps the client to externalize the problem. The questions render the problem an adversary. For example, "When were you last able to hold Depression at bay? Who helped you to do this? What time of year is Depression most likely to attack?"

Having externalized and personified the problem, the narrative therapist looks for exceptions to the dominant story. White sought to develop with the client an alternative story that enhances the client's ability to author her own life (White, 2007). He helps the client strengthen and detail those alternative stories ("thicken" in White's vernacular) so that eventually an alternative story that is less problematic, and in which the self is more powerful than the problem, is found or created. The new story is grown by written as well as verbal means. For example, the narrative therapist may send to the client copies of her session notes on the client's crafting of a new story, or issue a certificate or award for finding a different story. This revised story becomes the client's life story, and significant family and friends are invited to witness the changed narrative.

A further step in cementing the new life story is what White referred to as "bringing-it-back" practices. These may involve, for example, meeting with the therapist and a new client who shares similar problems to share how the client found and developed the new story.

White was very concerned about the deleterious effects of power imbalances. Thus, it is very important in White's narrative therapy to establish an equal power relationship with the client where the client is the expert on her life and the therapist acts as consultant, striving to listen more than speak. The meta-narrative in White's approach is a war story. The client is encouraged to fight the dominance of the problem saturated story not by direct confrontation, but more by waging guerrilla warfare, developing and sewing together snippets of alternative stories.

White took a somewhat radical approach to psychology, eschewing diagnosis as an example of a "totalizing story" that, by pathologizing, maintains a person's problems. He was quite sensitive to how dominant stories maintain a power imbalance that serves to create and continue problems. Both identities and problems are stories for White.

Dan McAdams (1954–)

Sherlock Holmes contended that the best place to hide something was in plain sight. Psychology has a long history of studying drives and needs and traits and reinforcement schedules and intelligence quotients and other rather arcane and constructed concepts, while ignoring the primacy of narrative that surrounded it. Dan McAdams has been a central figure in turning that around.

McAdams is a personality theorist and chair of the Department of Psychology at Northwestern University outside of Chicago, and the author or co-author of at least 19 books. He is the winner of the Henry A. Murray Award from the American Psychological Association, and has spent virtually his whole career since the early 1980s studying stories and narrative. Of necessity, his research has integrated not only personality theory, but developmental psychology and cognitive psychology with forays into clinical psychology as well. His work incorporates the fields of hermeneutics, biography, and autobiography. McAdams' consistent message has been that narrative can be studied, and that it is crucial to do so.

Much of McAdams' research has entailed in-depth interviews with hundreds of adults about the narrative of their lives. In his prototypical research, McAdams and his colleagues and students attempt to identify—and help the respondent identify—his or her personal myth that McAdams believes forms their identity (McAdams, 1993, 2001, 2006a). The interview begins with having the person divide his or her life into between two and eight chapters, giving each chapter a name and summary, much like a table of contents. The second question inquires about specific stories, what McAdams calls "nuclear episodes." He sees these nuclear episodes as the climax or turning point in life chapters (and are thus some of what I have termed "foundational stories"). The nuclear episodes assessed are the person's peak and nadir experiences; a major turning point; the earliest memory; and one story each from childhood, adolescence, and adulthood.

He then moves from events to people for the third question, asking the respondent to describe four important people in his/her life. McAdams then moves in the fourth question to asking about future plans, dreams, and ambitions.

The fifth question concerns inquiring about two major current conflicts, problems, or stressors. Finally, he moves to the person's fundamental beliefs and values, including spiritual, political, and overall beliefs. In the seventh (last) section he returns to the chapter delineation of the first question to ask if the person can now discern an overall theme or message that runs through his or her life. The interviewer acts as an interested witness throughout, offering no counsel or suggestion, but helping the person expound.

Although developed for research, the above outline can make for a wonderful clinical history in the early stages of therapy.

For McAdams, identity is a life story. McAdams has integrated his research findings by noting that people's narrative identity tends to relate to relative strength on two general themes: that of agency and that of communion. These themes are especially revealed in the interview section that inquires about nuclear episodes, or stories. A person who is high in agency tends to have higher needs for achievement and power. Related story motifs include that of strength or impact; status and recognition; autonomy and independence; and competence and accomplishment. A person who is high in communion tends to have greater needs for intimacy. Motifs that predominate in their nuclear stories are those of love and friendship; communication and sharing; care and support; and unity and harmony.

The section of the interview that inquires about important people relates to the central characters in a person's life story. McAdams refers to these characters as "imagoes." The concept of character combines with theme in that some imagoes tend to be agentic and others communal. There can be both common and individual imagoes in a person's life story, and each individual will populate the more universal imagoes in her or his unique way. Common agentic imagoes include the Warrior, the Traveler, the Sage, and the Maker. Common imagoes of communion include the Lover, the Caregiver, the Friend, and the Ritualist. Some imagoes are both agentic and communal, including the Healer, the Teacher, the Counselor, the Humanist, and the Arbiter; some tend to be low in both agency and communion: the Escapist and the Survivor.[4]

A life story identity, according to McAdams, cannot be created until late adolescence. This does not mean that children have no sense of self; rather, they have no autobiography.

McAdams' approach to personality is three-tiered. Each tier is overlaid on the one below, and all three are important in describing the adult personality.

The first tier is that of traits. McAdams calls this level that of "actor," for traits describe one's characteristic way of interacting in the social world. Even small infants have proto-traits, so there is likely an inherited component in addition to factors such as the inter-uterine environment and early attachment. The infant's temperament, such as activity level or fussiness, becomes the well-researched "big five" traits by young childhood: conscientiousness, openness, autonomy, neuroticism, and extroversion. A young child's personality can be well described by reference to traits. "She is very quiet, but curious." "He likes to do things on his own and is the kind of kid who would pass the marshmallow test (a famous experiment concerning young children's ability to delay gratification)." Traits describe enduring qualities that are manifested in the present time. Although McAdams does not directly state it, young children—like little yogis—live mostly in the present. There is a short term past, mostly scaffolded by the adults in her life ("remember when we got that ice cream cone yesterday?") with a few isolated episodic memories; and only a vague sense of future which is conflated in a dichotomous fashion: in the next moment or forever.

By middle childhood a description of traits is necessary but inadequate to describe children, for now they have particular intentions and ways of coping (but see some conflicting research in Chapter 4 which suggests preschool children understand intention, as well). They have gone from being only actors to being agents, which might be thought of as the protagonist in episodic stories. I believe this also is a way of saying that the child has gained a (mostly) short-term future.

It is only in mid-to-late adolescence that the young person becomes capable of an autobiographical identity. This is what McAdams refers to as "authoring;" it is authoring one's own lived autobiography. In authoring one's identity, one is tying together past, present, and future. Finally, the young person has full range of access to the entire time spectrum of her life (McAdams, 2006b). Following from within McAdams's ideas is the notion of a change in the perception of time over the growing years, from being rooted in the present with memories of the recent past that are supported by adults in the child's life, to being able to access in late adolescence a chronological self extending into the future.

With his research authored and co-authored in books and numerous articles, McAdams has done for the recognition of the importance and ubiquity of narrative what Judith Herman did for the recognition of the significance and ubiquity of trauma (see Part 5). Both narrative and trauma are such widespread aspects of the human condition that for much of our clinical and scientific history they were hidden in plain sight.

Let us turn now from the giants of narrative in therapy to the aspects of narrative itself.

Notes

1. One can only speculate from Freud's own early history at being what he called an "Oedipal victor;" and what Alfred Adler would later call "pampered." Freud was the firstborn of his father's third wife (she would have seven other children), and overwhelmingly his mother's favorite. For example, when his sister's piano playing bothered Freud, his parents removed the piano from the apartment (Storr & Stevens, 1998).
2. If this sounds like Freud's Superego, Ego, and Id, one can see the roots. Berne argued that his three parts were all part of Freud's Ego and thus technically different.
3. Virtually all opposition is merely a contrasting style of dealing with the same issue and thus not a qualitative difference.
4. Note the similarity of McAdams' imagoes with some of the Jungian character archetypes described by Pearson and Marr (2007). Agentic archetypes, for example, would include Warrior, Seeker, Sage, and Creator. See Chapter 8.

References

Adler, A. (Ansbacher, H. L., & Ansbacher, R. R., eds.). (1956). *The Individual Psychology of Alfred Adler: A Systematic Presentation in Selections from His Writings.* New York, NY: Basic Books.

Berne, E. (1964). *Games People Play: The Psychology of Human Relationships.* New York, NY: Grove Press.

Berne, E. (1976). *Beyond Games and Scripts.* New York, NY: Grove Press.

Carr, A. (1998). Michael White's narrative therapy. *Contemporary Family Therapy, 20*(4), pp. 485–503.

Epston, D. (2016). The corner-Re-imagining narrative therapy: A history for the future. *Journal of Systemic Therapies, 35*(1), pp. 79–87.

Evans, R. B., & Koelsch, W. A. (1985). Psychoanalysis arrives in America: The 1909 psychology conference at Clark University. *American Psychologist, 40*(8), pp. 942–948.

Feinstein, D., & Krippner, S. (1988). *Personal Mythology: The Psychology of Your Evolving Self.* New York, NY: St. Martins Press.

Feinstein, D., & Krippner, S. (2006). *The Mythic Path: Discovering the Guiding Stories of Your Past-Creating a Vision for Your Future.* Santa Rosa, CA: Energy Psychology Press.

Freud, S. (1896/1962). The aetiology of hysteria. In *The Standard Edition of the Complete Psychological Works of Sigmund Freud: Volume III: (1893–1899) Early Psycho-Analytic Publications*. London: Hogarth Press.

Freud, S. (Strachey, J., trans.). (1900/2010). *The Interpretation of Dreams*. New York, NY: Basic Books.

Herman, J. L. (1997). *Trauma and Recovery: The Aftermath of Violence-From Domestic Abuse to Political Terror*. New York, NY: Basic Books.

Jung, C. G. (Jaffe, A., ed.). (1961/1989). *Memories, Dreams, and Reflections*. New York, NY: Vintage Books.

Keen, S., & Valley-Fox, A. (1989). *Your Mythic Journey*. New York, NY: Jeremy P. Tarcher/Penguin.

Krippner, S., Bova, M., & Gray, L., eds. (2007). *Healing Stories: The Use of Narrative in Counseling and Psychotherapy*. Charlottesville, VA: Puente Publications.

McAdams, D. P. (1993). *The Stories We Live By: Personal Myth and the Making of the Self*. New York, NY: Guilford Press.

McAdams, D. P. (2001). The psychology of life stories. *Review of General Psychology, 5*, pp. 100–122.

McAdams, D. P. (2006a). *The Person: A New Introduction to Personality Psychology, 4th Ed.* Hoboken, NJ: John Wiley & Sons.

McAdams, D. P. (2006b). The problem of narrative coherence. *Journal of Constructivist Psychology, 19*, pp. 109–125.

Pearson, C. S., & Marr, H. K. (2007). *What Story Are You Living*. Gainesville, FL: Center for Applications of Psychological Type.

Sandhu, P. (2015). Step aside, Freud: Josef Breuer is the true father of modern psychotherapy. Retrieved from: https://blogs.scientificamerican.com/mind-guest-blog/step-aside-freud-josef-breuer-is-the-true-father-of-modern-psychotherapy/.

Sophocles. (Reprint 1991). *Oedipus Rex*. New York, NY: Dover Publications.

Steiner, C. M. (1984). *Games Alcoholics Play*. New York, NY: Ballantine Books.

Storr, A., & Stevens, A. (1998). *Freud & Jung: A Dual Introduction*. New York, NY: Barnes & Noble Books.

White, M. K. (2007). *Maps of Narrative Practice*. New York, NY: W. W. Norton.

Part 2

The Aspects of Story and the Foundational Story Model

Chapter 2

The Aspects of Story

As humans we converse in stories; we connect with stories; we remember in stories; we even dream in stories.[1] Our stories comfort us, they prepare us, they bind us, they divide us, and they heal us. We have a storied psyche.

Gregory Bateson once told an adaptation of the following story:

> There once was a computer scientist who became very curious about artificial intelligence and its relation to human intelligence. Accordingly he slipped into the lab late one evening, using his keycard and his voiceprint to access the research supercomputer. Very quietly he typed out his question: "Will computers ever think like humans?" Even the huge computer whirred and flashed for what seemed like ages, performing trillions of calculations. Finally the whirring returned to a hum, and the myriad of lights returned to their usual flashing pattern. The man heard the brief buzz of the printer. He ran to the out tray and eagerly pulled up the sheet of paper. There in neat letters was typed, "That reminds me of a story."
>
> (Adapted by the author from Bateson, 1979, p. 13)

As Bateson humorously reminds us in the above excerpt, it is our stories that make us human; and it is through our stories that we make meaning in an uncertain world.

We are born to a chaotic world, one in which entropy far exceeds order. In one of his many poignant essays, Gregory Bateson (2000) poses the question, "why is it harder to build a house than to tear one down?" He concludes that there are millions upon millions of pathways to destroying a house, any one of which results in destruction, whereas there is only one way to build a house according to a particular architectural plan.

That chaotic world is dangerous, and ultimately deadly for us all. Joseph Campbell notes that the ultimate fact with which all religions wrestle is that life has to feed on life. Death is necessary for life. The Jains, according to Campbell (2004), attempt to avoid this by making as little impact on the world as possible; the Zoroastrians, and by extension, the Christians, either fight it by dichotomizing the world into Good vs. Evil, or deny it by believing this world does not count except as it relates to the world to come; and the Buddhists attempt to transcend it. He notes some indigenous religions that embrace it through their rituals which maim or kill participants. Different approaches, same issue.

In an unpredictable and dangerous world, stories create order. They bind and comfort us, so we need not face the Dark alone. They teach us by examples of success and examples of failure, passing hard-earned wisdom down through generations. In short, stories are perhaps our primary tool for survival.

What is a story? One of the simplest definitions of story is intent expressed over time. But consider the following:

> Turn the crockpot on high. Place in the crockpot a large can of red kidney or chili beans and a small can of black beans, including the juice. Add a large can of whole tomatoes and a small can of diced tomatoes with the juice. Alternatively you may substitute one bottle of beer for the bean and tomato juice (any alcohol will evaporate in the cooking process). If using ground turkey, begin to lightly fry ¾ of a pound in a pan; if using tofu "ground beef," place it directly in the crockpot. Add a half package of matchstick sliced carrots and a bay leaf. Now dice and add one green pepper and one medium onion. Crush and add one garlic clove. Spice with a tablespoon of chili powder; a tablespoon of sugar; and a teaspoon each of sea salt and of pepper. If using, add the lightly fried ground turkey, stir, and replace the top. Cook for three hours on high, then turn to low for an additional four hours. After the first hour, taste and adjust the seasoning accordingly.

The above has implied intent (to make chili), and it takes place over time. Yet a three-year-old child can tell the difference between a recipe and a story.

Now consider this:

> Which is the water without any sand?
> And which is the king without any land?
> Where is no dust in all the road?
> Where is no leaf in all the wood?
> Which is the fire that never burnt?
> And which is the sword without a point?
> Which is the house without a mouse?
> Which is the beggar without a louse?
>
> (Give up? Here are the answers, in order: Water in the eyes (tears); king in cards; the milky way, or a river; firewood; a painted fire; a broken sword; a snail's shell; a painted beggar.)
>
> From James Francis Child (1882/2014)

Here again we have no story. But consider this rendition:

> The son of a merchant passes by a garden where a young lady is picking flowers. He greets her, then asks: "Shall I ask thee riddles, beauteous maiden?"
>
> "Prithee ask them, ask them, merchant's son," replies the young lady. The young man proceeds to ask six riddles. "Well then, maiden, what is higher than the forest? Also, what is brighter than the light? Also, maiden, what is thicker than the forest? Also, maiden, what is there that's rootless? Also, maiden, what is never silent? Also, what is there past finding out?"
>
> "I will answer, merchant's son, all the six wise riddles will I answer. Higher than the forest is the moon; Brighter than the light the ruddy sun; Thicker than the forest are the stars; Rootless is, O merchant's son, a stone; Never silent, the sea; and God's will is past all finding out."
>
> "Thou hast guessed, O maiden fair, guessed rightly. All the six wise riddles hast thou answered; therefore now to me shalt thou be wedded. Maiden, shalt thou be the merchant's wife."
>
> (Child, 1882/2014, p. 3)

What makes the difference between a series of riddles and the story containing riddles? As a way of organizing the world, stories have their own intrinsic order. It is an order that we implicitly grasp, having heard millions of stories. We know when a story conforms to the implicit order and when it does not. When it does not, we may sense that something is off, and that the tale does not move us. Some well-told stories are able to transcend the implicit order. Then despite, or precisely because something is off, the tale does move us. Like a Jackson Pollock painting, it can break the rules, but it does so in a manner that references the rules.

What is that implicit order that we listen for in stories? Stories have universal elements that riddles do not. These elements are related by certain rules. The elements and their rules make up virtually every folktale, myth, and oral tradition story from every culture, and the vast majority of all other stories. Although the content of the tales can differ widely, the basic structure remains the same. Even more than the structure of music, this structure of story is truly archetypal in the Jungian sense.[2] These universal elements and rules make up what narratologists have called a "story grammar" (Mandler, 1984) because, like language grammar, it consists of universal parts connected by rules. The internalization of story grammar begins around age two or three. Even young children remember items or events better if they are ordered in story format, and they will naturally organize events in story format (Mandler, 1984). That internalization of story grammar is what is referred to as a "story schema."

Perhaps our earliest narrative theorist, some of whose works survive, is Aristotle. *Poetics* is a little book about drama and tragedy, but it applies to all stories. In it, Aristotle (trans. 2015) notes that stories have three parts: a beginning, a middle, and an end. In tragedy he labels these as Beginning, Complication, Unraveling (Denouement).

In the late 1800s, the German novelist Gustav Freytag (1895/2012) expanded upon Aristotle's three-act understanding to develop a story arc of tragedy that became known as "Freytag's Pyramid." The pyramid had five components: Exposition, Complication, Climax, Falling Action, and Catastrophe. In the exposition, the setting (time, place, and emotional climate), protagonist, and some of the other major characters are introduced. We may be given some of the back story, and the protagonist's desire is introduced along with the beginning of dramatic tension.

In the Complication phase, the conflict and the drama build until they reach the Climax (now often termed the "midpoint"). The climax is both the crescendo of the action and a point of no return for the protagonist. Whether she will succeed or fail, the die is cast.

Following the Climax is Falling Action wherein the choice at the Climax plays out. There are reversals of fortune such that the tragic hero almost succeeds; and the comedic (remember comedy for the Greeks is a happy ending, not necessarily a funny story) hero almost loses everything.

Finally, the Catastrophe is the resolution, the demise or ruin of the tragic protagonist, or the victory for the comedic hero.

Note for Freytag, as for Aristotle, stories have an inherent symmetry. For Freytag there is the beginning (Exposition) and ending (Catastrophe) with rising action (Complications) on one side of the pyramid and falling action on the other, with the Climax (midpoint) as the fulcrum (or as the top of the pyramid).

Let us look at how this structure applies to tragic ballads. Francis Child was a Harvard professor who, in the late 1800s, begin collecting ballads from the British Isles. We have already met with one of the ballads he collected in the story of the merchant's son and the young maiden. Child ultimately collected over 300 ballads, together with numerous variations of each, thus preserving a fragile folk art form. Unfortunately, Child was not a musicologist, so the tunes to most of these ballads have been lost. Here is a narrative (as opposed to poetic) rendition of Child's Ballad #281 (1882/2014):

> There once was a lofty British ship named the Golden Vanity which commenced to sail on the Lowland Sea (an old term for the Mediterranean Sea). There she encountered a Spanish enemy ship. The cabin boy stepped up to the captain and asked, "what would you give me if I sink the Spanish ship?"
>
> The captain replied, "Why, I would give you silver and gold and the hand of my daughter in marriage!"

"Very well, Sir!" cried the cabin boy, and with that he stripped off his clothes and sprang over the side of the vessel. Carrying a brace and auger (this is an old hand drill and bit—no power tools), he swam undetected to the Spanish ship and bored holes in the wooden hull. Immediately the Spanish ship begins taking on water and lists, finally sinking in the Lowland Sea with all hands.

The cabin boy swims back to The Golden Vanity amid the uproar of cheers from the crew. But the captain immediately regrets his promise, and so turns his back on the swimming cabin boy and orders the crew to set sail. The cabin boy shouts, but his screams grow dim as the ship leaves him in the Lowland Sea.[3]

We can easily see how this old ballad follows Freytag's pyramid precisely. In the Exposition, we are introduced to the nautical setting of a tall British ship sailing the Lowland Sea. We are shown the main characters—the cabin boy, the captain, and the crew; and introduced to the seeming adversary, the enemy ship. Complications involve rising tension. There is an enemy ship within sight, and we worry about possible peril. The lowly cabin boy comes up with a plan, and the captain enthusiastically agrees. Tension mounts and events accelerate as the cabin boy jumps into the sea and swims toward the enemy ship. In the midpoint, or Climax for Freytag, the boy bores holes in the enemy ship and the ship begins to sink. In Falling Action, the cabin boy swims back; as in most tragedy, at this stage there is a point at which it seems the hero will emerge victorious. Like the crew, we believe he will be saved and cheer. But tragedy for both Freytag and Aristotle has reversals. The captain refuses to take the boy back on board, making for the Catastrophe and resolution.

Now let us consider the ideas of Joseph Campbell, the famous mythologist and disciple of Carl Jung. In his first and perhaps most famous book, written in 1949 and called *The Hero with a Thousand Faces*, Campbell shows an astounding breath in his knowledge of myths and folktales from all over the world: from the Americas and western Europe to Pacific islands, Africa, Indonesia, India, China, Australia, and the Middle East. He integrates this vast literature by describing the ubiquity of the hero's journey. And what is the hero's journey? In essence it is a three-act story: separation, journey (initiation), and return; Aristotles's beginning, middle, end. Over the course of the journey, the hero must die to his old self and be reborn anew; in other words, it is a story pattern about change.

Campbell breaks his three stage/three act model into 17 subphases. The hero begins in a familiar setting; familiar, but inadequate in some fashion, whether or not the hero acknowledges it. The hero receives a call to set out on a new path—Jack's mother tells him they have no money or food left, and so he must take their cow to market and sell her. Often, the hero is reluctant to hear or to follow the call. Once having made an initial commitment to the quest, there is often supernatural aid (read: one's deeper wisdom) to cross the first threshold out of the familiar. In western European tales, Campbell notes this is often symbolized by stepping, like Hansel and Gretel, into a dark and mysterious forest; in Pacific Island tales, it is heading out to sea (and into the unconscious for Jung). The hero must meet and overcome many challenges before attaining the boon he sought, and he does so with the aid of various helpers. Having reached his goal, he may be reluctant to return, but having at last decided to return, he is often pursued or meets challenges equally harrowing to those he already endured. The giant thunders after Jack as Jack races for the beanstalk with the magic hen. Finally crossing the return threshold, the hero is now master of the old world and the new. Having faced death, or even having lost his life, the hero no longer fears death. This frees him to live in the moment with neither regret for the past nor fear for the future.

John Yorke (2015) summarizes the pattern as: 1. Either home is threatened or the hero has a problem or flaw. 2. He goes on a difficult journey to find a cure or slay the threat. 3. At the halfway point in the tale he meets the dragon or finds the elixir. 4. Journeying back, he must face the consequences of engaging the threat or taking the cure. 5. He suffers a literal or metaphorical death. 6. Returning home with the boon, he is reborn and home is saved.

Note the similarity of Campbell's overall journey model and that of Prochaska and DiClemente (1983) in their therapeutic stages of change model, which spawned motivational interviewing. Prochaska and DiClemente began by researching smoking cessation. They found early on that a significant portion of people who gave up smoking did so on their own without benefit of either medication or counseling. They became interested in how this process occurred in hopes of being able to apply some of the lessons to smokers who had not been able to quit. What they found, along with Miller's application to create motivational interviewing, became the single most significant revolution in substance abuse treatment since the 12 steps.

Prochaska and DiClemente's stages of change were: 1. Pre-contemplation. This is home before the calling; and "home" is inadequate in an important way. The client is not consciously aware or rejects that she has a problem. Often events or other people have tried to make the person aware, but she has refused the call. 2. Contemplation. This is ambivalence for Prochaska and DiClemente. Although the client now knows there is a problem, there is a tug to deny and refuse to change. She experiences an equally strong pull to make a change, even though this puts her in the woods, in unfamiliar and frightening territory. 3. Preparation/Determination. The client makes a decision to change and starts making plans, small steps. 4. Action. The client actually makes changes. She is open to receiving help from others. This is equivalent to grabbing the boon or slaying the dragon. Now she must face the return. 5. Maintenance. This is the return phase. She is pursued by the dragon of addiction, and must face trials equal or greater to those encountered on the way to sobriety. Many do not survive the trials and "slip," or relapse, and have to repeat the journey again, sometimes multiple times, before truly returning as a changed and sober person.

Much of the effectiveness in motivational interviewing (based upon the above steps) is in the counselor being an effective witness, and in helping the person master the phase in which they find themselves, rather than pressing them to be further in the journey than they are.

Having looked at how the arc or flow of a plot characterizes stories, let us now look at some of the specific and universal narrative elements that make up story grammar. No real surprises here, as it merely categorizes what we have been aware of since early childhood.

The first of these elements is that of exposition, or setting, which is usually described in the first line or two. The setting situates the story in time and place, introduces the main characters, and may also set the emotional tone. In the story of the merchant's son and the young maiden, the setting is outdoors in a garden. We are introduced to the young maiden picking flowers, and the merchant's son who is passing by. We know from the first utterance of the young man that he sees the maiden as quite pretty; and use of arcane words ("thee," "beauteous," and "prithee") suggests the story is set in some long-ago time.

The second element is that of character. There is almost always a main character, or protagonist, who has an intention or a problem. Here we learn of the protagonist's intention to test the young lady to determine if she might be marriage eligible. In addition to the protagonist, there frequently are one or more antagonists; there may also be companions to the protagonist, and helpers along the way.

The plot (a third element) is divided into "episodes;" these are similar to acts in a play. An episode begins with an event (the young man sees a potentially marriage-eligible maiden), followed by a "development"—the protagonist reacts (our young man chats up the young woman), followed by his setting a goal, stated or implied (to determine if the young maid is a potential marriage partner). A goal path follows, which includes an attempt to reach the goal, and the outcome of that attempt. In the ballad, the young man poses six riddles to test the young lady. In the simplest stories, there is a reaction to the protagonist's initial response, followed by an ending. The response to the posing of the riddles is that the young maid deftly answers them all, and the ending has the young man declare that he will marry her.

Each part of the episode is causally connected to the one previous. Chatting up the young woman is causally linked to the prior initiating event of spying her in the garden, and posing the riddles is causally linked to the intent of determining her eligibility. The setting, on the other hand, is not causally linked. It provides the context, with a sort of "and" linkage to the episode(s). These causal links between the aspects of a story episode make for a kind of horizontal flow of the story in time.

Now consider this early foundational memory:

> I am two years old, and it's my father's birthday. His cake had been left out on the kitchen table to cool. I climb onto a chair, and reach, trying to get the icing off my father's cake. I fell backwards off the chair and hit my head on the kitchen floor. I had to go to the hospital.

Once again, we have the setting in the first couple of lines: the story takes place in a kitchen with a table and chair. The time is her father's birthday, and her own age of two. Our young protagonist has the clear intent to eat icing from her father's cake. Her goal path involves climbing onto the chair and reaching for the cake. The consequence is falling, and the causal link to falling is to being injured and taken to the hospital. This foundational story was related by an 11-year-old girl, who was brought to treatment by her mother in part for difficulty with limits and with following instructions.

More complex stories have multiple episodes. Consider this tale, re-told and adapted by the author from Gates and Tatar (2018). The story is originally from *The Brownie's Book*, a 1920 magazine by W. E. B. DuBois.

> One day Br'er Rabbit went to see the King. "Your Highness," he said, "what is Trouble?"
>
> "Oh," responded the King, "you never want to ask after Trouble."
>
> But Br'er Rabbit was curious by nature; and he had heard of this mysterious thing called Trouble. The King's refusal made him even more curious. So, he persisted. "Your Highness, all the other animals speak of Trouble. It's not fair that I don't know what it is!"
>
> "Br'er Rabbit, you are so fortunate not to know Trouble. Do not ask me again!" ordered the King.
>
> "Please, Your Highness! I simply MUST know what Trouble is!" pleaded Br'er Rabbit.
>
> The King relented. He handed Br'er Rabbit a large box. "Take this box with you, but don't open it until you have crossed the wide meadow and you are almost at your home in the briar patch."
>
> Delightedly Br'er Rabbit skipped into the meadow. The box was heavy, and as he grew more tired, he also grew more than a little curious. He stopped. Surely it wouldn't hurt just to peek at Trouble.
>
> A loud voice thundered behind him. "Br'er Rabbit, I told you not to open the box of Trouble until you were almost home!" The King had followed him.
>
> "Oh, I wouldn't do that, Your Highness! I was merely stopping to rest, as the box is heavy." With that the rabbit hopped on.

Soon the box grew even heavier than before. And now Br'er Rabbit thought he heard a faint scratching from inside the box. Surely a little peek wouldn't hurt. He looked behind him. The King was no longer in sight, so Br'er Rabbit sat on an old log and raised a corner of the box.

Out of the box bounded two hounds, barking and yelping as they viciously tore after Br'er Rabbit. Terrified, Br'er Rabbit ran as if his life depended upon it, for indeed it did. And he ran all the way across the meadow until he was safe in his home in the briar patch.

This is a story with three causally related episodes (some stories have episodes that are connected by time but not causation, as when a hero has multiple adventures). In the first episode Br'er Rabbit approaches the King with the intent to learn about Trouble. The Rabbit's request forms the initiating event (often the initiating event comes instead from outside the main character). The King responds and the Rabbit persists. The first episode ends with the King relenting. The second episode is the Rabbit's journey carrying the heavy weight of Trouble while observed by the King. In the third episode, the Rabbit's curiosity overwhelms him, and we have the climax, falling action, and ending.

The main characters are introduced early on, but the place of the setting is scattered later in the story where we learn about the meadow and the briar patch where Br'er Rabbit lives. If the setting is given short shrift, there is another element that is well developed, and that is the element of a moral: "do not seek trouble, for you may find it."

These elements are important to understand because both foundational and life stories consist of the same structure. If we change any of the elements—for example, change the characters so the Rabbit is less curious and the King less wise, we might have a story, for example, where the King orders the Rabbit to take Trouble, which changes the theme and the moral. A change in any one or more of the story elements changes the story. So, too, as we shall see, with foundational and life stories. *If a person can change any element, they can change their story.*

Let us review the elements of a complete story:

1. Author—Each of us has authorship in our own foundational and life stories. That authorship may be more implicit or more explicit. Those with implicit authorship do not feel they author their story at all. Life happens to them; they feel victims of circumstance. This is the story version of the Julian Rotter's social psychology concept of "external locus of control" (Rotter, 1975).
2. Voice/Narrator—A story may be told in one of several voices. Most foundational stories are told in the first person from the perspective of the protagonist. Most folktales and myths are told from an omniscient third-person stance. Occasionally a foundational story will also be told

from this omniscient third-person viewpoint. What might it mean that a person has this degree of removal from the experience of themselves in their own story? A third common voice in stories is that of a more minor character narrator—think Scout and Jem in *To Kill a Mockingbird*; or even from the point of view of the antagonist—think *Wicked*, where *The Wizard of Oz* is told from the perspective of the witch. Where a foundational story is spontaneously told from a non-protagonist perspective, one might wonder what it means to not be identified with the hero in one's own story. We will see later that shifting the voice in a person's story can be used as a technique for better understanding and changing one's story.

3. Context—Here I refer to all of the context: both the external context within which the story is told, and the "exposition," which is the context internal to the story.

   The external context includes the witness(es) to the story, and the time, place and emotional atmosphere where the story is told. This external context can be more or less important. Think of *The Arabian Nights*, where the external context was that of Shahrazad telling compelling stories in order to distract the king from killing herself and other young women. Here, the external context forms a story itself (she ultimately tames and marries the king). The stories she tells are embedded in this larger story; even more complex, some of the stories she tells have stories within them, making for three levels of embeddedness. This is an example of a story that is organized vertically as well as horizontally in time. The external context is crucial in psychotherapy, as it includes the therapeutic relationship, the witnessing by the therapist, and the emotional tone in the consulting room.

   The context within the story—the internal context—is called the "exposition." The exposition is usually contained in the first few lines of a brief story and is a kind of concise introduction, giving the setting (i.e., the time, place, and emotional tone of the story) and introducing the main characters.

4. Character and Roles—Stories have characters who assume certain universal roles, the more common of which include a protagonist and an adversary. The protagonist often has companions as well as helpers.

5. Plot—Plots are almost always about conflict. In general, plots flow from past or continuing present toward the future. The plot begins with an initiating event (which may include a calling in a journey story) and a problem or goal. The protagonist responds, and this leads causally to a response from others or from the environment. After the initiating event, the plot continues to rising action, including conflict; crisis; falling action; and resolution/ending. This pattern is what has been called the "story arc," and, as mentioned above, was first popularized by Gustav Freytag (Freytag, 1895/2012).

6. Theme—The theme of a story may be conceived of in differing levels, from very close to the actual descriptions to much more abstract and generalizable.
7. Moral or Lesson—Many stories contain an explicit or an implied moral. This is an important connection between many foundational stories and an individual's life story.
8. Overall (Meta) Characteristics of the Story—There is a plethora of general story characteristics. One of the major of these we have already met with is the concept of stories being either tragic or comedic. As applied to life stories, the more modern terms are "redemptive" and "contaminated" (MacAdams, 1993, 2001). In the contamination story, a potentially positive outcome turns sad, or tragic. The Child ballad mentioned earlier about the cabin boy is one such example. Alfred Adler had a particularly graphic metaphor for this; he called it "spitting in the soup."

In the redemption story, an important positive lesson is taken from even very difficult events. This is the overall goal of psychotherapy: to turn potentially contaminated life stories into redemptive stories.

A second major meta story characteristic relates to plot movement. The protagonist has only four overall ways (or a combination) for dealing with impediments or adversaries and for moving in one's life story. The three most well-known of these movements were delineated long ago by the early female analyst Karen Horney (1937): toward, away, and against. These make for, respectively, a love story, a journey story, or a battle/war story.

We are reminded now from trauma work of a fourth movement, that of "surrender" ("fight, flee, and surrender"). That fourth approach of surrender also makes for the "freeze," which is the genesis of most trauma symptoms. We also see the freeze in the life stories of people who feel they are not able to approach the next developmental phase; for example, a felt inability to gain a vocation or to make a relationship commitment. We will see later that surrender can also be used to heal.

I would add that the extension of toward is "embrace." Embrace effectively describes much of what we think of as resilience. I will return to these story movement characteristics with examples in later chapters.

There are other overall story characteristics which have been identified, as well. All can be useful in understanding a person's stories and his personal characteristics as well as some of his trouble. Due to space, we will not elaborate much on them, but some are: the continuum of story organization (from loose to rigid) (McAdams, 2006); the complexity of stories (brighter and more complex people are capable of telling more complex stories); the logic of the story flow (related, as we will see, to the developmental stages of storytelling and a person's own logic); story specificity (in general, people with greater difficulty, particularly depression, tell more general and less specific stories); degree of polarization in stories; and the centrality of a particular foundational story to a person's life story. Many of these (organization, complexity, logic, and polarization) relate to earlier or later developmental narrative ability.

We will meet these story characteristics in greater detail as they apply to clients' foundational and life stories in Part 3: *Life and Foundational Story Assessment*.

They are again described together with approaches and techniques from a variety of therapeutic modalities that address each particular element in Part 4: *Changing Foundational and Life Stories*.

Notes

1. Some have argued that we dream in images which we then connect into story upon awakening. No matter; either is an expression of the ubiquity of story.
2. As noted in Chapter 1, archetypes are templates that structure how all humanity across all cultures and all times perceive the world. While there are certain tones and overall structure that is universal in music, our Western system of 12 tones arranged in groups of eight (keys) and six modes (of which two are almost exclusively used—what we now call "major" and "minor" modes) is common, but not universal. Thus, the structure of story is even more widespread and perhaps older than the structure of music.
3. I have re-told the tale here, choosing details from among the various versions. The ship has names other than *The Golden Vanity*; in some versions, the enemy is not Spanish. The various versions even state, and disagree, upon the number of holes bored in the enemy ship. The basic plot and characters remain the same.

References

Aristotle. (Butcher, S. H., trans.). (2015). *Poetics*. New York, NY: Start Publishing.
Bateson, G. (1979). *Mind and Nature*. New York, NY: E. P. Dutton.
Bateson, G. (2000). *Steps to an Ecology of Mind*. Chicago, IL: University of Chicago Press.
Campbell, J. (1949). *The Hero With a Thousand Faces*. New York, NY: Pantheon Books, © Bollingen Foundation.
Campbell, J. (2004). *Pathways to Bliss: Mythology and Personal Transformation*. Novato, CA: New World Library.
Child, F. J., ed. (1882/2014). Ballad 1: Riddles wisely expounded. In *The Project Gutenberg EBook of The English and Scottish Popular Ballads* (Volume I of 5). Urbana, IL: Project Gutenberg. Retrieved May 15, 2019, from: www.gutenberg.org/ebooks/44569.
Freytag, G. (2012; orig. pub. 1895). *Technique of the Drama: An Exposition of Dramatic Composition and Art*. London: Forgotten Books.
Gates, H. L., Jr., & Tatar, M. (2018). *The Annotated African American Folktales*. New York, NY: Liveright Publishing.
Horney, K. (1937). *The Neurotic Personality of Our Time*. New York, NY: W. W. Norton.
Mandler, J. M. (1984). *Stories, Scripts, and Scenes: Aspects of Schema Theory*. Hillsdale, NJ: Lawrence Erlbaum Associates.
McAdams, D. P. (1993). *The Stories We Live By: Personal Myth and the Making of the Self*. New York, NY: Guilford Press.

McAdams, D. P. (2001). The psychology of life stories. *Review of General Psychology, 5*, pp. 100–122.

McAdams, D. P. (2006). The problem of narrative coherence. *Journal of Constructivist Psychology, 19*, pp. 109–125.

Prochaska, J. O., & DiClemente, C. C. (1983). Stages and processes of self change of smoking: Toward an integrative model of change. *Journal of Consulting and Clinical Psychology, 51*, pp. 390–395.

Rotter, J. B. (1975). Some problems and misconceptions related to the construct of internal versus external control of reinforcement. *Journal of Consulting and Clinical Psychology, 43*(1), 56–67.

Yorke, J. (2015). *Into the Woods: A Five Act Journey Into Story*. New York, NY: The Overlook Press.

Chapter 3

The Foundational Story Model

Every day we engage in thousands of interactions, and have millions of thoughts and feelings, as anyone who has ever tried to meditate will attest. We cannot possibly remember all of this, mostly detritus.[1] Why do we remember the events that we do?

Studies have shown that our memory for life story episodes is not evenly distributed throughout our lives. Freud first remarked on what he termed "childhood amnesia." Subsequent studies bear him out on this point; people remember a dearth of stories before the age of three and virtually none before the age of two. Studies of college students show their earliest memory to be at about the age of three (Pillemer, 2001). In part, this is due to the lack of language skills. Early memories are marked by memory for isolated events with little continuity between them.

The other point of uneven distribution is what has been termed "the reminiscence bump," occurring in late adolescence and early adulthood in Western societies. Here there is a plethora of stories. This is a time of major life transition from prolonged dependence on one's family of origin to the establishment of vocation and relationship, and studies show an increase of episodic memories during times of transition (Pillemer, 2001). This transition occurs in the context of fully developed cognitive and story capacity.

But this only tells us that there are periods in life where we commonly remember more stories, and periods where we remember fewer. It still does not tell us why we remember the particular stories we do.

In the middle of Missouri there is a large lake known as "Lake of the Ozarks." Recently the lake has achieved notoriety as the backdrop of the Netflix series *Ozarks*. One of the lake's claims to fame is that it contains more coastline than the state of California. Now, it is a large, irregularly shaped lake, but it is minuscule compared to the smallest of the Great Lakes. How can it contain more coast than California? Is this just hype from the Missouri Department of Natural Resources?

The answer, I suspect, is fractals. Fractals are a visual pattern that emerges in a chaotic system. A chaotic system has pattern but minimal predictability. The weather is a chaotic system. Although we see recurring patterns we are unable to predict weather more than a few days out, and it has been theorized that even if we had a weather station every three meters over the entire Earth's surface, we still could not predict the weather much more than a few days further out than we do now.

A fractal is a shape that recurs similarly at different levels of magnification. A coastline or a lakeshore is a fractal pattern. Take a satellite picture of a coastline, and it will have twists and turns that look very similar to the twists and turns you would find if you zoomed in on one inlet. That, in turn, would be similar to the pattern of twists and turns if you zoomed to a square yard of shoreline, and so on, down to the microscopic pattern between water molecules and sand grains. Zoom in close enough and any coastline measures astoundingly long. Similar patterns within patterns within patterns.

From early adulthood on, everyone has a story of his/her life that defines who they are, how they relate to others, and what they expect from the world (McAdams, 1993, 2001). That life story is composed of many examples of smaller stories (Ribeiro et al., 2010), each with a similar cast of characters, plot, moral, and theme. Fractals—similar patterns within patterns.

There is a synergistic relationship between the smaller stories and one's life story, such that the smaller stories make up the life story, while at the same time our life story helps us select and remember particular smaller stories. This process can range from rigid to flexible. In the more rigid process, a person entertains and remembers little outside a limited cast of characters, plots, or themes; this is, in general, indicative of greater emotional problems.

A given smaller story can also be more or less central to a person's life story. Those that are central, and especially those that are formative, are what are here called "foundational stories." There is a foundational story behind every symptom. Changing those smaller stories, especially the foundational stories, is one way of altering the trajectory of one's life story. Thus, *psychotherapy is the co-changing of a person's life story, and is often performed by a change in foundational stories.*

Note the following foundational story:

> Nathan 3.1 was eight years old when he wrote and colored a small book. He carefully stapled the edges. When it was done, he wrapped it and placed a large stick-on bow on it, then carefully placed it under the Christmas tree. The tag read "Merry Christmas to Dad."
>
> A week later Nathan was playing with his toy cars on the floor of his father's office. Under the desk he happened to peer into the trashcan. There was a large bow and the book he had so carefully crafted. Nathan felt a pain so intense that he thought he might die. He thought to himself, "whatever made me think I could do anything that was worthwhile?"

Would you be surprised to learn that Nathan's presenting problem was social anxiety and lifelong depression? Can we say that his father's insensitivity caused his depression? I think not. Of course, there is no way to definitively test, to grow a control group Nathan exactly like Nathan 3.1, but without the Christmas book experience. It is equally plausible to assume that a depressed Nathan selected this and similar early stories to remember by looking back through a depressed lens. I suspect it is some of both, with the scale tilted more towards the causal impact of a remembered event where that event would be more overwhelming or traumatic to most people; and the scale tilted more toward the depressive life story lens in instances where the story would not likely be universally traumatic and where the depression is more pervasive.

Fortunately, we do not have to decide. It is the synergy between the foundational story and the life story that is important. If a person changes their life story, they change their lens; they will then select different foundational stories, or place a different, more positive and agentic spin on the stories they remember. Alfred Adler showed this many years ago (Adler, 1956). At both the beginning and the end of psychotherapy, he would ask a person for her earliest memory. Often the two stories were of completely different events; but even where they were of the same event, the story was modified in a manner which reflected the changes made over the course of therapy.

Life stories show how we view ourselves, others, and the world around us, and are ultimately composed of foundational stories. Most of us can readily see our lives in "chapters" (Schneiderman, 2015), and each of those chapters are composed of foundational stories with a similar take on ourselves, other people, and context. Thus, change enough foundational stories, or change one or more very central foundational stories, and a person has altered her life story.

John Yorke, in his perceptive and accessible book on narrative theory (*Into the Woods*, 2015) observes that story contains conflict. The protagonist must confront the antagonist, who represents whatever the hero is most lacking, like Winston Smith in George Orwell's novel *1984* where the ultimate torture is housed in Room 101. And what does Room 101 contain? Based on extensive review of all your data and communications over your life, Room 101 contains whatever it is that you fear the most.[2]

The antagonist, then, represents whatever the hero is not—the Shadow for Jung. The hero must leave the familiar and step into an alien environment to pursue what she wants, rarely realizing that what she must gain is what she lacks. What she wants is to buff up her image, her *persona* in Jungian terms. If she just has more wealth, or more acclaim, or the right relationship, then surely she will no longer be bothered by fears of abandonment, or low self-esteem, or unbidden thoughts.

Of course, this is most often how people enter therapy, seeking what they want in their lives, rarely understanding that what they want is a simple, untenable fix that will hide what they lack. Just help me get rid of this depression without having to consider what part of me I am depressing; help me stop drinking without seeing the alcohol as a temporary salve for a deeper wound.

If our psyches are storied, then how does change take place in narrative, and what might that tell us about personal change? Aristotle gives us a hint:

> Reversal of the Situation is a change by which the action veers round to its opposite, subject always to our rule of probability or necessity. Thus in Oedipus the messenger comes to cheer Oedipus and free him from his alarms about his mother, but by revealing who he is, he produces the opposite effect.... Recognition, as the name indicates, is a change from ignorance to knowledge, producing love or hate between the persons destined by the poet for good or bad fortune. The best form of recognition is coincident with a Reversal of the Situation as in the Oedipus.
> (Aristotle, 2013, Part XI)

Peripeteia, or reversal of fortune, is accompanied by *anagnorisis*, which is recognition or discovery—literally re-cognition. It is the reversal of fortune which leads to insight. A situation is confronted by its opposite, leading to insight.

At its heart, a story is a particular way of organizing. It is change through conflict. Change occurs in story precisely *because* of conflict. Yorke spells it out for us. The process is dialectical; act one is thesis, act two is antithesis, and act three is synthesis. The narrative way we learn and grow is by confronting what we reject and disown, ultimately integrating it to form a new platform from which we confront what we then exile. *Dialectical change is built into our narrative being.*

If stories are overwhelmingly dialectical (thesis, antithesis, synthesis), this would seem to imply a three-act story with each act bounded by a turning point. Yorke's insight is that this is so. A story is a dialectic consisting of three acts. Each act is itself bounded by a turning point and consists of three scenes arranged as a dialectic. Further, each scene consists of what are called "beats," also arranged dialectically. Each part has the same shape at all levels; it is dialectical all the way down (fractals, again).

Indeed, as Joseph Campbell (1949) shows (see Chapter 2), three acts are ubiquitous in all of folklore and mythology (home, separation, return; familiar, struggle with the Other, integration). This symmetry of three is what we intuitively expect in a story. If the story differs too much from this, the story feels somehow "off" or wrong. It is the way we see and place order on the world around us.

But what about Shakespeare and the five-act tragedy? How does this fit our model? Yorke notes that a five-act play (e.g., Shakespeare) is actually a three-act play with the second act extended and divided into three. The symmetry continues such that the first and last of the story mirror each other, as do the second and fourth acts; the first half of the third act prior to the midpoint reflects the last half of the third act. Yorke diagrams this in what he calls "the 3-D Roadmap of Change," relating to stories where the protagonist changes. Act One and Act Five are reflections of each other, as are Acts Two and Four. Act Three is bifurcated around the midpoint of the story. The second half of the story is a reflection of the first, making for symmetry within the story.

This understanding makes for many implications for therapy. The problematic story will be similar at differing levels. We have to decide at which level to focus our therapeutic attention: vignette, chapter, or life story; past stories or present unfolding, currently authoring stories. If currently authoring story, where is the person in the dialectic of that story? Are they at "home," in Prochaska and DiClemente's (1983); and (Miller's (2013)) Pre-Contemplation phase (see Chapter 2)? What is their call, and how have they responded to it? As noted in the last chapter, there are four overall ways of responding to a call or to a conflict: approach/embrace, fight, flee, or surrender.[3]

Or perhaps they are on the journey. Are they wrestling with exiled forces, parts of themselves that seem "other?" Have they gotten what they need and are now struggling to integrate it (the Return)? What is our best role as therapist in this moment? Is it witness, companion, purveyor of hope, or midwife?

We conceive of our life story as a three- (or five-) chapter dialectic, as well. Separation, journey, return. Home, battle with alien forces, return. Thesis, antithesis, synthesis. Each chapter is part of the dialectic of that larger story; and each chapter consists of smaller vignettes, each of the same dialectical pattern. Those smaller vignettes are the Foundational Stories. They will share a theme, or introduce a theme that is related to the themes of the current chapter and of the larger life story.

In sum, our very notion of Self is a lived story. Our life story consists of chapters, which, in turn, contain remembered vignettes. These vignettes are remembered through the lens of our life story; that lens either screens out stories that are too dissimilar, or refracts the stories remembered so that their plots and themes and morals are highlighted in a manner consonant with the life story itself. In turn, stories which contain high emotion, and/ or which occur in important contextual times, and/or which are similar to other stories in plot, characters and themes are formative of our life stories.

Each of those stories at every level consists of the same elements: external and internal context; characters, minimally including a protagonist and an antagonist; a plot, which is a problem and its intended solution across time; a theme; and a moral.

The plot of those small and large personal stories moves forward by conflict followed by integration—in short, a dialectical process. Just as between every breath there is a moment of calm, in every one of our stories there is the possibility of change. We carry both moments of calm and the potential for change with us every day.

The foundational story lens does not create a new approach to psychotherapy (although it does offer some new tools and techniques); rather, it provides a context for understanding and utilizing many extant approaches. This narrative understanding is easily integrated into a therapist's given approach while broadening the clinician's awareness and acceptance of other techniques and theories.

The next chapter, Chapter 4, expands on the above ideas, delving into both the parts of story and how we develop our storying ability, providing additional clinical and literary examples.

Notes

1. There have been some famous exceptions. The seminal Russian neuropsychologist, A. R. Luria (1968), penned the book *The Mind of a Mnemonist* about a man who could recall the smallest detail—the weather and what he wore on a particular date, etc. Such a phenomenal memory was an equally phenomenal curse, as his memory was not at all selective. The mnemonist was haunted by his inability to synthesize, plan, or organize the most basic of tasks.
2. Unfortunately, in the novel *1984*, the room contained rats for Winston. Torture, for sure, but very literal.
3. Halstead (2007) has a useful little book where he looks at the client's overall tendency to fight, flee, or surrender, combining this with the areas of Self, Other, and World; and with Jeffrey Young's schemas.

References

Adler, A. (Ansbacher, H. L., & Ansbacher, R. R., eds.). (1956). *The Individual Psychology of Alfred Adler: A Systematic Presentation in Selections from His Writings*. New York, NY: Basic Books.
Aristotle. (Butcher, S. H., trans.). (2013). *Poetics by Aristotle*. The Project Gutenberg E-book of Poetics [E-book #1974].
Campbell, J. (1949). *The Hero With a Thousand Faces*. New York, NY: Pantheon Books, © Bollingen Foundation.
Halstead, R. W. (2007). *Assessment of Client Core Issues*. Alexandria, VA: American Counseling Association.
Luria, A. R. (1968). *The Mind of a Mnemonist: A Little Book About a Vast Memory*. New York, NY: Basic Books.
McAdams, D. P. (1993). *The Stories We Live By: Personal Myth and the Making of the Self*. New York, NY: Guilford Press.
McAdams, D. P. (2001). The psychology of life stories. *Review of General Psychology, 5*, pp. 100–122.
Miller, W. R. (2013). *Motivational Interviewing: Helping People Change*. New York, NY: Routledge.
Pillemer, D. B. (2001). Momentous events and the life story. *Review of General Psychology, 5*(2), pp. 123–134.

Prochaska, J. O., & DiClemente, C. C. (1983). Stages and processes of self change of smoking: Toward an integrative model of change. *Journal of Consulting and Clinical Psychology*, *51*, pp. 390–395.

Ribeiro, A. P., Bento, T., Goncalves, M. M., & Salgado, J. (2010). Self-narrative reconstruction in psychotherapy: Looking at different levels of narrative development. *Culture and Psychology*, *16*(2), pp. 195–212.

Schneiderman, K. (2015). *Step out of Your Story: Writing Exercises to Reframe and Transform your Life*. Novato, CA: New World Library.

Chapter 4

Foundational Stories
Russian Dolls and Magic Mirrors

Foundational stories from early in our lives remain formative in our psyches. Thus, there are developmental layers of story which are built upon in subsequent life phases. Some aspects of life story have roots in pre-verbal meanings. Using life stages as a general template for the influence upon one's story, this chapter elaborates on the following periods and their influence on life story:

1. Infancy: Tone, body theme, and attachment.
2. Toddlerhood: Fragmentation and lack of logic (early pre-operational).
3. Magical—pre-operational: It is during this period that many foundational stories develop, and so they incorporate the naiveté and the irrational logic of the young child.
4. Middle childhood: Linear logic and increased complexity (concrete operational).
5. Adolescence: Identity stories and the protagonist in the world.

These first five phases scaffold our adult stories where story areas include stories of work, stories of love, and stories of parenting. Story devices used include meta-story, flashback, and other devices (formal operational). In addition, they form the templates for the reflections so crucial to our late life stories.

As you read the above summary of how one's story is elaborated over a life, note that, in general, the elements of one's story are crafted in early developmental periods. In later periods, from adolescence on, the stories may become increasingly complex, and different life content areas become elaborated (e.g., one's place in the group and the world in adolescence; the content and one's place in the work world in early to middle adulthood, etc.). These later elaborations in content and complexity are scaffolded upon the story elements *that are already crafted in early childhood*. Imagine a set of Russian dolls, one inside the other. The shape and painting of the very smallest doll at the core of the set is a miniature of all the outside, larger dolls. You might say they are each patterned on the smaller ones inside. Or, think of it like the lens correction in eyeglasses. I got my first pair of glasses when I was seven. I was quite nearsighted; I still remember the wonder of being able to put the glasses on and see the individual leaves on a tree. Now, decades later, I do not have the same prescription I had as a child; but my prescription now is an elaboration on that early one. I am still nearsighted; I will never develop astigmatism, nor become farsighted. Those early glasses were the template for all of my eyeglasses.

Infancy

There is some evidence that certain proto-traits are present from very early: traits that will become introversion or extraversion; optimism or pessimism (McAdams, 1993). The optimistic story is the Greek comedy; the pessimistic story is the tragedy. Thus, the ending of one's life story is, in a sense, present from the very beginning.

Just as there is a developmental progression for humans' physical, cognitive, emotional, and ethical ways of functioning and abilities, there is a developmental progression of our ability to tell and understand stories (Giampaolo et al., 2004). This evolves from a basic clustering of mental images to more complex, "proper" stories with characters that interact with one another in both an internal scenario and in the external world. Chaotic representations coalesce progressively into increasingly consistent narratives. Like the developmental progression in other areas, our narrative development is an iterative process full of regressions and detours. Giampaolo and his colleagues identify a first narrative organizational level as "pre-narrative." This level includes nonverbal bodily states, images of objects both outside and inside (thoughts, memories, sensations) and the representation of relations between aspects of the environment and bodily state. It includes wordless sequences of what happens to the person in her environment.

In effect, this is a pre-story level that generates perceptions of environmental tone and bodily states and sensations which become linked to certain stimuli. Repetitive environmental tone (e.g., nurturing, dismissive, hostile, etc.) forms the basis for the tone of the context of one's later life story. Initially *in utero* and in infancy, the tone is the dyadic tone of the infant's relation to his mother. This tone and the infant's response form a circle that becomes the basis of one's attachment style (Wallen, 2007). Thus, for example, when the mother is all too frequently distracted or otherwise unresponsive to the infant's needs, the child may turn away, becoming avoidant. The mother may feel then that she gets even less from her interactions with her baby, which reinforces her distraction and lack of response (why bother?!), which in turn reinforces the baby's avoidance. This dismissive/avoidant cycle can become inculcated into the growing child's story in the form of the narrative's contextual tone, the expectations of other characters, and one's primary response to others.

Attachment theorists hypothesized two basic attachment patterns: secure and insecure. Insecure attachment was divided into pre-occupied (anxious) and dismissive, later adding disorganized. There is a vast experimental and research literature on attachment, to which Wallen's book is a good entrée. A person's attachment theme has been found to recur in adulthood, and to predict the attachment style of one's child.

The attachment style of adults is frequently measured using a structured interview called the Adult Attachment Interview (AAI). The intriguing aspect of the AAI is that it is scored not just by scoring the particular content answers, but also by looking at the meta-characteristics of how one answers. These have correlates in the meta-characteristics of the foundational stories one tells. Thus, for example, persons with a dismissive style tend to tell shorter and more generalized stories, downplaying the impact of events.

Both the secure theme and the various styles of insecure attachment become inculcated in both the tone of one's life story, and in the expectations one has of how the world is and what one can expect from others. These latter two aspects form what attachment theorists term "internal working models," templates of what one may expect in relationships (read: "story").

The pre-story level can be evidenced in interview with clients of all ages (Ivey, 1986, 1993). In *Developmental Counseling and Therapy*, Ivey notes that some adults remain fixated at a sensorimotor level, while others regress to that level in times of crisis or in early grief. Clients at this level tend to speak in disorganized fragments with a short attention span. The client *is* her feelings and perceptions with no perspective; there is little ability to separate oneself from others or from events. Stories are disjointed and incomplete, lacking the formal sequencing of events we have come to expect in plots. Ivey's approach to clients at this pre-story stage is to help ground them by asking about concrete perceptions: what do they see, hear, feel in the immediate environment and in their disorganized recounting. Ivey applies the developmental principle of working horizontally (that is, within the same developmental level) before helping the client move vertically to different developmental ways of organizing. Only when the client is solid in his own developmental level does Ivey begin to help them move to an adjacent level. He is careful not to skip levels. Thus, asking a client with a sensorimotor, pre-story organization what meaning they make of what they related (a formal operations task for Ivey; a conscious propositional narrative task level for Giampaolo) would make for a huge disconnect to which the client would be unable to respond, and may feel a momentary rupture in the therapeutic relationship.

As the infant's world expands, so too does the size of the environment that contributes to the tone that the baby experiences. As it expands to the other parent and other family members, the emotional tone of the parenting couple's relationship, then of the family, influences the tone of the young child's life story and that of the related foundational stories.

Toddlerhood

Toddlerhood is a time of accelerating abilities, initiated by walking (usually around 12 months of age). Soon those first few wobbly steps become the ability to scale a bookshelf, pull over a lamp, or knock a vase off a table. Young parents quickly learn the futility of "child-proofing" their homes. I remember my wife and I buying locking plugs to seal all the exposed electrical outlets in our house. One day our toddler twin daughters proudly approached us, each with two hands filled with the safety plugs they had collected from numerous wall sockets.

The prodigious increase in physical ability is matched by an increase in mental ability. At some point their vocabulary seems to explode from a few words like "mama" and "dada" (or, in the case of my son, "uh-oh!") to many. And they begin combining words, not always in the correct order, but in ways that make sense.[1]

Emotionally, they demonstrate that they can see themselves as a protagonist separate from the others around them. Certainly, this is evident in the fascination and over-reliance on the word "No!" "No" means that I am separate from you, and have different wishes; and I can sometimes even control your anger by conjuring it up with a "No!" How powerful! This separation and beginning of the notion of self as protagonist is also evidenced in another crucial milestone—the child's first lie. Although other animals, even crustaceans, lie (Laidre, 2009), children as young as two will lie to avoid punishment. This develops hand in hand with the ability to pretend play, and with the ability to recognize oneself in a mirror (Lewis, 2015). There is a budding distinction between me and you, complete with a nascent theory of mind.

At first the notion of me and you, inside and outside, is tenuous. The game of peek-a-boo delightfully plays with this, raising the delicious fear that by shutting off my eyes I can make you disappear. And then, to my repetitive relief and delight, I remove my hands and you are still there!

Beginning between the ages of two and three, children are able to describe linear scripts (first this, then that). For example, to make cookies you first have to get out the oatmeal, the raisins, the milk and egg, the flour, and the sugar. Then you mix them, and, finally, you cook them. With the parents' cueing, the young child learns repetitive actions appropriate to various settings: for example, here is what you can expect in a restaurant or a doctor's office, and here is how you behave. These scripts form what Giampaolo et al. (2004) refer to as the "procedural unconscious narrative." These linear scripts become a foundation for later stories.

The Magic Years

My wife and I and our (then) three small children had set out from the Visitor's Center through the dunes and the sea oats following a guided trail to the natural wonders and the lure of the beach. For our three-year-old twin girls, the world was still new and huge and awash in both excitement and terror. It was a world grounded by *Sesame Street* with the familiar faces of Oscar the Grouch, Cookie Monster, and Kermit the Frog. At a bend in the trail, we came across an old abandoned World War II concrete bunker left adrift in the sand. We read to the children from the Trail Guide about how this bunker for many years had been home to a hermit who had set up residence in it. Finally, the hermit had died as he had lived—alone in his bunker. Our daughter Rachael was unusually quiet. Finally, in a small sad voice she intoned, "I sure am going to miss that frog!"

The ages of three to six, called the "pre-operational period" by Piaget, were appropriately termed "the magic years" by Selma Fraiberg (1966). Those early years see the development of the young child's first stories (the "conscious propositional narrative" for Giampaolo et al., 2004). Those early stories, while disorganized, especially at first, are often crafted around the felt tone of the earlier attachment and family experience.

We tend to think of such incidents as that of Rachael and Kermit, cute though they may be, as errors in hearing and errors in logic. Indeed, there is a whole psychology (CBT) built upon identifying these "errors" and correcting them. But this misses the point that this was not an error on Rachael's part so much as a true expression of how she saw and understood the world. We could tell her that it was not her K(H)ermit who had died; but we could not explain that Kermit could not live both on television with his friends and at the beach by himself at the same time; nor that the odds were infinitesimal that if Kermit were at the beach it would be at the particular beach where she was vacationing; and certainly not that Kermit is not alive to begin with, but is a puppet in a scripted show. For, at Rachael's age, she lived much more in the world of meaning than in the world of objects. We all start incorporated completely in the world of meaning and only gradually—and forever incompletely—enter the world of objects.

Take a look at the following list of "errors of thinking." You will no doubt recognize it as similar to many such lists:

- **Jumping to conclusions** when the evidence is lacking or even contradictory.
- **Exaggerating or minimizing** a situation (blowing things way out of proportion or shrinking their importance inappropriately).
- **Catastrophizing** or over-focusing on the worst possible outcome of a situation.
- **Disregarding important aspects** of a situation.
- **Oversimplifying** things as good/bad or right/wrong.
- **Over-generalizing** from a single incident (a negative event is seen as a never-ending pattern).

- **Mind reading** (you expect other people to know what you're thinking or want; or you assume people are thinking negatively of you when there is no definite evidence for this).
- **Emotional reasoning** (your logic is clouded by your feelings).

The cognitive behavior therapy approach is to teach clients to recognize these "errors," then to develop a logical comeback, which they then work to integrate into their self-talk. For example, "my wife is fixing fish yet again for dinner. She should know by now that I'm tired of eating fish. Hmmm—perhaps I'm mind reading and she doesn't know I don't want fish again. I need to call her."

But look at the list of "errors" again. Let us let go for the moment of the stance of judging everything by the standard of how well or poorly it conforms to the principles of formal logic. When do I make conclusions without "evidence;" lack any notion of grey, seeing the world in a dichotomous, either-or fashion; and know that important people in one's life know what I'm feeling or thinking? When, in other words, am I at the center of a simplistic universe?

It is, of course, in that pre-operational period between three and five or six where Piaget famously demonstrated that young children believe the moon follows them down the street. Jungian analyst Dr. Julie Bondanza remembers visiting her sister's family when her nephew was three or four years old. One evening he ran excitedly into her bedroom and pointed out the window. "Look, Aunt Julie—I made the moon rise!" (Bondanza, 2018). What from one viewpoint were errors, from another are a pretty good list of how the pre-operational child sees the world.

And how do we best work with the pre-operational child? Any parent can tell you the severe limitation of pointing out the logical "errors" in the child's thinking. At worst, it can make her feel as if she is held to a standard that she has no way of comprehending; at best, it is just ineffective. So, when the young child awakes at night terrified of the monster under the bed, the logical parent turns on the light and opens the closet door. Then has the child look with him under the bed. "See! What did I tell you? No monsters there. Now go back to sleep!"

Anyone who dares to remember being a small child him or herself knows that monsters hide from lights and parents. Of course, no one could see the monster when mommy and daddy were in the room, for that's when they were hiding. But as soon as the light goes out and the door closes. . . .

A far more effective approach is to present the child with a magic stick (a yardstick will do) or a jar of bubble stuff. "When the monster returns (because he will), blow these magic bubbles in his direction (or touch him with this magic stick) and the monster will either leave, or he will sit down for a chat. And if he sits down for a chat, please remember all that he tells you so that you can tell me tomorrow morning."

The magical way of organizing does not just morph (magically!) into a rational way of organizing. Rather, we develop a rational way of understanding the world layered on top of the magical. Under the right circumstances, we are all still quite capable of viewing the world through this older lens. In fact, the majority of emotional symptoms were formed from some aspect of a pre-operational story that we still retain, and that awaits only the proper trigger to unfold yet again.

> For example, Harriet 4.1 was loved at work. She would always take on the extra project, stay late to finish, and never complain. Bosses could not ask for an easier employee; that is, until one late fall when she became seriously depressed after a project was late. The depression would come in waves, the waves finally becoming smaller in the late spring. Her husband, a political scientist and academician, worried terribly for his wife, but had no concept of how to help. He thought a vacation away might brighten her mood, so the following fall he rented an isolated mountain cabin for the two of them. Harriet's depression returned with a vengeance.
>
> Harriet had spent her first five years in the same small town in Ohio where her great grandparents had settled. Her grandparents, all of her aunts and uncles, and a gaggle of cousins—as well as her parents—surrounded and embraced her in the early years. Then, in the late fall when Harriet was six, her parents struck out for western Oregon hoping to shed what they considered the shackles of small town Midwest in search of the beacon of personal and sexual freedom and expression reputed to pervade the West Coast of the early 70s. As her parents began to "express themselves," jealousy and misplaced rebellion tore into their marriage. Harriet laid awake late into the night listening as her parents shouted and cursed at each other. In the daytime, Harriet worked even more diligently at school, but to no avail. Her father moved out, and her mother was host to a succession of boyfriends. Trying desperately to be no trouble, Harriet got herself to the school bus most mornings while her mother, groggy from booze and sex, slept in.

Remember that the moon follows young children down the street, and their world—how they understand the world—revolves around them. Little wonder that Harriet's pre-operational story was that she must have done something horribly bad to cause her parents to take her precipitously from the bosom of extended family to a strange land and a new school where she knew no one. And her neediness must have caused the rift between her parents. It was on her to keep what small family she had left together; and she could do this only by displaying no needs, making no waves—by being the "perfect" child. Since her parents fought even more and ultimately separated, she must have failed horribly at being good enough. This was further proof of her badness.

56 Foundational Story Model

The combination of timing (late fall) and "failure" (missed deadline) had triggered the depression she felt when uprooted as a child. The vacation became yet another uprooting. Treatment consisted not of convincing her that her depression was illogical (which would only be further proof of her imperfection and failure), but in identifying and helping Harriet change the little girl's story.

In the pre-operational period, the child now has moved beyond the linear sequencing of events in scripts to a concept of intention and goals. For a long time, narrative theorists believed that the stories of pre-operational children showed characters only as actors with no mental life. The development of intention that was not just inferred from a character's action was thought to take place only in middle childhood, at age eight or nine (Piaget's concrete operational stage; see for example, Chapter 1 on Dan McAdams). In an innovative study, Nicolopoulou and Richner (2007) show that agency is common in the stories of four-year-olds; it was the methodology that prevented earlier researchers from seeing this.[2] The stories of three-year-olds are, by and large, those of actors, but they likely understand intentionality and have just not yet learned to craft it in a story. Here is an example story from Nicolopoulou and Richner, 2007 (Table 1, page 418):

> Once there was Peter Pan and then a knight came, and Captain Hook. He fighted and the knight and Peter Pan fighted. Cat Woman and Joker fighted too.

By five, children integrate personhood into their stories—the reciprocal impact of internal states on the external world (see the Introduction re: the function of story in integrating the internal and external worlds). Look at the following story by five-year-old Edgar, from Nicolopoulou and Richner (2007, p. 426):

> Once there was Robin Hood. Then a bear came. But the bear was nice. And Robin Hood thought the bear was evil so he shot an arrow at the bear. But the bear knocked the arrow out of the way. The bear didn't fight Robin Hood. So he shot another arrow at the bear. But the bear again knocked the arrow out of the way. After that the bear didn't run at Robin Hood. Bear was a nice bear. So then that told Robin Hood that the bear was a nice bear. So they were friends. Then a bad guy came. The bear and Robin Hood fighted the bad guy. And the bad guy died. And Robin Hood and the bear won the fight. The end.

This is a sophisticated story that not only recognizes internal states, but explains actions by the acknowledged false belief that the bear was one way (evil) when the bear was really another way (nice).

It is during this pre-operational period that many children have an imaginary playmate, and the two craft numerous adventures together. The imaginary playmate is the dawning of the character of the companion—Robin to Batman, Sancho Panza to Don Quixote, Samwise Gamgee to Frodo Baggins.

The stories told and remembered during the magic years have a developmental significance for both later development and for adult personality (Mulvaney, 2011). It is in this period that many crucial foundational stories originate, replete with all the "faulty logic" and egoism of the small child.

Middle Childhood

Middle childhood constitutes what Piaget termed "concrete operations." Logic tied to the concrete, observable world gradually replaces magic. At first it is quite rigid and rule bound. I remember as a child playing "Boy Come Across" with neighborhood friends. This was a simple game played with two lines about 50 feet apart. All the children except one stood behind one of the lines. The lone child stood in the middle. At a signal, the other children ran across the space between the two lines while the child in the middle attempted to tag them. Anyone he tagged joined him in the middle for the next round. The game continues until all children have been tagged.

If a new child moved into the neighborhood who played the game in a manner that anyone tagged by the person in the middle was out, and had to sit out of play until the next game, no one would have thought that he had learned a variation of the game. They would just believe that he did not know how to play. There is only one way to play the game, and that is our way.

Although younger children can order events sequentially, this ability becomes better developed. For the first time, the child is able to organize events by the season of the year.

The length, breadth (e.g., including Who, What, and When in a story), and thematic coherence of children's autobiographical stories increases throughout childhood from ages four to ten (Bauer & Larkina, 2017). The stories become more complex, coherent, and flexible (Mulvaney, 2011).

Despite this increase in autobiographical storying ability across middle childhood, even the ten-year-olds' ability paled in comparison to the length, completeness, or thematic coherence of adult women. This lends further support to McAdams' view that true autobiographical ability does not emerge until adolescence. Children can tell increasingly complex stories of individual incidents, but even this ability to narrate a particular story does not approach that of adults. We will see that the ability to combine autobiographical stories into a thematic whole awaits the next phase: adolescence.

Adolescence

While storying ability develops somewhat quantitatively and progressively over early and middle childhood, adolescence sees a qualitative change in narrative ability (Mulvaney, 2011). In adolescence, the young person is at last able to combine foundational stories into an overarching story of her life. Molding these stories into a meaningful whole is what Habermas and Bluck (2000) refer to as "autobiographical reasoning." According to McAdams (1993), it is only in adolescence that a person becomes able to develop a life story and the reflective identity that emerges from it. Habermas and Bluck (2000) agree, noting that the creation of a life story involves the ability to create a fully coherent story of one's own life. Of the four forms of story coherence they identify (temporal, causal, thematic, and cultural), the thematic and the causal develop only in later adolescence. The thematic coherence allows the budding adult to connect stories seemingly disjointed by time (past occurrences from various periods, future hopes) and by storyline to become thematically integrated into "events that shape who I am." While the idea of protagonists having intent, and of one event leading to another, develops in earlier childhood, it is not until late adolescence that the young person is able to apply this to himself. Now he can see that choices he made or incidents he experienced have affected who he now has become.

It is also in adolescence that Giampaolo et al.'s verbal interactive narrative level is realized. This ability goes beyond the ability to understand and tell a consistent story to the ability to develop a mutual story through dialogue. The ability to create a shared story is the basis of a long-term satisfactory relationship, including marriage. How many couples have you seen where one or both are temporarily or chronically unable to create a shared narrative? Each may experience the other as an intruder or obstacle in one's own story; or they may co-exist amicably, living separate lives and separate stories, but never creating a shared story of the two of them as a couple. Often the work of the couple or marriage therapist is to promote the development of just such a shared story, not just the story of you and of me, but the story of us.

As in all developmental theories, the previous ways of organizing are neither completely subsumed nor lost. Under stress (Ivey, 1986); or in personality disorders (Giampaolo et al., 2004) a person's stories may regress to a former level of story organization. Further, a change in early organizations (e.g., a change in basic emotional tone from threat to safety) can ricochet through the more developed stories of the self.

Culture

> Nathan 4.1 was an executive in a large multi-national governmental organization. He had very different roots than his colleagues in his Western European and American controlled establishment, even though the organization is one known for its diversity. Nathan grew up in a small rural African village. One day when he was but a small child, the village elders visited his parents' shack. It seems they had been informed in a dream that Nathan would be the next Chief. In a place where

few could read and write, the village found the money to send him to school in a medium-sized city some hundred miles distant. Nathan did well, and when he graduated, the village raised the funds to send him to faraway Oxford University in England. Nathan traveled the world for the multi-national governmental organization he joined after Oxford; he never returned to live in the village where he was born. But the village never left him, either. The village sported one telephone, a pay phone near the center installed years earlier by some aid organization. Nathan would get collect calls, sometimes, depending upon where he was, in the middle of the night his time. People would ask him to settle land disputes and marital squabbles; he was called upon to decide on amends for thievery and to resolve family arguments. After all, he was Chief.

Culture is collective story (Howard, 1991). In a sense, culture is the meta-story within which one's foundational and life stories form. This meta-story provides a list of acceptable roles, story characters, themes, and primary plot lines for the individual. It also provides normative time slots for certain important transitional events (going to school, getting married, having children, working, etc.) (Bohn & Berntsen, 2008). The timing, and sometimes even the events themselves, vary from one culture to another (for example, "retirement" is not a phase in many cultures).

In an eloquent and humorous essay in the *New Yorker*, Rebecca Solnit (2014) contrasts her mother's culturally derived view of perfection with that of several California Native American tribes. She notes her mother's view is based on the Biblical story of Adam and Eve where anything short of perfection becomes sin and is punished by banishment—even talking with snakes and having unapproved fruit snacks. The Native American story, by contrast, is that of Coyote—unpredictable, quixotic, lecherous and creative. The contrast is between a world where misfortune is the result of never measuring up; and a world that is itself messy, beautiful, cruel, and unpredictable. What different life stories are crafted from such differing cultural narratives!

Let us now enter into the importance of cultural stories.

> The room was furnished mostly with antiques. There were velvet chairs with little claw feet and a matching velvet couch with a spool side table. Crystal prisms hung from the lamp on the table, and they turned the afternoon sunlight into sparkling blues and reds and purples. A large gilded mirror hung over the couch where Alice lazed stroking the white kitten. For a while he was content to cuddle and purr, but presently he became restless. After batting at one of the prisms, he climbed onto the back of the couch. Alice wondered lazily if she should corral him, but the effort seemed rather monumental. Instead she watched with half closed eyes as the white kitten walked along the top of the couch

staring intently at the kitten in the mirror. As she watched drowsily the smooth, hard mirror glass began to swirl slowly like a languid pond. Suddenly the white kitten leaped through. Alice sat bolt upright. The kitten was nowhere to be seen, not in her drawing room nor in the mirror room. Alarmed, she climbed up on the back of the couch and, holding her breath, jumped into the mirror.

(Re-written and adapted by the author from Dodgson, 1991, update 2016)

Whether it is passing through into the mirror room, or going down the rabbit hole, or entering the wardrobe, or walking through the wall in the train station, each of these stories describes passing through some wormhole into a place that not only is unfamiliar and peopled with unaccustomed characters, but into a place where even the rules of how things operate have changed. All of us have or will experience this in each of the four great life transitions[3]: 1. Coming of age—moving from decades of dependency to taking our place as a responsible adult part of society. 2. Marriage—joining not just our lives and our legality with another person, but intertwining our stories in a way of which only identical twins have any pre-cognition. 3. Childbirth—now we have gone from two to three parts in a manner that no experience with babysitting or with younger siblings can ever prepare us for. 4. And, finally, sickness and death, the final magic mirror. Each of these transitions is similar in that we must let go of how our lives have been and of our former stories, even though we cannot know what the experience is like on the other side. Each of these is a qualitative change in our life course entailing a profound loss followed by movement into the unknown. More and more, the wreckage of those who have failed successful passage is strewn all about us: the child-man who cannot hold a job, who still depends on parents to bail him out, who perhaps still remains playing games in the basement; or the couple who, like all couples, after two or three years in, struggles with what is me vs. what is us in the face of the fading glow of that one-dimensional shiny projection of the ideal man/woman. Instead, you wake up beside another human, one who refuses to replace the cap on the toothpaste. And instead of combining their stories, they divorce, searching again for that ideal mate, never realizing they are only serially cramming real people into the one-dimensional ideal in their heads. Or the couple who neglects their child by holding him too close for too long, rendering him vulnerable to not holding a job, continuing to depend on his parents to bail him out, or hiding in the basement with his games.

Besides giving us rules by which to live, and helping us distinguish who is in and who is out, and who is up and who is down, cultures provide rituals (a ritual is an enacted myth) and witnesses for those great life transitions.

In our Western cultures there are major problems associated with the uber-mobility of our society, such that families are scattered across time zones and few people live in the same place long enough to find or establish cultural roots, and religious membership is declining.

These factors leave people alienated from the very resources that could help them navigate life's major transitions. In this vacuum, a significant number turn to psychotherapists. A major therapeutic role becomes acting as a substitute culture, complete with witness and shaman to steer people through coming of age, marriage, birthing, and death. We cannot do this by attacking the symptoms people express from their strain, but by helping them find the stories, the guides, and the hope that allows them to build a new story, one that allows them to thrive on the other side of the mirror.

Notes

1. This understanding was one of the coups in the famous debate between the linguist Noam Chomsky and the behaviorist B. F. Skinner. Skinner argued for language acquisition as a product of gradual accumulation by reinforcement. Not only does that not explain the sudden vocabulary explosion in toddlers, but, Chomsky noted, it does not explain how toddlers combine words in the wrong order, but in an order that nonetheless makes sense.
2. Earlier researchers cued stories with pictures or story stems, and worked in a laboratory setting. Nicolopoulou and Richner worked in the children's familiar school environment and did not prompt children by asking them to tell a story to a picture or to a particular topic, but instead had them freely tell stories on any topic they chose.
3. A fifth transition is, of course, birth itself. If you have not given or witnessed birth, there are YouTube videos of natural, healthy childbirth. It will give you a sense of how radical and traumatic is that transition. Cultural rituals around birthing may welcome the newborn, but are largely focused for the parents.

References

Bauer, P. J., & Larkina, M. (2017). Predictors of age-related and individual variability in autobiographical memory in childhood. *Memory*, pp. 1–16.

Bohn, A., & Berntsen, D. (2008). Life story development in childhood: The development of life story abilities and the acquisition of cultural life scripts from late middle childhood to adolescence. *Developmental Psychology*, 44(4), pp. 1135–1147.

Bondanza, J. (2018). Personal Communication.

Dodgson, C. (AKA Lewis Carroll). (1991, update 2016). *Through the Looking Glass*. Urbana, IL: Project Gutenberg. Retrieved June 7, 2019 from: www.gutenberg.org [EBook #12], Chapter 1, Looking Glass House. (no page numbers).

Fraiberg, S. (1966). *The Magic Years: Understanding and Handling the Problems of Early Childhood*. New York, NY: Scribner.

Giampaolo, S., Giancarlo, D., & Semerari, A. (2004). A model of narrative development: Implications for understanding psychopathology and guiding therapy. *Psychology and Psychotherapy*, 77(Pt. 2), pp. 231–246.

Habermas, T., & Bluck, S. (2000). Getting a life: The emergence of the life story in adolescence. *Psychological Bulletin*, 126(5), pp. 748–769.

Howard, G. S. (1991). Culture tales: A narrative approach to thinking, cross-cultural psychology, and psychotherapy. *American Psychologist*, 45(3), pp. 187–197.

Ivey, A. E. (1986). *Developmental Therapy: Theory Into Practice*. San Francisco, CA: Josey-Bass.
Ivey, A. E. (1993). *Developmental Strategies for Helpers: Individual, Family, and Network Interventions*. North Amherst, MA: Microtraining Associates.
Laidre, M. E. (2009). How often do animals lie about their intentions? An experimental test. *American Naturalist, 173*(3), pp. 337–346.
Lewis, M. (2015, Mar–Apr). The origins of lying and deception in everyday life. *American Scientist, 103*, pp. 128–135.
McAdams, D. P. (1993). *The Stories We Live By: Personal Myth and the Making of the Self*. New York, NY: Guilford Press.
Mulvaney, M. K. (2011). Narrative processes across childhood. *Early Child Development and Care, 181*(9), pp. 1153–1161.
Nicolopoulou, A., & Richner, E. S. (2007). From actors to agents to persons: The development of character representation in young children's narratives. *Child Development, 78*(2), pp. 412–429.
Solnit, R. (2014). Coyote. *The New Yorker*, December 22 & 29, p. 76.
Wallen, D. J. (2007). *Attachment in Psychotherapy*. New York, NY: Guilford Press.

Part 3

Life and Foundational Story Assessment

Chapter 5

Gathering Stories

The most important and ubiquitous technique for gathering stories is that of being attuned to the client's tales. Clients constantly tell stories to describe their experience, their memories, their wishes, their feelings. Like all of us, they connect, explain and justify with stories. With a focus on the stories, the clinician is in a better position to help the client expand on partial narratives and identify together the themes and extracted meanings. This focus not only improves the therapeutic relationship, but begins to modify the stories themselves, and helps identify foundational stories that may require more intense focus. As David Berger (1989, p. 249) said, "Knowing more about the stories that rule us not only makes our lives richer but it makes it possible not to be as influenced by them as one had been in the past."

It is helpful not just to take note of a client's stories, but to ask for specific, narrative examples. Thus, the clinician approaches each interview with a storied attitude—always listening for stories, and asking for story examples.

Clients most often tell stories spontaneously as well as in response to direct questions. Two stories that form useful starting points are *The Instigation Story* and *The First Occurrence Foundational Story*. The Instigation Story is the story of the recent occurrence of symptoms that had the client decide to seek help. A person's attitude toward the problem (away, against, surrender, or embrace) is often highlighted. The client's stage of change also becomes apparent (a brief explanation of DiClemente and Prochaska's Stages of Change as it models the story arc is included earlier in Chapter 2).

The First Occurrence Foundational Story is the client's first remembered episode of having anything like their current symptoms.

> Nathan 5.1 came to therapy in middle age for help in maintaining sobriety. Nathan had been diagnosed with pancreatic cancer to which alcohol was a contributor. For years he had gone to a bar after work, telling his wife he was working late; or had, on occasion, even slipped out of work to drink. He remembered the story of his first use of alcohol. It was at age nine; he and a buddy were playing at his friend's house. They snuck into the garage where his friend's father kept cases of beer

in stacks. Nathan and his friend broke into one of the cases and stole two beers. They managed to open them and begun to drink. Nathan found the taste was awful, and he remembers throwing up in the friend's backyard. However, when asked what part of the story stood out for him, he said it was tearing open that case. They chose a beer case that was toward the back so the crime would not be immediately evident. Asked how he felt, Nathan replied, "Excited—almost exhilarated." The excitement continued as the boys searched for a means to open the bottles without being seen by the friend's parents.

Note that alcohol was associated not with the bad taste, but with the thrill of not getting caught. Without inquiry, this might have been taken as a story of *drinking leads to bad consequences*, and Nathan's alcoholism to the point of endangering his life would seem inexplicable. *It is not what happens as a result of the story, but the moral or lesson one takes that determines the impact.* As with Nathan, the consequences and the moral may be unrelated. We will return to this observation later. For both the First Occurrence and the Instigation stories, it is important to get the setting; the plot, including lead in, sequence, and consequences; roles and characters; and the moral (often revealed by what stands out in the story).

Symptoms are often not just problems, but are also solutions to untenable situations or to feelings in a larger story. In listening to the First Occurrence and Instigation stories, the clinician can begin to ascertain whether this is the case; and, if so, what the function of the symptom might be in that larger story. It is for this reason that the Instigation and First Occurrence stories are included in the Foundational Story Interview, covered in the next chapter (Chapter 6).

In order to gather stories, it is important to have methods that allow the clinician to enable the client to travel from a feeling, a symptom, or an expression of speech to the stories they represent. This is an important supplement to listening for and asking directly for stories. Sometimes a Foundational Story is dissociated from the symptoms that are part of it such that the client experiences symptoms that are unexplained or "out of the blue." This occurs especially in trauma, but in other circumstances as well. Accordingly, three techniques for uncovering hidden foundational stories are described next. The first is the Bridge, originally delineated by John and Helen Watkins (1997), but with important modifications and variants by Mark Lawrence (Personal Communication, February 11, 2009), Richard Kopp (1995, 1998), and others. The second technique is the use of spontaneously produced metaphors to unpack, and at times help change, the connected story. The Invented Story, where a client is asked to make up a story that might account for the symptoms, is yet a third procedure. Finally, dreams are stories we tell ourselves about our lives, but space does not allow for suggestions on working with dream stories. Explanations of these techniques follow.

The first of these practices is called the Bridge. Various authors have referred to an Affect Bridge, an Emotional Bridge, or a Somatic Bridge, or even a Cognitive Bridge, but these are all really the same technique applied in differing circumstances. It is an extremely useful and powerful tool for unearthing foundational stories, and the interested clinician is encouraged to practice it. The Bridge is helpful in connecting a feeling or symptom to its associated story. It can be applied in cases of trauma where dissociation may prevent access to part or to all of the traumatic occurrence.

Both the Affect and the Somatic Bridge techniques were first described by the hypnotherapist husband and wife team of John and Helen Watkins (1997). In the Watkins' version, the client was first placed in a hypnotic trance. The client was then asked to experience the troubling affect (or sensation for the somatic bridge) in the session. She is then told that the affect will take her back to the first time she had the feeling. Another image that the Watkins use is that of traveling back in time as on a train with the track being the problematic affect. Inevitably the present is linked in memory to the past foundational story through the affect. While having the client in a trance state can be helpful in using the technique, the bridge can be applied without using hypnosis (Kopp, 1998; Noricks, 2011; M. Lawrence, Personal Communication, February 11, 2009, agree).

M. Lawrence (Personal Communication, February 11, 2009) makes the point that it is important for the client to experience the affect sufficiently and to remain with it for a few moments. After respectfully asking the client for permission to work on an issue, he would help the client gain as clear an experience of the involved affect as possible, including its bodily manifestations. "How do you experience that feeling? Is there an image, a feeling in your body, or something else?" If a bodily feeling was involved, he would ask about the nature and location of the sensation. Then he might ask how large it was, and even what colors and textures were involved and whether it moved or was stationary. If the client reported an image, he might ask her to describe the image with enough clarity that he could draw and color it.

After the client has described the image or sensation as clearly as she can, Lawrence would ask, "I wonder if you would be willing to make that (sensation/affect) a little more intense? Now I'd like you to increase the intensity so that it is just short of unbearable. Don't let it shade into unbearable, just bring it right up to the brink. Stay with it for a few moments. Now let that (sensation/affect) take you back to the first time you experienced it. Don't try to remember; just let the feeling take you back."

Kopp's (1998) variation is to have the client engage in the sensation or affect, then warn her that he is about to ask a bit of an odd question. He then says he would like the client to tell him the earliest memory that comes to mind, a memory of a specific episode. The memory will, of course, be related to the affect or sensation of focus.

The key steps, then, to bridge from a current somatic experience or affect to the foundational story that either initiated the experience or which encapsulates the experience are:

1. Ask permission to focus with the client on the sensation or affect.
2. Have the client focus on the affect or sensation. If the experience is already intense, you can proceed to #3; if not, encourage the client to increase the intensity, but not so much that it exceeds her tolerance and becomes unbearable. Failing to take sufficient time and to make the experience sufficiently intense is the most common clinical error.
3. Either encourage her to let the feeling take her back to the first time she experienced it, or ask her to recall an early memory.
4. In most cases, this will result in a foundational story. Asking the client to tell or re-tell the story in the first person will make the episode available for any of the techniques described in Parts 4 and 5 for changing stories.

A second method for accessing foundational stories that may not be in the client's immediate awareness—or which may even be dissociated and unavailable—is through the use of metaphor. A metaphor is a connection between two things. A story also connects two or more states; the protagonist transitions from one state to another: that, in effect, is the bare bones of plot. Because it relates two perceptions, a metaphor is, in effect, an encapsulated story. The encapsulated story can be productively expanded. In the very accessible and practical clinical book *Metaphor Therapy*, Richard Kopp (1995) describes a method of working with metaphor that can be used to expand the foundational story condensed within the metaphor.

Much of our language is metaphorical, and Kopp would have us tune in to the important metaphors that clients use. Our speech is replete with metaphors if we only listen for them. In just recent days clients have told me, "my husband is so walled off I don't feel I can reach him," and "there's this big hole in my life that terrifies me" and "sometimes I feel not so much like I'm drinking, but like my beer is swallowing me."

The following is an integration of Kopp's technique with an emphasis on story. After noticing a metaphor, help the client expand the imagery. "When you say that your husband is walled off, what is the image that comes to mind?" Once the client describes a scene, help her enlarge it without introducing your own imagery. Ask open-ended questions and perceptual questions (how large is the wall? Tell me about any colors. How would you describe the texture?). Get the protagonist's position: are you in the scene, and if so, where?

With the expansion of the scene you can begin to help the client unpack the story. "What do you imagine happened before that might have led up to this scene? What might happen next? What is the feeling? If you and I were watching a video of this story, what would we see?"

The next step is to inquire about change: "how would you like to change this story?" Have the client imagine living the changed story. "What is the feeling like now?"

Finally cycle back to the initial life situation. "How is that story about the wall like your situation with your husband?" And then, "how might the change you made in the story inform you about the situation with your husband?"

The steps are:

1. Notice your client's metaphors. Pick a metaphor that seems relevant to your client's current concern.
2. Underline the metaphor by repeating it: "you say you feel as if the beer is swallowing you."
3. Begin unpacking the metaphor by asking for the associated image.
4. Help the client expand on the image without introducing your own imagery.
5. Having expanded on the scene, help unpack the associated story by introducing time—what occurred before and after the scene.
6. Ask the client if he would like to change the story, and if so, how.
7. Have the client live the altered story in imagination.
8. Bring the story back to the current life situation that led to the metaphor. See if the change in the story has any wisdom for the client's concern.

The Invented Story is another technique useful when the client has emotional or physical symptoms of unknown origin. It relies on guided imagery, so it is important to obtain the client's permission before beginning. You might say something like "there is an exercise that may give you and I some useful direction to help with your (symptom). It involves guided imagery. Would you be OK with trying it?"

Having obtained permission, have the client uncross arms and legs, settle into his seat, then take several deeper, calming breaths from the stomach. I usually say something like, "you may want to leave your eyes quiet and unfocused; or you may wish to close them, whichever seems more calming." Some people who have been traumatized and people who may have either weaker ties to reality or suspiciousness can become more tense, even agitated, in closing their eyes. Therefore, I give the client the choice. Often someone who has opted to keep his eyes open and unfocused will later close his eyes spontaneously.

If the client has already established a calm place (see Chapter 19), help him return there, becoming aware of the range of sensations in the scene.

Then tell the client, "we're going to the movies. I'd like you to pick a very comfortable theatre, one with large, reclining chairs. Find a favorite seat and settle in. Push the button to recline the chair to the most comfortable position for watching the screen. Now let the lights dim, and the projector begin. It is a scene showing a man much like yourself, and he, too, is experiencing depression. Where is he? Watch as the camera pans around his surroundings. What do you see? Describe the scene. Who else is there? What are the sounds? How does the man show his depression; how can you tell just by watching this scene, that he is experiencing depression? If there is dialogue, what is it? "

"Now allow the projector to shift back in time one scene. What do you see and hear? What if anything is different in the man's actions or demeanor?"

"Now let the projector go back to the scene immediately before this man's depressive episode. What do you see and hear?"

"The next scene is immediately after the depression begins. I wonder how it starts, what the very first signs might be, what is happening around him. I wonder what might trigger the depression this time. Now let the film continue to roll, all the way up to the episode we initially saw. Still the film continues to roll, catching the next scene and the next, until this period of depression has stopped or run its course. You may watch it silently, remembering what you see; or you may describe it, as you wish. Let the movie roll all the way to the end, until you see the credits."

"Take a moment to absorb what you have witnessed. When you are ready, push the button on your chair to return to upright and gently return here, to this space and time, still retaining both the feeling of calm and the memory of all you have witnessed."

When the client has returned, remain in silence. Let the client speak first. Despite the client's seeming oriented and ready to resume, many people need a few moments before they are ready to communicate with another.

By having the client change roles from protagonist to witness he is able to see his problem from another perspective, one that is not so close to the affect and the experience. The imagery starts with an imaginary rendition of his symptom, then helps him create a story about it—a story which includes some of the triggers to his symptom. It also embeds the idea that most symptoms occur in episodes, and episodes have ends as well as beginnings. His depression will not last forever.

Having looked at some ways to gather foundational stories, in our next chapter we will look more closely at some ways of understanding them.

References

Berger, D. M. (1989). Developing the story in psychotherapy. *American Journal of Psychotherapy*, *43*(2), pp. 248–259.

Kopp, R. R. (1995). *Metaphor Therapy: Using Client-Generated Metaphors in Psychotherapy*. New York, NY: Brunner/Mazel.

Kopp, R. R. (1998). Early recollections in Adlerian and metaphor therapy. *The Journal of Individual Psychology, 54*(4), pp. 480–486.

Noricks, J. (2011). *Parts Psychology: A Trauma-Based, Self-State Therapy for Emotional Healing.* Los Angeles, CA: New University Press.

Watkins, J. G., & Watkins, H. H. (1997). *Ego States: Theory and Therapy.* New York, NY: W. W. Norton.

Chapter 6

Understanding Foundational Stories

This chapter is a primer on analyzing stories to understand how the story might relate to symptoms, and how the story may be a synergistic template for the way a person views him or herself, important relationships, and the world.

Let us begin with general methods for understanding the skeleton of a story. By skeleton, I mean the major elements internal to the story itself. By reducing the plot to its bare movement and denoting characters by such generalities as gender, age, and position relative to the client, we can often derive a functional means-end template which we can then see if it applies to other stories in the client's life. This is a method long used in the narrative analysis of text. Alexander (1988, p. 278) gives the following example:

> My boss called me in to discuss a report which I had just finished after a week of productive and satisfying effort. He chose to dwell on a minor point which he thought might contain an error. This made me very angry and I sat there dumbfounded.

This story can be abstracted as: Independent effort → productivity and satisfaction. Male authority interrupts with unwarranted, picky criticism → anger and inactivity. By reflecting on the essence of a client's stories in this way, hypotheses can be made about patterns (does this plotline repeat in other settings and times for the client?); and important questions can be raised (e.g., What impact does the pattern have on continued effort and productivity? Does the client anticipate criticism from females, as well? In situations where the client reports feeling angry or stymied, is there often a perception of being criticized?).

Of course, by abstracting the story in this manner, we are choosing to temporarily ignore the important element of context. We will discuss more about context in Chapter 11, but as stories become more problematic, they tend to infect more of the client's life contexts in a similar manner. When the child who has trouble cooperating and doing her chores at home begins to ignore assignments at school, the problem has worsened. It now crosses two contexts in her life.

Adlerian Approaches to "Early Recollections"

What he called "early recollections"—actually early storied memories—was one of the four aspects of a person that Alfred Adler believed the clinician needed to grasp in order to understand a person's "life style," or life story.[1] The life style represented the person's movement through the world toward often unconscious goals (which he termed "fictional finalisms") in a manner largely influenced by "mistaken" beliefs and "faulty logic." Although for Adler both the beliefs and the logic were particular to each individual, common patterns like over-generalization and catastrophizing presaged the cognitive behavioral therapists by many years. It is rare that cognitive behaviorists cite Adler or recognize the debt they owe him. So many insights are not so much discovered as re-discovered.

The mistaken beliefs and faulty logic emanated from childhood for Adler. However, even in the early 1900s, long before careful memory studies and sophisticated scans, Adler understood that memory is contextual. An early recollection is not so much a report of a childhood occurrence as it is a comment on a person's current life.

Given that Adler put so much emphasis on early recollections as one of the important pathways to understanding life story, Adlerians have developed numerous helpful methods for understanding storied memories. Many of these are similarly useful for understanding Foundational Stories.

In asking for early recollections, many Adlerians collect three to ten specific stories of a client's first memories. For each recollection, they ask the age at which it occurred (helpful for understanding the context in the story); the overall feeling of the incident; and the part that most stands out, together with the feeling associated with that vivid aspect.

Adler himself gave only very general guidelines for understanding early recollections. Some of his followers delineated useful open-ended methods that help the therapist and client understand the story. Some of these methods follow.

An initial, easy method is helpful in determining the theme of a story. Called the "Headline Method" (Kern et al., 2004), it calls for the client to imagine that the particular story is to be published in the newspaper, and asks what the headline would be. Headlines are usually pithy, and written in present tense and active voice. The task helps the client gain enough perspective that she can most often derive the relevant theme of the story.

A second method, devised by Kaplan (1985), consists of ten questions that the therapist might ask herself about a given story. The order and wording has been changed here to cluster the questions thematically. The first questions involve the characters in the story and the narrator's reaction to them:

- Who is present in the story?
- Who is remembered with affection?
- Who is disliked?

The next questions have to do with the plot:

- What problem(s) are confronted?
- What are the implied goals?
- What special abilities are revealed? This question gets at the manner in which the protagonist attempts to solve the problem or reach the goal.
- What does the story suggest about the client's social interest?

The final questions are overall questions about the story:

- What is the protagonist's level of activity in the recollection?
- What are the emotions?
- In general, is the story pleasant or unpleasant (i.e., redemptive or contaminated)?

Having answered the above questions, the clinician is then asked to summarize the overall view of self, others, and goal of each recollection. Perhaps an even more useful format for the summary I have modified from Kopp's rendition of Shulman's summary (Kopp, 1998):

> I am _____; other people are _____; life is _____; therefore _____.

The conclusion ("therefore . . .") forms the moral of the story, and is quite important, as we will see in Chapter 17. Eckstein and Baruth (1996) point out that hints to the conclusion or moral can be garnered from what part stands out or is most vivid for the client (and it is often not whatever part you might expect).

Powers and Griffith (2003) have a very helpful way of looking at early recollections. They begin with empathy, encouraging the therapist, when listening to an early recollection, to put oneself in the situation of the child in that setting—that age, size, etc. Then you can move forward in the story, acting, being acted upon, or observing as the client does.

They then listen for five categories for interpretation, arranged here to refer to differing aspects of a story.

1. Context—What was the external context of the client's life at that time/age? What is the context in the story? Does it take place outside or inside?
2. Protagonist and her movement through the story—This movement of the protagonist is one way of describing the plot. Remember that Adler's theory is teleological, so importance is placed upon moving forward in time toward a goal which may be both unacknowledged and no longer useful. What are some characteristics of the protagonist in

the story that show how she moves through the narrative? Powers and Griffith identify five aspects:

a. *Effectiveness/ineffectiveness*—how effective is the protagonist? Are there gender differences in effectiveness?
b. *Relative position*—Eckstein and Baruth (1996) talk about vertical and horizontal views (they attribute this to Lidia Sicher). In a vertical view, the person is concerned with who is on top. They may view themselves as above others, or beneath others in worth, power, effectiveness, etc. Each position implies the other: if someone is higher, that is because someone else is lower. In the horizontal view, others are seen as peers. There is not the comparison concerning who has or does more or less.[2]
c. *Degree of activity and initiative*—how active or passive is the protagonist? Does she take action and initiative, or is she a recipient of action, or an observer? Does this change over the course of the story?
d. *Extent of participation and cooperation*—what role does the protagonist have with others?
e. *Sensory aspects*—neurolinguistic program therapists pay particular attention to a person's primary sensory modality orientation (Grinder & Bandler, 1976). Is the person primarily visual? Auditory? Kinesthetic? You can get a sense of this from sensory details in the early recollection. Knowing this primary modality can be useful in understanding the person's world and in structuring comments and interpretations so that the person is more likely to grasp them. In yet another way of reflecting on the sensory aspects of a story, Jung (followed by Isabel Myers and Katherine Briggs) in his personality typology, saw some people as oriented toward the sensory details and practicalities of life (so-called "Sensing"), while others are more oriented toward big-picture understandings and intuitions (so-called "Intuition"). While the theory of types is much more complex than this, it is useful to understand a person's primary orientation toward Sensing or Intuition, again as a way of structuring interpretations and better grasping the psychological world in which they dwell.

Overall aspects of the story:

3. Content—what is the content of the story? Are there small details that are given that do not move the plot forward? In general, the more extraneous a detail, the more important it is.
4. Gender—are there only men in one's early recollections? Or only women? Are men noble and women evil, or vice-versa?
5. Evaluation—this seems to include both overall feelings (feelings as evaluative) and the overall story moral for Powers and Griffith.

Powers and Griffith go on to offer three guidelines for evaluating a series of early recollections together. First they look for *sequence*. What does having these particular themes in this order suggest? Next they look for *similarity*. Do the stories have a similar theme or similar plot line? Is the protagonist similar in characteristics from one story to another? Finally, they look for *symmetry*. Does one story capture one side of an issue, and a second story the other side?

The Adlerians offer excellent ways of understanding the protagonist and the movement within the story, then helping apply these to a person's life story. Narrative theorists offer ways of wording characters and their roles that make them more generalizable to one's larger life story. Neither do much with the symbols that may occur in Foundational Stories. Psychodynamic theorists look almost exclusively at the symbolic, but only through the narrow lens of sex, aggression, and their derivatives. It is here that the Jungians come into their own. A full grasp of the symbolic from this perspective is more than a treatise in itself, and well beyond the scope of the current work. However, one need not have a full grasp of the symbolic to benefit one's understanding of foundational stories. To that end, I recommend the following:

1. Notice the objects or processes in the story which may have a larger meaning. Ask the client to expand upon these. A useful wording is "what comes to mind when you think of (a filling station, a black Plymouth, a lamp—these are all examples from foundational stories which follow)." Try to get several ideas ("what else?"). This more Jungian approach proves more useful for Foundational Stories than the Freudian chain of associations (i.e., psychodynamic therapists get the association to the association. While useful, this takes the person away from the story and its significance. Jungians return each time to the symbol: "what else occurs to you about 'lamp'?"). This gives some clues about the personal meaning of the object or process.
2. Next, get some idea of the universal or archetypal meanings of the object in question. While the personal meaning is what is important for the client, knowing some of the universal meanings can give you a larger context through which to understand the symbol. Here, it is important to note the difference between a sign and a symbol. A sign has a one-to-one correspondence with its meaning. For example, an octagonal road sign means "stop" and nothing else. A circle or a mountain, on the other hand, can have numerous meanings; it is more evocative than equivalent. To begin understanding symbols, I recommend you consider purchasing two books (see references): *The Book of Symbols: Reflections on Archetypal Images* (Archive for Research in Archetypal Symbolism (ARAS), 2010) and *Animal-Speak: The Spiritual and Magical Powers of Animals Great and Small* (Andrews, 2002). The former can tell you how

Understanding Foundational Stories 77

hundreds of symbols have been used through the ages, and *Animal Speak* is an excellent work for understanding animal symbols. Keep a small notebook or computer file to record symbols and the understandings you encounter in client work.

Let's see if we can combine some aspects of the above, then apply to a couple of Foundational Stories. Read through the first foundational story, then think to yourself how you would answer the questions that follow:

I was three, because we had just moved to the house where I grew up and I was three at the time we moved. I had just met the little girl "Cathy" who lived behind us, and she had come over to play. There was a pile of old bricks in the back of our yard, and Cathy was helping me stack the bricks to make a filling station. The brick filling station got to be almost as tall as I was. I put one more brick on top, and all the bricks fell down. One of them hit me on the back of the hand. It must have cut a vein, because the blood poured out. It did not hurt badly, but when I saw all the blood, I got scared and began to cry. I got up and ran toward the house. Mother came out and wrapped my hand in towels, then put me in the back of our old black Plymouth and drove me to the doctor's house. The pediatrician did not believe in stitches, so he closed the wound with a butterfly bandage; consequently, I had the scar for decades. It seems afterward that my father told me you had to stack bricks flat so they would be less likely to fall. It was a bit disappointing, because that meant I couldn't build as high.

Feeling: Excitement, then fear.

Part that stands out: Running toward the house with blood pouring from my hand.

Feeling: Frightened.

Tell me about "filling station." When I was small, filling stations were intriguing. I think the first word I learned to spell was "Gulf," a brand of gasoline. Cars could get what they needed to run; and if they had problems, they could be repaired. It was comprehensive.

How about "black Plymouth?" It was the car my parents had through much of my childhood. Boxy, with two bench seats, one in front, one in back. The fabric was frayed. Of course, metal dashboard and no seatbelts.

Let's begin with the story context by placing ourselves imaginally in the protagonist's position. You are a three-year-old boy (think for a moment about what that may entail developmentally). You have recently moved to a new house. You are playing in the backyard (suburbia?) with a new friend. Seeing a pile of bricks, you decide to build a *filling station* (not a house or a fort; this is one of the small details that Powers and Griffith note may have significance). What is the world like for this little boy? How might he feel? What do we already know about what sort of person he may be? Recognize that your own sense of being in this experience may be different from how it is for the client.

1. Context:
    a. What are the "facts" of the environment and of the little boy's station in life? What is the emotional climate in the beginning of the story?
2. Characters:
    a. Beginning with the protagonist, what is important to him? What is his problem or goal? How active or passive is he? Does he show initiative? Is he alone or connected to others? In what way does he relate to female peers? To those in authority? Is he cooperative? Competitive? Does he move toward, away, or against others? What special abilities does he show in moving toward his goal? What are peers like for this boy? What is authority like for him? What are females like? Males?
    b. There are four other characters in the story; what role does each play? What sort of person is each? Anyone remembered with affection? Anyone disliked?
3. Plot:
    a. Make a scene by scene plot skeleton, substituting position, gender, and role for each character. What happens in scene one? Scene two? Etc.
    b. What is the primary problem or goal?
    c. How does the plot unfold and end? Is it a happy or tragic ending?
4. Overall:
    a. What is the author's primary sensory modality—visual, auditory, kinesthetic, unknown? Is he more Sensing or Intuitive?
    b. What are the emotions?
    c. If this were a newspaper story, what would the headline be (put it in present tense, active voice)?
    d. What is the moral or lesson learned?
5. Summarize the story in the form of *I am* _____; *other people are* _____; *life is* _____; *therefore* _____.
6. What additional hypotheses do you have?

Most of the answers to the above questions can be summarized on the Foundational Story Diagram, found in Appendix II. For title, use the newspaper title you developed. When you summarize each scene, use the more

Understanding Foundational Stories 79

general role/position/gender of each character to make hypothesizing from the story easier. The story summary (I am, other people are . . .) can be placed on the theme line. Try your hand at completing the Foundational Story Diagram before peeking at a suggested answer, below.

Here is one possible set of answers:

1. Context:
    a. Three-year-old boy in new house, neighborhood. The atmosphere is one of a sense of freedom to explore, excitement, but unknown danger (the bricks, the car).

2. Characters:
    a. *Beginning with the protagonist, what is important to him? What is his problem or goal?* What is important is creating his project. *How active or passive is he? Does he show initiative?* The protagonist is active and shows initiative. Even when injured, he runs for help.
    b. *Is he alone or connected to others?* Others are in his life and help him, but his focus is on his project. *In what way does he relate to peers?* Peer girls are enjoyable helpmates. *What is authority like for him?* Authorities play a helpful role when the protagonist extends beyond his reach. *Is he cooperative? Competitive?* Cooperative with the mother and the doctor. *Does he move toward, away, or against others?* Focus is on project rather than relationship. *What special abilities does he show in moving toward his goal?* Constructive abilities; also logic ("I was three . . . because I was three when we moved"). *What are females like?* Females are unflappable and helpful in a crisis, or enjoyable helpmates. *What are males like?* Males are kindly.
    c. *There are four other characters in the story; what role does each play? What sort of person is each?* The boy (protagonist); Cathy, peer, companion; Mother, unflappable helpful crisis manager; the doctor, kindly healer; and Father, permissive advice giver. *Anyone remembered with affection?* All characters. Cathy is a fun playmate, Mother can take charge in a crisis, the doctor is kindly, and Father gives good advice without restricting creativity.
    d. *Anyone disliked?* No one is actively disliked. There is some ambivalence toward the doctor, with the sense that by trying to avoid pain he prevented fast healing.

3. Plot:
    a. *Make a scene by scene plot skeleton, substituting position, gender, and role for each character. What happens in scene one? Scene two? Etc.*

       Scene 1. Little boy is building higher than is sustainable. Female peer is helping.

Scene 2. Unsustainable creation injures boy. Scared, boy seeks help.
Scene 3. Female authority takes charge, seeks male healer.
Scene 4. Male healer helps, avoids hurting boy.
Scene 5. Male authority offers advice.

    b. *What is the primary problem or goal?* The goal of the protagonist is how to create a "high" achievement; the problem is the physical limits in the objective world, and getting injured when he exceeds them.

    c. *How does the plot unfold and end? Is it a happy or tragic ending?* The story contains unpleasant elements, but has a happy resolution.

4. Overall:

    a. *What is the author's primary sensory modality—visual, auditory, kinesthetic, unknown?* Likely visual ("saw all the blood," "black Plymouth"). *Is he more Sensing or Intuitive?* Focus is not on details, so possibly intuitive.
    b. *What are the emotions?* Excitement, then fear, then disappointment.
    c. *If this were a newspaper story, what would the headline be (put it in present tense, active voice)?* Icarus in the Backyard: Boy, Striving for Self-Sufficiency, Hurt By Falling Brick.
    d. *What is the moral or lesson learned?* If you build too high you can get hurt. You need help to be self-sufficient.

5. *Summarize the story in the form of "I Am, Others Are, Life Is, Therefore:"* *I am* creative; *other people* are helpful; *life is* interesting and surprising; *therefore* I take on too much.
6. Hypothesis: It may be that the family environment, while permissive, for this boy may not provide all that he needs in a comprehensive way to fill and sustain him (the filling station); and there are unseen dangers (the backyard and the car). His response is to creatively build what he needs on his own, soliciting peer help. But he overreaches and gets hurt. The adults then help him and offer advice about working within the limits.

Let's look at one more example, this time three stories, each from the same author. We will use Powers and Griffith's suggestion for understanding a series of stories (similarity, sequence, symmetry). First, make a brief individual interpretation of each story. Read the stories, and, as before, place yourself in the protagonist's situation. Consider the setting; the protagonist and his goal; the other characters; and the plot. What is the theme of each story? The moral?

Feel free to look up any possible symbols you find in the story (we do not have the author's associations), then list any additional hypotheses you may have. Here are the stories:

> (Age 2) I remember being at the beach with my family. I was sitting on the sand because I had a bone disease that made movement quite taxing.

Understanding Foundational Stories 81

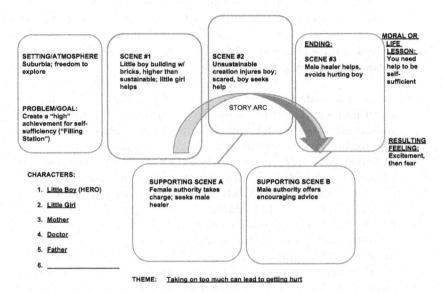

Diagram 6.1 Example Foundational Story Diagram

My older brother was healthy, so he could play and run and jump. My mother and father, indeed everyone, did all they could to help me.

(Age 5) My friend's father, a craftsman, once asked me what I wanted to be when I grew up. "I want to be a doctor," I said. "Then you should be strung up to the nearest pole!" he replied. His answer did not dissuade me in the least. I just thought, "he's someone else who had a bad experience with doctors; but I will be a different kind of doctor."

(Age Unknown) In order to get to school you had to take a path through a cemetery. The other children paid it no heed, but I was frightened and horrified. It annoyed me that I was not as brave as the other children, so I decided to end this fear of death by hardening myself. Accordingly, I lagged behind the others and put my school bag down. I then ran back and forth across the cemetery until I felt I had overcome my fear. Afterwards I could traverse the path easily with no fear.

Here are some ideas about the stories:

Story 1: I am a sickly child and moving is a strain; peers are mobile and athletic, adults are nurturing and kindly; life is unfair; therefore ??

Story 2: When adult males decry and even threaten me for my choices, I stand firm. I rationalize that they do not understand how I will realize my aspiration.

Story 3: A fear of death prevents me from doing what I need to do; peers are more courageous than I. I take action to overcome my fear.

Now let's look at these Foundational Stories through the Powers and Griffith lens of sequence, similarity, and symmetry.

Sequence: These three stories can be seen as a progressive sequence about illness and its cure. In the first story the protagonist is sickly and cannot "stand up for himself." He is passive and others have to care for him. In the second story he is determined to compensate by becoming a "real" healer. Verbally, at least, he is now "standing up for himself." We can now hypothesize about the "therefore" in the first story: I am a sickly child and moving is a strain; peers are mobile and athletic, adults are nurturing and kindly; life is unfair; therefore *I will try and remedy this by becoming a doctor*. In the third story he is even more active, and we get more detail about the nature of the illness he is interested in and his efforts to be a "real" healer to himself. While in the first story the illness was a physical disease caused by a vitamin deficiency (rickets), in the third, it is emotional (death anxiety). He develops a version of exposure therapy, which he applies with success, having become even more active. Another sequence is that of relation to authority. His perception of authority goes from nurturing to conflictual to non-existent.

Symmetry: Under the theme of illness, the protagonist shifts from one pole to the opposite: from patient to doctor.

Similarity: All three stories are about illness and healing. His relations with peers, noted in the first and third stories, remain vertical, and he compares himself with others, only to come up wanting. Once again, they are more competent than him due to one illness or another. If we move to the realm of speculation, we look for the potential deeper "red thread" which thematically connects the stories. We might infer that all three stories are about death. In the first story, the protagonist may have endured such sickness that he feared he would die. This created a determination to overcome or at least postpone death by becoming a healer. Although speculative, it explains how his wish to be a doctor was so powerful that it would stand up to the vehemence of a grown man. In the final story, he almost directly names and wrestles with death anxiety (anxiety cutting through a graveyard). Because this theme is removed from the data, we have to relegate it to hypothesis only. But if this man were in treatment, we would listen to his other stories with an ear tuned to the possible theme of death anxiety and reactions to it.

The man is, of course, Alfred Adler.[3] We can see in these stories how he might have coined the phrase "inferiority complex" ("complex" was a Jungian term, but "inferiority complex" was Adler's own), and how sibling position might play a role in his theory. We might also note how among the harmful reactions that parents have to their children for Adler is that of "pampering." Over the course of the stories, as noted above, his relation to authority figures goes from being nurtured and appreciative to standing up to authority to the absence of authority and developing his own method for healing. We might wonder if this parallels the progression of Adler's relationship with the older Sigmund Freud.

Interestingly, concerning the graveyard story, Mosak and Kopp (1973) note that in later years, Adler returned to the town where he grew up and attempted to find the graveyard that had paralyzed him so. Not only could he not find it, he could find no record that it ever existed. Adler's experience is a striking example of how we see the world through the lens of our stories.

Notes

1. The other three were: a dream; a person's ordinal position in the family; and the current problem and its impinging external circumstances. Of the four, two were objective (position in the family and current problem circumstances); and two were subjective (a dream report and an early recollection) (Adler, 1956).
2. This use of horizontal and vertical to refer to an orientation toward peer versus status comparisons is different than the use of horizontal and vertical in Chapter 4 to refer to the developmental concept of moving vertically between developmental levels versus moving horizontally as consolidating gains within the same level.
3. The accounts are adapted and re-written from Mosak & Kopp, 1973, pp. 158–159; the third is also found in Adler, 1956, pp. 199–200.

References

Adler, A. (Ansbacher, H. L., & Ansbacher, R. R., eds.). (1956). *The Individual Psychology of Alfred Adler: A Systematic Presentation in Selections from His Writings*. New York, NY: Basic Books.

Alexander, I. E. (1988). Personality, psychological assessment, and psychobiography. *Journal of Personality*, 56(1), pp. 265–294.

Andrews, T. (2002). *Animal-Speak: The Spiritual and Magical Powers of Animals Great and Small*. St. Paul, MN: Llewellyn Publications.

Archive for Research in Archetypal Symbolism (ARAS). (2010). *The Book of Symbols: Reflections on Archetypal* Images. Los Angeles, CA: Taschen America.

Eckstein, D., & Baruth, L. (1996). *The Theory and Practice of Life-style Assessment*. Dubuque, IO: Kendall/Hunt Publishing.

Grinder, J., & Bandler, R. (1976). *The Structure of Magic II*. Palo Alto, CA: Science and Behavior Books.

Kaplan, H. B. (1985). A method for the interpretation of early recollections and dreams. *Individual Psychology*, 41(4), pp. 525–532.

Kern, R. M., Belangee, S. E., & Eckstein, D. (2004). Early recollections: A guide for practitioners. *Journal of Individual Psychology, 60*(2), pp. 132–140.

Kopp, R. R. (1998). Early recollections in Adlerian and metaphor therapy. *The Journal of Individual Psychology, 54*(4), pp. 480–486.

Mosak, H. H., & Kopp, R. R. (1973). The early recollections of Adler, Freud, and Jung. *Journal of Individual Psychology, 29*(2), pp. 157–166.

Powers, R. L., & Griffith, J. (2003). A Q&A on lifestyle assessment. *Journal of Individual Psychology, 59*(4), p. 488.

Chapter 7

Assessing the Impact of History and Context

The Foundational Story Interview and Family of Origin Mapping

Foundational Story Interview (Reproduced as Appendix I)

The Foundational Story Interview is a template for collecting story vignettes in psychotherapy. There have been a number of client history questionnaires that either include, or to some extent focus on, collecting stories (see, for example, Andre Marquis' *The Integral Intake* [2008]). Most famous is the Adult Attachment Interview (George et al., 1996), which asks for example episodes (read: stories) to demonstrate each of the descriptors, and scores not only by content, but by how the stories are told. In 1989, Arnold Bruhn self-published a workbook called *The Early Memories Procedure* which asks clients to write different types of early memory stories and reflect on them. Dan McAdams' study interview protocol was briefly explained in Chapter 1 (McAdams, 1993, 2001). These and numerous other sources have been the inspiration for the *Foundational Story Interview Procedure*. You may wish to review Appendix I as you read the following explanations.

Begin with the initial orienting questions: Who lived with you growing up? Where did you mostly live? What did your parents do for a living? What was your family's ethnicity and religion? How devout were they? What is the family story about your name and how your parents chose it? What is the family myth or story of your birth? Record the stories as close to verbatim as you can.

Now record the story of the client's first memory, which is her first foundational story. It should be the tale of a particular time, a particular incident—not "I remember in the summers we would go to the beach;" but "I remember playing pirate and hiding among the sea oats when a big dog broke away and ran right toward me." What was the feeling? What part stands out for the client? What was the feeling in that part? Now record the same for a second recollection.

The next task is for the client to think of his life as if it were a play or story in either three or five acts or chapters. Often it is helpful to have a whiteboard and easel available with four columns for chapter number, age, title, and predominant feeling. Ask the client: from what age to what age would define each chapter? In what chapter are you currently?

Have the client tell an important story from each chapter they have lived, again making it about a particular remembered episode (you may choose to use the two early stories already collected to represent the first chapter).

Now look at the list of other possible stories from the Foundational Story Interview (Question 11 on the template in Appendix I). Pick two or three of the topics and have the client tell the stories, again telling about a particular episode and including the feeling and the part that is most vivid to her.

When done, you will have recorded at least eight foundational stories, and possibly more: the family story of the client's birth; the story of her name; two early memories; a story from each of one to four additional life chapters; and two to three additional stories. Explain to the client "we have discussed a number of incidents and memories from throughout your life. I would like to go back to the stories in turn to see what insights we gain together." Read the first story aloud (likely the story of the client's birth or name). "Did I get down how you remember it?"

If you have not already done so, ask for the feeling and the part that stands out. Then ask "how would you title this story? If this story appeared in a newspaper, what would the headline be?" Then inquire "what might be the moral or lesson learned from this story?" Stating the themes and morals of successive stories can often make both client and therapist aware of central or opposing themes and issues in one's life.

You can use the Foundational Story Diagram (Appendix II) to condense important aspects of the stories so that you can look at recurring patterns in settings, roles, themes, plotlines, and morals. Where is the client in her life trajectory—on the journey or in the return? Has she encountered a midpoint or central life crisis?

When you look at the protagonist across her stories, what would you say about her? Does she have some stable characteristics across all the stories? Does she have more of an internal locus of control where she takes the initiative, or does she tend to be buffeted by circumstance? How has she grown and changed? How has what she has sought in each story changed or remained the same?

What would you say about the primary or recurring antagonist(s)? How were they similar and different across stories? Were they primarily internal or external? If external, might they also symbolize an internal part of the client? How did the protagonist most frequently deal with the antagonist? Was it by battling, avoiding, surrendering, or embracing?

What would you say about the helpers in the client's life, both within and without? Any similarities among them? Was the client able to accept their help?

Can you yet see an overall life theme, moral or synthesis?

Any of the above may become a focus of treatment as an outgrowth of discussion with the client. Example foundational stories may be processed using the storyboarding from Chapter 16, or by using any of the methods delineated in Part 4 or contained on your own workbench. In the next chapter we will look at additional techniques for diagramming life and foundational stories.

Family of Origin Mapping

Family of Origin Mapping (FOOM) is a method of diagramming and analyzing the impact of one's early family context upon one's life and orientation in the world. It includes most of the factors deemed important by various theorists, and is laid out in a manner that allows the client to recognize patterns and to synthesize many of the results. It is also a way for the therapist to synthesize influential family information and dynamics about her client. The skeleton of the map can be a template for the therapist's notes when inquiring about the client's early history; as such, it is a reminder of important areas to explore and a visual for remembering them. Finally, the map is an excellent starting point for finding and telling foundational stories. As one therapist put it after drawing her own map in a workshop, "this is like three years of analysis condensed into an hour session."

By now I have assisted hundreds of people in drawing their maps. Although it began with a partial hospital clientele, it has been used in pre-marital workshops (by having each partner draw their map, then discuss it and its possible implications with their fiancé); with private practice clients; in marriage therapy (I will discuss a modification that makes it especially useful in this modality); and in professional workshops for therapists.

Look now at Figure 7.1, an example of a Family of Origin Map (FOOM). Note that it is oriented around the large circle in the center, which represents the client. It is about the client's perspective; a sibling, even a twin, will draw a completely different map. While squares are used to represent the males in one's family of origin and circles represent the females (from a convention used in Murray Bowen's Genogram; see McGoldrick & Gerson, 1986), the center figure representing the client before the age of eight is always a larger circle. Carl Jung spoke of the circle as a mandala symbol, originally from the ancient Hindus, and representing the self (Jung, 1964).

Recall from Chapter 4 that many foundational stories occur in the pre-operational "magic years" (from the classic book of that title by Selma Fraiberg, 1966) between the period of three to six. Ideally this is the period referenced in the FOOM, but because many clients have few memories before the age of seven, they are told to draw the map as they remember things before the age of eight.

Almost all clients can draw the map from their memories before the age of eight. Where a client protests that they have no memories from this early, ask them to draw it from as early as they can remember. Make a note in your mind, as the lack of early memories may be a sign of a traumatic and dissociated childhood.

88 Life and Foundational Story Assessment

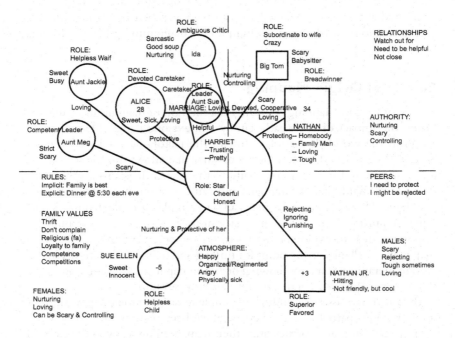

Figure 7.1 Example Family of Origin Map (FOOM)

Give the client a large sheet of paper, a variety of colored markers, and a table or easel on which to work. I explain to the client that I will walk them through the process step by step. Working at an easel, I demonstrate each step, sometimes using examples from my own map. If presenting to a group, I use a PowerPoint of the procedure.

It is helpful to draw your own map before using the procedure with clients. You may follow the procedure here and in Appendix III; or you may wish to have a friend or colleague read the instructions from the Appendix to lead you through the procedure.

You may wish to refer to Appendix III, which has step by step instructions, as you read the following overview of the mapping procedure and its variations. The first step is to draw the basic skeleton of the map, beginning with the large center circle (see again Figure 7.1). This both creates the scaffolding for the map and provides intrigue about just how this process will unfold. The center circle and the four surrounding smaller circles and squares (each eventually connected to the center circle by a line) are all labeled with the names of family members: the client in the middle, the two parents in the top circle and square, and brother and sister in the bottom square and circle respectively. Of course, very few families consist of two parents and a male and female sibling, but the map begins with this because

Assessing the Impact of History and Context   89

we are interested in the client's template perception and relationship to male and female peers and parents.

The client is next told to write the name s/he was called as a child in the center circle. Once again, the perspective of the child is emphasized. They are then to place the name of their mother under the top smaller circle, and their father under the small top square as in Figure 7.1. You then deal with variations. If the client grew up with only one parent and no contact with the second, they put an X through the circle or square of the absent parent and write the date that the parent died, or left, as best they know it. If there are one or more stepparents, each of those is represented by another small square or circle (depending upon gender) above those of the parents. If the client was adopted, the names of the biological parents (if they know them) also go under a small square or circle above those of the primary parents.

The name of the client's brother goes under the small square below and to the right of the center circle, and the name of her sister goes under the small circle below and to the left of the center circle. In Figure 7.1 the client had one brother and one sister. If the client grew up without a brother or sister, the name of the closest childhood peer of that gender goes under the respective square or circle and hash marks are drawn on the circumference of the circle or square to signify this was not a family member. If the client has multiple siblings of one gender, they create additional small circles or squares below. The sibling in the topmost circle or square if there are multiple siblings of the same gender is the sibling that most stands out for the client for any reason. It may be the sibling she looked up to; it may be the one that picked on her the most; it may be the one that was a companion. The other siblings are listed in age order from top (oldest) to bottom (youngest).

The client is then asked if there were any other people who lived with him, or with whom he lived growing up, or who were otherwise very important in the young years. Note on Harriet's map (Figure 7.1) that she had three maternal aunts and paternal grandparents who were important in her life. As on Harriet's map, adults (say a grandparent) would be designated as a small circle or square above the parents, males on the right and females on the left. Likewise, non-sibling children who lived with the client would go in a circle or square (according to their gender) below the siblings.

Now that all family members are represented, the client places in the circles or squares representing siblings the age of that child *in relation to him/herself*. Everything on the map is in relation to the client. Thus, a brother one year younger gets a -1; a sister eight years older would be +8; and a twin would be 0. Notice in the example map in Figure 9.1 that Harriet's brother is three years older and her sister five years younger.

In the circle or square representing each of the parents, the client next places the parents' respective ages at the time of his or her birth. Note in the example that the client's father was 34 and her mother was 28 at the time of her birth. Often clients will have to pause and calculate at this stage, as they have not considered how old their parents were when they were born. The age of the parents at the client's birth can raise a lot of hypotheses about the person's childhood context. Was this a teen mother ill-equipped to handle a baby while missing out on friends and school? Was the client a late-life baby, perhaps at a time the parents had less energy and interest in a newborn? Was one parent much older than the other? If so, how did this play out in their relationship and parenting? Does it play out in the client's choice of partners? The numbers become a window into possible contexts for her life story.

In discussing her map, Harriet related that her brother was likely conceived while her father was on leave from World War II where he was an army lieutenant in the Pacific theatre. So her mother was at home raising an infant. Note on the map that Sue is a "caretaker;" and her relationship with the client was "helpful." Possibly this was also Sue's role with Alice in those years while her husband was away at an especially brutal theater of war. She could not know if her husband would return; she is left only with his namesake, Nathan, Jr. Then the war ends, Nathan returns, and they immediately conceive the client, Harriet, who is born a year later. No wonder Nathan, Jr. was "not friendly" and would hit his sister. Thus, the client's perceptions recorded on the map begin to expand the understanding of her early context.

The next step is the first of what I call the "heavy lifting" steps. The client is to write one to three adjectives beside each circle and square on the map that describe what that person was like when the child was growing up. Clients needing help (and it is almost always needing help describing the parents; most of us are very attuned to the characteristics of our competition/siblings) can be told to think about how neighbors and friends, even local shopkeepers, might have responded to the person. If it is still difficult, they can put in descriptors from later in life.

Be sure to give clients time for this step. Watch for any signs of a client either spacing out (dissociating) or showing great affect. This step begins to bring the client back into the past stories, some of which may have been painful. After the step, I pause the client and ask how the process has gone so far. This gives them a chance to settle and re-focus, and gives me an opportunity to see how they are impacted.

After describing all the people on the map, I have the client draw connecting lines from each circle and square to the center circle, and a line connecting their parents. Having a very concrete and rather curious step here also helps with calming and re-focusing. On each of those lines I then have the client describe briefly the nature of his/her childhood relationship with that person. I want them to avoid generalizations like "good" or "pretty bad," as this tells little. I will ask "what kind of good? How would you describe it?" or "what makes it pretty bad?" Other questions that can help are "what was the primary gift and the major hurt you felt in the relationship with that person when you were a child?" (See Brenner & Martin, 2000 for creative use of gifts and hurts. I will expand on this in the chapter on themes). I often check in with clients after this step, as well, for this can also bring back memories. Both these relationship descriptors and the adjectives describing each person are potential starting points for later finding foundational stories following map completion (e.g., "you described your mother as 'all business' when you were growing up; can you give me an example?").

I then explain that, like a business organization, families place members in particular roles. I give a list of roles (also in Appendix III as Table III.1) and ask the client to place under each circle and square the primary role that person played in the family. This, of course, refers to the role in the family story or drama. Defining what may have been implicit pulls on the client can be freeing, and it helps her or him make a distinction between character and role.

All families, all organizations, and all stories have an emotional atmosphere or climate. A family may feel stifling; or it may feel frenetic and chaotic; or light and upbeat; or any of a myriad of other descriptions. The client is asked to describe in one or two words the emotional climate of her/his family of origin. On Harriet's original map (digital copy is Figure 7.1) she seems to have first written "Organized/regimented, Angry, Sick" as descriptors of the family atmosphere. She seems to have added "Happy" and then modified "Sick" with "Physically." Inquiring of Harriet, the "physically sick" seems to derive from the fact that her mother had an auto accident early on in Harriet's life, which left her with limited mobility and in chronic pain, and later in life confined her mother to a wheelchair.

Anomalies are best explored after the map is completed. Here we may wonder in a family described as "organized/regimented, angry, and (physically) sick" why Harriet added the adjective "happy." Doubtless there is a story there!

Even if the atmosphere is unpleasant, it becomes familiar so that it is common for people to find themselves working in an organization or continuing with a relationship with a similar climate to that in which they grew up. Harriet recognized this immediately when she reviewed her map. She spent her career as a psychiatric nursing director at a large Veterans Administration hospital where she worked with physically and emotionally sick people in a place that was regimented and had its share of anger. It was a very familiar atmosphere.

Rules help define a system and delineate how it will operate. Families, like other systems, have rules. Rules tend to be of two types. Overt rules are spoken, often repeatedly, such as "you must be home for Sunday dinner no matter what else is happening." Implicit rules may never have been spoken. They are part of the operational fabric of the family, the way things are done. No one is told explicitly, "Never speak of Aunt Matilda who moved away with the boyfriend no one liked" or "Don't bother Uncle Buck when he's been drinking." If you live in the family, you just know this. These implicit rules are often examples of prohibitions resulting from stories that must not be uttered. In this next segment, the client is asked to begin a list of the major family rules, both explicit and implicit. Of course, the implicit rules are harder, both because silence is often an aspect of the rule itself, and because it requires reflecting on things taken for granted, rarely observed, then translating them into a verbal form.

For the next item, family values, a prompting list of common family values (also available in Appendix III as Table III.2) is given the client. This is usually an easy item, for, just as children know who is the favorite, they also know what are the major values (no matter how much or how little they may adhere to them).

I usually pause the process again here to allow clients to take stock. I explain, "you have done the difficult work; the rest of the steps involve pulling together and summarizing what you have done." We then discuss again what the process of mapping has been like for the client.

The first step in synthesizing involves making a vertical dotted line directly through the center of the page. This divides the page into two halves with the males on the right and the females on the left. Beginning with the males, the client is asked to read through how they described each male on the map. What are the characteristics the males share? Is there a "red thread" that runs through the descriptions, or an overarching descriptor that would fit? I often ask clients to imagine these are the only males in existence (as indeed they were for the client in her young years). If these were all the males, how would you describe "male"? The client is asked to put a one- to three-word description somewhere on the left of the map. The process is repeated for the females on the left. How we describe and understand (even implicitly) maleness and femaleness often colors what we expect and how we interact with those of the same or different gender.

Next the client divides the page in half again, this time with a horizontal dotted line through the center. Below the line are people in the same generation as the client—her peers. Above the line are those in authority. She is asked to read through the descriptions of the people at the top of the map. If these are the only people in authority, and if the ways they wield authority are the only ways, what could one say about authority? The client is asked again to summarize in one to three words.

The process is repeated for the peers. What can you expect peers to be like?

The client is then asked to read through all the relationships and summarize what they would say about relationships from the map. The final step is to read through all the descriptors of family members and summarize what people are like. What can you expect from them?

This completes the basic map. The client is given a camera and asked to take a picture of the map, which is printed for use in subsequent sessions so that the client can take the map with him. Often clients elect to take a picture on their cell phones, as well. At this stage, the client is asked to look over their map for patterns and insights which are then discussed. It is only after an open-ended discussion that the clinician brings more focused questions. Examples are: How are important people in your life now similar or different than you have described the family members on your map? What characteristics do you share with others on the map? Do you find yourself still playing the same role in settings in your current life? How has your view of authority changed/remained the same? Where in your life have you found a similar atmosphere? How does your early experience with males and females jive with the men and women in your life now? When you came here you complained of (anxiety); I see on your map that you describe your (grandmother) as (anxious). Is there any connection? Each question can be the impetus for a storied example.

Several modifications are in order for special circumstances. In marriage or couples therapy the spouses can draw their own map simultaneously, then, in a subsequent session, take turns describing their map to their partner and the therapist. Often much of her partner's material will be familiar, but there are almost always surprises. I have each partner listen to her partner's description without comment. Afterward I will ask the person if s/he is able to entertain questions and comments from the spouse (almost all will). The mapping becomes an empathy building tool wherein partners come to learn not only what is important to the other, but why.

A modification that can aid in couples therapy is to add a small circle horizontal to and on the right of the large middle circle. That circle is given the partner's name and a brief personality description. At the appropriate time in the procedure that circle, too, is connected with a line to the center circle, and the relationship is briefly described. It then becomes possible to see how the partner fits into the person's family of origin view. Does the partner have characteristics of a brother? Of the mother? Are the qualities of the relationship with the spouse similar to another relationship on the map? Or do they provide a needed balance to other relationships on the map?

The FOOM can also be used in a group setting. All members of the group draw their map simultaneously, then take turns describing and discussing it with the group in subsequent sessions. Here, too, it builds empathy, but it also begins to lay out the group dynamics.

With more disturbed clients, the mapping process may need to be slowed and completed over several sessions instead of over one. This is especially the case if calling to mind early figures or relationships is triggering. Ultimately, putting those characters and those relationships on paper becomes healing. Seeing on paper that, yes, my sister was abusive to me growing up can be incredibly confirming of a person's experience. Also, the fact that all of this fits on one large sheet of paper, and is bounded by the edges, gives the implicit message that what happened is, in some important sense, limited.

The procedure is especially helpful in a group setting with more disturbed clients. There they see in a convincing manner that others experienced great difficulties growing up as well. One helpful entry into Family of Origin Mapping in a group setting, especially with more disturbed clientele, is to have the group watch a movie together, then do a FOOM on one of the characters in the movie and discuss it together. This creates an easy bridge to doing their own FOOM and discussing it in the group.

Some people view their childhood experience and the characters therein as all negative. There are people who have been subjected to horrific circumstances as children, but there is always some seed, some gift in what they might have taken from what they lived. In these cases, I ask the client to record one negative descriptor and one positive descriptor or gift they might have received from each character on the map. If they cannot think of a gift from the character, they are to leave the descriptors of that person blank; they can go back and add at any time in the process. This procedure is not necessary for the majority of clients, as they will have some characters viewed positively on balance, and some viewed neutrally, in addition to a few viewed negatively.

One modification with which the clinician must be very careful, especially with more disturbed clients, is that of drawing a map wherein all characters and relationships are the way the client would have liked them to be. While this can open a discussion of "how would you be different if this had been the case," and, then, "how else could you get there," the contrast between what the person lived and how the person would have wanted it can be overwhelming and depressing.

So often our view of the characters, roles, values, rules of operation, expectations, and emotional setting of our youth re-cycles or influences the stories of our current lives. The process is synergistic, because the selection of remembered characterizations is in some sense influenced by the story of our current life. Either way, it lays out some of the dynamics of our life story. I encourage you to first do your FOOM, then offer the process to a potentially willing client. See what you can learn.

References

Brenner, P., & Martin, D. (2000). *Seeing Your Life Through New Eyes: Insights to Freedom From Your Past*. Hillsboro, OR: Beyond Words Publishing.

Bruhn, A. R. (1989). *The Early Memories Procedure*. Bethesda, MD: Arnold R. Bruhn & Associates.

Fraiberg, S. (1966). *The Magic Years: Understanding and Handling the Problems of Early Childhood*. New York, NY: Scribner.

George, C., Kaplan, N., & Main, M. (1996). *The Adult Attachment Interview*, 3rd Ed. Unpublished manuscript, University of California at Berkeley.

Jung, C. G. (1964). *Man and His Symbols*. New York, NY: Doubleday.

Marquis, A. (2008). *The Integral Intake: A Guide to Comprehensive Idiographic Assessment in Integral Psychotherapy*. New York, NY: Routledge.

McAdams, D. P. (1993). *The Stories We Live By: Personal Myth and the Making of the Self*. New York, NY: Guilford Press.

McAdams, D. P. (2001). The psychology of life stories. *Review of General Psychology, 5*, pp. 100–122.

McGoldrick, M., & Gerson, R. (1986). *Genograms in Family Assessment*. New York, NY: W. W. Norton.

Chapter 8

The Seminal Importance of Roles

Many years ago, I signed up to participate in a modified training group, or "T Group." "T Group" has since come to be confused with "encounter groups." Encounter groups were a variety of small, intense, experimental groups wildly popular in the mid-1960s to mid-1970s that focused on baring your soul—and sometimes your body—to complete strangers.

A T Group was different from encounter, as it focused upon understanding small group dynamics. The "T" in T Group stands for Tavistock, which is the name of a famous London psychiatric clinic. The original T Group was also called a "Bion Group" for its roots in the work of Wilfred Bion (who came to work at Tavistock). Bion was a British psychoanalyst who in World War II developed a method of studying the dynamics of small group process by placing people in a leaderless group observed by "consultants" who would refuse to lead, just periodically make provocative observations about the group as a whole. Think *Lord of the Flies* for adults.

The group in which I participated was modified to study intergroup processes. It took place on the weekend in an empty office building with about 25 or 30 participant strangers. In the beginning of the group, the consultants chose five of the participants and requested that everyone else give their car keys and shoes to these unfortunate selectees. Then the consultants stepped back. Now even though this was an era before cell phones, there were plenty of telephones in the office building, and the building was on a major bus route. Plus, whatever happened, you knew you had to get your keys and shoes back at the end of the day. That was the external situation. That was not the psychological situation.

Flash forward to the end of the day. The group of five have barricaded themselves in an office. The other 20 or so are outside screaming and pounding on the door. I am pounding on the door, all the while thinking "this is crazy!" If the door had given way before the consultants stopped the process, I shudder to contemplate the fate of the five.

This of course calls to mind Zimbardo's famous Stanford prison experiment (Drury et al., 2012) where some students were randomly selected to be prisoners and others guards. The study had to be stopped. Such demonstrations show the power of roles. Any of us (yes, even you, and as shown above, definitely me) can be placed in a role that overwhelms our usual stories and our authorship of those stories.

This realization suggests at least two things: 1. Sometimes the problem with which people present can, at base, be a problem of overwhelming or conflicting roles; and 2. changing one's role can be a powerful way of changing one's story.

A role is a particular function in the plot of a story. Any number of different characters may play the same role, giving the expression of the role differing nuanced qualities based on how the particular character performs in the role. Thus, the same role can be performed by many characters. The most basic of stories requires only two roles: the protagonist and the adversary. Schneiderman makes the point that adversaries may be of four types: another person, nature, society, or the self (Schneiderman, 2015).

As stories increase in complexity, the number of roles increases from the two roles of protagonist and adversary. The increase in roles often begins with the addition of supporting roles to the protagonist.

Few therapies make role understanding and role changes a central aspect. Without naming that he is working with roles, Milton Erikson was a master at helping clients change through changing their dominant roles. In one case, Erikson was called on to evaluate a young man hospitalized for acute schizophrenia. The young man suffered from the delusion that he was Jesus Christ. Since he was Lord, it was not fitting for him to participate in any of the ward activities or groups. Erikson walked into the young man's room and greeted him by saying: "So, I hear that you are a carpenter." The hospital had a woodworking shop, and the young man agreed to participate. From there he was able to transition to additional activities and eventually to leave the hospital (Haley, 1973).

Many have pointed out how Erikson used the double bind, but it is a double bind of *roles*. Erikson looked for a sub-role that is a dominant part of a problematic defensive role and used that sub-role as a resource. Presumably the role of Jesus protected the young man from the vagaries and potential rejections inherent in participating in life. If he denied he was a carpenter, then he was not really Jesus, and the protective edifice would have a major chink; on the other hand, if he admits to being a carpenter, then he must logically participate. Erikson does not give him the option to not change.

In the 1960s, Stephen Karpman (1968/2011) asserted that if the roles are identified in a person's favorite childhood story (they can even be diagramed by writing them around a central circle), there will be a correspondence with the roles she takes in her current life. This was almost a footnote in a paper that first described the drama triangle (explained below). The idea was well worthy of an expansion that, to my knowledge, never occurred. Note the roles identified in a FOOM (see Chapter 7). Are these roles still in the person's life? In Harriet 7.1's FOOM from the last chapter, she identified her family role as "Star." As an adult she received numerous awards for her hospital work, and was on the board, then elected president of the state nursing association. Sometimes people will take a primary role in later life that is different from the family role they held as a child, but it will almost always be a role that occurs somewhere on their FOOM, a role that occurs in their childhood family.

Karpman also distinguished between two types of roles: identity roles and action roles. Identity roles are roles like parent, attorney, neighbor, etc. Action roles are roles defined by having a function within a drama (protagonist, supporting character, adversary, etc.). It is this latter use of roles that corresponds to my use of "roles" in foundational stories.

Roles and the Drama Triangle

Karpman identified three ubiquitous roles that occur in family dramas, and thus in our internal stories. While three legs make for a very stable stool, we know from group process that three is an unstable group which tends to devolve into two allies and one outlier. This, of course, was Freud's Oedipal template, with the boy child wishing to join the mother and eliminate the father. The three roles for Karpman are Persecutor, Victim, and, intriguingly, Rescuer. The Rescuer joins the Victim, leading to the Persecutor becoming the outlier. For Karpman, the same character may take any of the three roles, and the quicker the characters switch roles, the more exciting the drama. When any one of the roles is missing, there is the equivalent of a casting call to find a character who can fulfill the missing role in the drama.

Understanding these three roles elucidates so many foundational and life story plotlines. In some dramas, the characters alternate in playing the roles; in still others, a given character is relatively wedded to one of the roles. The dynamic among the three can play out in relatively harmless stories; or it can play out in destructive and tragic stories. Once keyed in to the three roles and their interaction, we all find numerous examples in our clients and in our own lives.

Here is how the three roles play out in the tragic Child ballad (Child, 1885/2014) called "Maddie Groves" in folk music. In Child's research, there are 15 different versions of the ballad, but the plot—and the roles—are essentially the same.

> Little Musgrave has gone to church on a high holiday, not so much to pray as to check out the ladies. And many of them are quite beautiful, but most beautiful of all is Lord Barnard's wife. Upon spying each other, they are immediately in lust. Lady Barnard tells Little Musgrave that her husband is away, and she has a place where they can rendezvous. Here Lady Barnard has become the betrayer—and thus Persecutor—to her husband, Lord Barnard, who is the as yet unaware Victim. Lady

Barnard's foot page overhears the conversation and determines that his allegiance is to his lord rather than to his lady. Thus, as Rescuer, he sets off on a fast horse to rescue Lord Barnard by informing him of the looming tryst. Lord Barnard, now would-be Persecutor, gathers his men and races toward the bower.

When Lord Barnard and his men are within earshot of the lovers, a friend of Little Musgrave who is in the employ of Lord Barnard blows his bugle as a warning. Here the friend has become the Rescuer. Little Musgrave, soon to be Victim, hears the bugle, but Lady Barnard tells him it is merely the horn of a shepherd, and they should go back to sleep.

When they awaken, Lord Barnard (Persecutor) is at the foot of the bed. Little Musgrave (Victim) protests that he has no clothes and no weapon. Lord Barnard tells him to get dressed, then offers him the better of his two swords and challenges him to strike the first blow. In this unusual turn, Lord Barnard voluntarily offers to go from Persecutor to Victim. Little Musgrave (now Persecutor) swings the sword as hard as he can and wounds Lord Barnard "quite sore." Now it is Lord Barnard's turn to be Persecutor. After he strikes Little Musgrave (Victim), Little Musgrave "strikes no more." Enraged, Lord Barnard turns to his wife and asks her how she likes being with Little Musgrave now that he is dead. Defiantly Lady Barnard states that she would rather be with a dead man than with Lord Barnard or any of his kin. She has embraced the role of Victim, and, accordingly, Lord Barnard stabs her in the heart.

The ending varies. In some versions, a saddened Lord Barnard, becoming belated Rescuer, has the lovers buried. In other versions he becomes a Victim, either being hanged for his crime, committing suicide, or finding that Lady Barnard was pregnant and he will be left without an heir.

Having seen a tragic melodramatic ballad version of the drama triangle, let us look at a relatively benign example with which many of us can identify, either as parent, or as childhood memory. Imagine a car trip with the mother driving and the two children in the backseat. Bored, little Harriet sticks out her tongue at her brother Nathan. Here Harriet takes the role of persecutor and Nathan, the role of victim. In response, Nathan escalates to an arm punch. Now Nathan has become the persecutor and Harriet the victim. What does little Harriet do? She screams bloody murder. "Mom! Nathan hit me!" This is a bid for rescue. Mom turns around in the seat to answer the call for rescue, but quickly shifts from Rescuer to Persecutor. "Nathan! How many times have I told you to NEVER hit your sister! Just wait until we get home—there'll be no screens for you!" Nathan, now abject Victim, whines, "I'm sorry Mom." With the roles of Persecutor and of Victim so masterfully filled, one role is yet open and, like a vacuum or a magnet, tugs on anyone not otherwise committed to the drama who may happen to be within reach. That, of course, would be Harriet. "Don't take him off screens, Mom. He didn't mean to do it" (Rescuer).

The same drama can be played in a dangerous and potentially tragically high-stakes fashion when the issue is partner abuse. A potential victim may need rescue before bodily harm or even death ensues; yet the rescue rarely stops the drama, it only continues the story.

Pearson's Archetypal Roles

Carol Pearson was a Jungian-oriented literature professor when she began thinking of how different archetypes commonly influence people at differing points in their lives. Archetypes, you may remember from the section on C. G. Jung in Chapter 1, are universal templates for perceiving and living in the world. They have a spiritual or numinous quality that can be evoked (but never captured) by symbols. Each archetype is individual in the manner in which a particular person expresses it. Thus, for example, each person's mother is different and mothers in her individual way; but "mother" is a universal experience to which people from all cultures and all times relate.

Pearson identified six (1986), then 12 archetypes (1991) that inform particular phases of a person's life journey. Following Joseph Campbell, Pearson sees the hero's journey as a three-act metaphor for one's life story. The first act (preparation) is about making one's way in the world. It begins in the innocence of early childhood (the Innocent), soon enduring the existential betrayal of life being unfair and quite unlike the young child's fantasies (the Orphan). Making one's way as a young adult requires the twin energies of protecting and setting goals and boundaries (the Warrior); and caring for others, especially younger siblings or an early child of one's own (the Caregiver).

The second act (the journey) sees the need to find one's identity in the world (Seeker) and learn to make intimate connections with others (Lover). Following one's path entails both creating (the Creator) and letting go (the Destroyer). Having established an outer life with a sense of one's identity and a connection with others one enters the third act, the Return. There one's tasks include taking ongoing responsibility for systems, organizations, and people (the Ruler); and managing the perceptions of others (the Magician). It is best done by continuing to learn (the Sage) and by being able to laugh at oneself and at the irony in the world (the Jester).

Pearson has devised an elegant and practical blend of Jung and Campbell's ideas. Her concept of archetype is more that of a protagonist's role than the ephemeral and mystic tendencies of Jung's archetype. Pearson's system is both intuitive and easy to grasp, yet retains complexity with the addition of two ideas. The first is the notion that encountering these 12 archetypes is an iterative process. While certain archetypes typically attain prominence at each of the three journey/life stages, one may need other archetypes at any time. For example, while establishing one's career in early adulthood, one needs to be responsible for one's home environs and for the projects at work (Ruler, a later-life archetype); and must learn to approach tasks with optimism (Innocent, an early-life archetype) and humor (Jester, another later-life archetype).

The second concept that adds depth and complexity is the idea of levels. Each archetypal role may be performed at one of several levels. For example, Shel Silverstein's delightful if dark children's book *The Giving Tree* (Silverstein, 1964) tells the story of a tree who befriends a little boy. As the boy grows, the tree gives more and more of herself, beginning with letting the boy climb in her, then build a tree fort, and ending with taking her branches and trunk until there is nothing left but a stump. In this example, the tree is performing Caregiver tasks at the lowest level where she completely depletes herself in the process. A higher-level Caregiver would also care for herself, which shortcuts not only depletion but also over-control and resentment.

Dr. Pearson and the current author developed and validated an instrument to help people determine which of the 12 archetypal roles were most and least active in their current lives. Called the "Pearson-Marr Archetype Indicator," or "PMAI," it formed the basis of the book *Introduction to Archetype* (Pearson & Marr, 2002). Pat Adson (1999) showed how the system could be used in psychotherapy in her book *True North*.

The concept of the archetypal protagonist role was extended to identify storylines that contained each of the 12 archetypal protagonists in the co-authored book *What Story Are You Living?* (Pearson & Marr, 2007). The book drew on myths and folktales, as well as current life examples, to demonstrate each of the 12 storylines and some of their variations. Both the PMAI (now available online) and *What Story* are in the process of updating and revision, with three of the archetypes being re-named, but the concepts of a particular universal protagonist role that defines a genre of story remains.

Marriage and Roles

When we marry, we make two simultaneous contracts: one overt (in sickness and in health, until death do us part, etc.), and one covert. That covert contract is based upon the role in the marriage that we expect to play, and the role that we expect our partner to play—often complementary roles derived from our family of origin. The covert contract, like the covert rules in a family, is always the more powerful.

> Harriet 8.1, after a brief early marriage, was single until her mid-forties. Nathan 8.1, of similar age, had never been married. Harriet and Nathan were long-time friends, and never considered either romance or marriage until Nathan was diagnosed with terminal cancer. It was at that point that these longtime friends married. The covert contract was that Harriet would assume the role of nurse to Nathan's role of dying patient. This unacknowledged contract was stable, as both parties

tacitly agreed. Until it was not. In Greek mythology, even the gods are subject to the Fates. Shortly after the marriage, Nathan's cancer went into unexplained total remission, and he remained cancer-free. The couple bought a condominium together, and as Harriet was carrying a box down to the basement, she slipped and tumbled down the steps, breaking her back. Now Harriet was bedridden for weeks after surgery. Suddenly the roles were reversed: Nathan, now healthy, had to be the caregiver for his invalid wife. Neither could tolerate this. It was not like Nathan to have anyone depending on him, and it was not acceptable to Harriet to need anyone—her job was to care for others, not require care herself. This could have become an opening for each to integrate the other pole of their primary role, but it was a bridge too far for them, and they divorced.

Roles are an essential part of any story. The familiar roles from early foundational stories tend to recur throughout our lives. Roles can be powerful magnets to draw us into even stories that are not our own.

Roles are inhabited by characters, and it is to a method for mapping characters to which we will turn in the next chapter.

References

Adson, P. (1999). *Finding Your Own True North and Helping Others Find Direction in Life*. Charleston, SC: Type & Archetype Press.

Child, F. J., ed. (1885/2014). Ballad 81: Little Musgrave and Lady Barnard. In *The Project Gutenberg EBook of The English and Scottish Popular Ballads* (Volume 2 of 5). Urbana, IL: Project Gutenberg. Retrieved May 15, 2019 from: www.gutenberg.org/ebooks/47692.

Drury, S., Hutchens, S. A., Shuttlesworth, D. E., & White, C. L. (2012). Philip G. Zimbardo on his career and the Stanford prison experiment's 40th anniversary. *History of Psychology, 12*(2), pp. 161–170.

Haley, J. (1973). *Uncommon Therapy: The Psychiatric Techniques of Milton H. Erickson, M.D.* New York, NY: W. W. Norton.

Karpman, S. B. (1968). Fairy tales and script drama analysis. *Transactional Analysis Bulletin, 7*(26). Reprinted in (2011). *Group Facilitation: A Research and Applications Journal, 11*.

Pearson, C. S. (1986). *The Hero Within: Six Archetypes We Live By*. New York, NY: HarperCollins.

Pearson, C. S. (1991). *Awakening the Heroes Within: Twelve Archetypes to Help Us Find Ourselves and Transform Our World*. New York, NY: HarperCollins.

Pearson, C. S., & Marr, H. K. (2002). *Introduction to Archetypes: The Guide to Interpreting Results From the Pearson-Marr Archetype Indicator Instrument*. Gainesville, FL: Center for Applications of Psychological Type.

Pearson, C. S., & Marr, H. K. (2007). *What Story Are You Living? A Self-improvement Guide for Discovering the Unconscious Influences That Drive your Life Story*. Gainesville, FL: Center for Applications of Psychological Type.

Schneiderman, K. (2015). *Step out of Your Story: Writing Exercises to Reframe and Transform Your Life*. Novato, CA: New World Library.

Silverstein, S. (1964). *The Giving Tree*. New York: Harper & Row.

Chapter 9

Assessing the Life Story Plot and Characters
Plot Diagramming and Character (or Ego State) Mapping

Diagramming

Having a method of diagramming together with the client the common problematic plot in one's life story—or, alternatively, a method of mapping the characters in a person's life story—gives both client and clinician the ability to recognize recurrences. It helps make important aspects of implicit stories explicit so that the client has greater capacity to make choices about whether to continue the story in the same manner. The procedure is flexible, allowing for alterations as the client proceeds.

Because plots occur in time, in the Plot Diagram the client begins with a foundational story or scene, then proceeds to map what happened in time before and after that occurrence. The larger plot often reveals itself to be a repeating cycle. In the Character (or Ego State) Diagram, the client visually identifies not only the important characters, but their relative importance to one another; then shows their groupings and interactions. When combined with sandplay figures*, the client develops a symbol for each state or scene in the Plot Diagram, and for each character in the Character Diagram. These symbols can be used as therapy proceeds to call up that character and the stories each holds.

> Nathan 9.1 was 17 and a high school senior when his distraught mother brought him for help. The situation had become unglued, and they were desperate. Although he was doing well in school and had friends, his parents had been extremely worried about his marijuana use. Also, they had noted periodic bouts of depression, and had taken him to a psychiatrist who had tried him on a variety of SSRIs, all to little avail.
>
> And then the bottom fell out. Nathan and his friends had learned that the parents of one of the group were going to be out of town and leaving the young man in charge of the house. What would a high school senior do with the use of a house for the weekend? I don't know about you, but I know what I would have done. Of course, that was the plan.

Unfortunately, at the last minute, the parents thought better of it and insisted their son accompany them. The group refused to let this minor detail deter their arrangements. After all, the party had already been scheduled.

Knowing the house would be vacant, the young people opened a basement window and started the party. Unbeknownst to them, the next-door neighbor was the neighborhood watch lady. She knew the family was away, so when she looked out her window and saw what she thought were numerous men entering the vacant house, she called the police.

The police did not send a couple of patrolmen to check out the situation. Instead, they sent the SWAT team. The SWAT team surrounded the house and demanded on the bullhorn for everyone to come out with hands on their heads. One by one the young people emerged, all except my client who, frightened, hid in a closet. After the other young people emerged, the police sent in the dogs.

By the time they reached Nathan, he had been dragged out by the leg, which had been bitten to the bone and half of his ear had been gnawed off. It would require plastic surgery and months to heal.

Of course, this was a traumatic incident for Nathan; we will take up trauma and story in Part 5. For now, our focus is on diagramming the plot.

As I often do when I work with someone who struggles with drugs or alcohol, I asked Nathan what his experience was like when he was high. It is almost always a state that the person seeks, and/or a way of avoiding some other more noxious state. If you then inquire about the setting and the sequence of occurrences and experiences before, then after the high state, using a recent drug use event, you get a drug use foundational story.

Usually when clients are asked this about marijuana they say something like "I'm more calm; I don't get so flustered and angry," or, "I don't worry about stuff; I don't care if I have a test the next day," or, sometimes, "it's pleasant at first, but then I start getting suspicious. I worry we'll get caught, or I think my friends are out to get me." Nathan surprised me. His answer to his experience when he smoked pot was, "I don't know how to put it into words exactly. I know it sounds weird, but I feel *connected*. It's almost, like, spiritual." I suggested that we map his experience together. The result was the first Plot Diagram (see Figure 9.1).

To create the original plot map, we used a white board and circles of paper to represent self states. Just rendering it as a drawing becomes frustrating, as it is difficult to change in the moment. A better alternative for diagramming the internal states experienced by the client is to use circles of magnetic white board. The writing on the circles can be easily erased and changed, and the heavier circles photograph easily. You can order whiteboard online that is thin and flexible enough to be cut with scissors. If your whiteboard sheets are not magnetic, you can purchase magnets online or at any office

Assessing the Life Story Plot and Characters 105

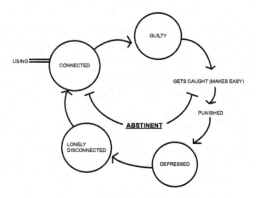

Figure 9.1 Example Plot Map

supply store. They are the kind of thin rectangular magnets, sticky on one side, that your realtor uses to mount her business card so you can keep it on the refrigerator. Some people use sticky notes, but it is difficult to get these in the shape of circles, which is preferable. The circle is an ancient symbol for representing the self (think mandala). Also, for more tactile clients, the heavier whiteboard makes for an easier emotional connection.

Nathan always smoked with friends, never alone. That experience of getting high with friends was the major emotional bond in his life. Nathan also knew that his parents greatly disapproved of his smoking, and in many ways Nathan was a cooperative young man who wanted to please authority, so he felt tremendous guilt after each instance of getting high. I asked Nathan how easy or hard he made it to get caught. He paused for only the briefest of moments before acknowledging, "Pretty easy. Last time I mistakenly left a pipe and some seeds on the table in my bedroom. I know that when Mom gets worried, the first thing she does is to toss my room." He would often "accidentally" leave paraphernalia or bits of marijuana in his room, knowing that his worried parents would periodically search it. Emotionally he believed he should be punished for his transgression, so he made it easy for his parents to learn of his pot use.

When his parents found evidence of his use, they would yell at him in exasperation, then ground him and restrict his use of electronics, confine Nathan to the house, and allow no contact with his friends. Punished, Nathan would become depressed. The depression and restriction would power feelings of loneliness and disconnection. The go to solution for that was getting high with his friends, and the cycle would repeat.

When Nathan's depression is seen in the context of this problematic life plot, it is easy to understand why anti-depressant medication was ineffective. It also becomes clear that the incident with the police was an escalation of the pre-existing cycle, with the traumatic injury becoming an over-the-top punishment.

The diagram offers not only understanding, but opens ways to proceed in therapy. Nathan became able to recognize the cycle and make better choices, especially when he was able to recognize the "connected" feeling and seek ways other than getting high to trigger it.

Below is a summary of the steps in creating a plot map.

Materials: One 2'x3' magnetic white board

> Set of colored whiteboard markers
> 6–8 white board rectangles, 2"x4" (optional, for depicting others' responses)
> 6–8 white board circles, 4" in diameter
> Box of business card magnets (for use with non-magnetic whiteboard material)

Preparation: Cut magnets in half, peel paper from sticky side, and apply one of the resulting smaller magnets to the back of each of the circles and rectangles

Step 1: Elicit self state of client's concern (e.g., what are you like when you are [high, depressed, anxious, angry, etc.]).

Step 2: Have client characterize that self state on one of the circles.

Step 3: Have client recall the last or a recent time s/he experienced that concern.

Step 4: Inquire about what was occurring immediately before the self state (sometimes it helps to have the client imagine a movie of the incident and freeze at the frame just before the concerning self state).

Step 5: If the occurrence in Step 4 was another self state, have client characterize it on another circle. If it involved a thought that the client had, have the client write that on the board before the self state (Step 2) circle. If it involved an action or words by someone else, have her write the action on a whiteboard rectangle and place it before the small circle from Step 2. Have the client then write any words or clarifying information on the board underneath the rectangle.

Step 6: Continue as in Step 5 to diagram the next prior occurrence (frame). Continue moving backwards in time several steps or until there is an initiating event or thought.

Step 7: Return to the Self State from Step 1 and follow the same process (Steps 4, 5, and 6) forward in time. Note with the client if the process is self-repeating or circular (as in the example).

Step 8: Discuss with the client. Is the sequence a familiar one? How so? How would she characterize the roles of any other people (characters)

involved? What roles in the drama are played by the self states? Where else do any or all of those roles recur in her life?

Internal Character Mapping

Nathan 9.2 was a playwright who wrote all of his drafts in various coffee shops. It was not that he preferred writing in coffee shops—quite the contrary. It was just that he felt he had no space to work at home. Nathan owned a small two-bedroom house where he rented out the basement to a friend and former lover. He and his roommate shared the first-floor kitchen and den. Nathan himself lived on the second floor in one of the bedrooms; the other bedroom he used like most people use their basement: a place to contain all the detritus from past apartments and marriages. In a word, a junk room.

One morning Nathan arose late. As he groggily headed for the stairs to the kitchen and the coffeemaker, he glanced into the junk room, then froze. The junk room was no longer a junk room. All of the boxes and old furnishings were gone. In their place was a new desk and computer, and a small bookcase neatly organized with the references he was using for his current play. Nathan later remarked that he did not believe in leprechauns, so he was simultaneously thrilled and freaked. How could this have happened? It was not until almost three weeks later that Nathan came across the receipts for the new furnishings and computer—and he had signed them!

Whereas Nathan represents an extreme, we all have internal characters, many of whom may represent themselves through the various voices in our minds, incessantly admonishing, negotiating, praising, and arguing. Unlike Nathan, we probably do not have internal characters of which we have no awareness. And it is rare that one of our characters seizes the microphone (called "blending" by Schwartz, 1995) without warning. Instead, we most often hand the microphone off to the character who best fulfills the upcoming role (the part of ourselves who comes out at the raucous party is not the one who completes the report for work). Like an Olympic relay team, the handoff is so smooth that we are usually unaware. Instead, we like to think we are the same person at the party who attends in the classroom or dines with our lover. This need for viewing ourselves as unitary and consistent can be so powerful that we do not notice when we change protagonists and narrators.

For most of us, a little reflection or self-observation of our internal voices or of how we color our various roles can easily reveal our consistent characters. These internal story characters and their common interactions can be diagrammed. It is both useful in planning treatment and incredibly affirming and normalizing for most clients who complete such a diagram. Nathan 9.2's diagram follows:

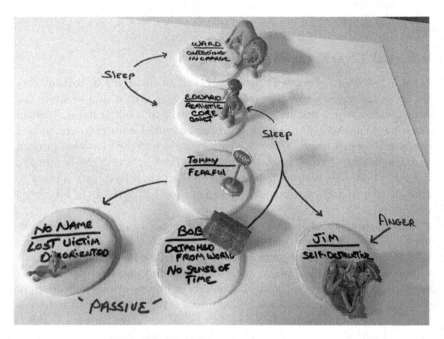

Figure 9.2 Example Character Map

I often ask clients what they might call a particular character. Nathan spontaneously volunteered the names of the diagrammed characters, having given many of them personified names (others will often refer to a character by its predominant mood—the "angry part"—or by its function or role—"the party girl"). Note the importance of what Nathan refers to as "sleep," by which he means a lack of awareness among characters. Thus "Ward" (character names have been changed, as well) only emerges when the quiet, everyday "Edward" is asleep. It was likely Ward who turned the junk room into an office. Edward usually experiences only himself, Tommy, and "No Name." As with many more dissociative clients, you can sometimes find other characters and other stories by having the client ask any characters of which he is aware if they know of additional characters. Since our focus here is on how to help a client create a character map rather than upon the case, I will mention the symbols only briefly. Note the Bambi figure for No Name, and, of course, the skeleton for Jim, who becomes self-destructive in response to anger.

While Nathan has a very clear map, the client need not be highly dissociative for the procedure to be helpful. The Character Mapping sequence is especially useful in conjunction with some of the ideas and techniques from Chapter 12 (Helping Characters Transform). Many of the materials and much of the procedure is similar to Plot Mapping (above). Here is the sequence of steps:

Materials: One 2'x3' magnetic white board

> Set of colored markers
> 3–4 white board circles, 6" in diameter
> 8–10 white board circles, 4" in diameter
> Box of business card magnets (if circles are not magnetic)
> Optional: Displayed set of sandtray figures

Preparation: Cut magnets in half, peel paper from sticky side, and apply one of the resulting smaller magnets to the back of each of the circles

Procedure:

Step 1: Obtain client's agreement to diagram the different parts or sides of himself/herself. The task is then to normalize and explain the process. You can explain that we all have different aspects or sides, only for many of us we do not attend to the phenomena. We are different in differing settings; for example, we are not the same at a large party as we are at work. You might say that different settings can bring out different sides of ourselves. Some parts may be characterized by emotion. We may have an angry part or a playful side. Also, most of us have a variety of recurring voices in our heads. The current task will be to map or diagram those major internal characters.

Step 2: Ask the client what is a major part of themselves of which they are aware. Only if the client draws a blank (an occasional, but not frequent occurrence), tentatively ask if the client is aware of some (more benign) part that you have observed. "For example, you told me that you had stood up to your sister when she wanted to borrow your favorite necklace. You also spoke up when your boss wanted that report on a very tight deadline. I wonder if there might be an assertive part of yourself? Is that what you would call it, or would you label it differently?" Have the client write the one- or two-word characterization on one of the small circles.

Step 3: Ask for additional parts, having the client write them each on a small circle. Continue until the client is not aware of other parts. Most people can identify six to ten parts, with brighter people usually identifying eight to ten. As the number approaches 12, it becomes more ungainly to work with, so I might ask the more obsessive client to limit themselves to eight or ten.

Step 4: If a client still has difficulty identifying more than one to three parts, I might show him a list of common characters (ego states), asking if any of these remind him of one or more of his own parts. I do not use the list routinely with clients who are easily able to identify their own parts, as it tends to have clients identify overly many parts that do not play a major role in the client's resources or difficulties.

Step 5: Say: "Many times people find that one or more of their parts loom so large or recur so frequently that they should be listed on a larger circle. Is that true for any of your parts?" As I ask, I show the client the larger circles. If the client identifies one or more "larger" parts, I have him replace the small circle with a large circle titled the same.

Step 5: Say: "Now I would like you to organize the parts in the way they work in your mind. Feel free to write on the white board if it's helpful to have arrows, connecting lines, etc." This is all the instruction most clients need, as they will know instantly and intuitively how their mind works. If a client does ask for clarification, you can tell her that sometimes people find parts are grouped together; other people find one part above another; or one part that leads to another. Encourage her to assemble it the way it works together for her. With this encouragement, it is extremely rare that a person—even small children—cannot organize the circles.

Step 6: Ask the client to explain the organization to you.

Step 7: (for those clinicians who have sandtray figures) Ask the client to choose a sandtray figure to represent each of the parts. This gives rich detail about the part and its meaning; gives a "handle" to refer to the part in future sessions; and helps solidify the client's memory of the particular self aspect.[1]

Step 8: Discuss with the client how he came to choose each of the figures.

Step 9: Have the client take a photograph of the map.

The two procedures, Plot Diagramming and Internal Character Mapping, reveal recurring aspects in a person's life story. Together they give a visual portrayal of a client's internal world, a world that the person, now more informed, can better decide whether and where to make changes.

Note

1. Sandtray is a method of assessment and therapy using a large collection of small figures (people, animals, and props like trees, bridges, and wishing wells) to make a scene in a small sandbox. It was originally developed by Margaret Lowenfeld (2005) after she read a little-known book by Jules Verne in which he describes using miniatures to play on the floor with his children. She called her assessment the "World Technique," as she asked the client to "make a world in the sand." Doris Kalff (2003) adapted the technique for Jungian-oriented assessment and therapy, calling it "sandplay." If you do not have a sandtray collection ("sandplay" for the Jungians), I encourage you to begin one, starting with just a few figures on a shelf. I have mine displayed in a bookcase in the office. Clients are often intrigued by the display, which helps mitigate some of the anxiety in using "toys." You can use the figures in formal sandtray therapy (there are many workshops countrywide), or you can use them creatively in all sorts of ways.

The tactile dimension of the figures is an added advantage over drawing or imagining. See Part 5 for more on this with trauma survivors. Besides, if you do not have small children in your life, it is a great excuse to roam toy and knick-knack stores!

References

Kalff, D. M. (2003). *Sandplay: A Psychotherapeutic Approach to the Psyche.* Cloverdale, CA: Temenos Press.

Lowenfeld, M. (2005). *Understanding Children's Sandplay: Lowenfeld's World Technique.* Buchanan, NY: Sussex Academic Press.

Part 4

Changing Foundational and Life Stories

Part 4

Changing Foundational
and Life Stories

Chapter 10

Introduction and Sources of Change

A variety of approaches to psychotherapy can be characterized by the dominant story element that the approach impacts. In subsequent chapters, we will briefly describe example psychotherapies and the story element upon which each focuses. For each particular theory we will include a delineation of techniques that the approach uses to transform one or more elements of a story, especially those techniques that can be adopted pan-theoretically. But first, it is important to outline the primary ways in which people change and, thus, the overarching change processes from which all psychotherapy draws.

Understanding the mechanisms of how people change life stories forms the underpinning for any intervention. Five most important sources of change in psychotherapy and in life are described briefly below with examples. Those five are:

1. Relationship
2. Memory Re-consolidation
3. Resourcing
4. Positive Trauma and Ritual
5. Dialectical Change

Some interventions combine mechanisms. Bruce Ecker (Ecker & Hulley, 1996; Ecker et al., 2012), in his Coherence Therapy, for example, uses memory re-consolidation with some reliance on relationship and dialectical change (more about Bruce later). Let's look at each of these mechanisms in turn.

Relationship: The relationship with the therapist forms the crucible for change. It is the current context within which stories are told, and the therapist is the understanding witness. The relationship with the therapist is the underpinning for all storytelling and all story change.

Most of us are familiar with the studies that show that the quality of the therapy relationship is by far the largest single factor in therapeutic change. For example, in a recent large meta-analysis of 295 independent studies involving some 30,000 clients, Flückiger et al. (2018) found a correlation between therapeutic alliance and outcome in adult psychotherapy of

$r = .278$. The correlation is consistent across alliance and outcome measures, treatment approaches, patient characteristics, and countries. Much of the rest of the variance is caused by non-specific factors (i.e., unknown factors)—not the therapeutic school, the degree or the experience of the therapist, degree of disturbance of the client, etc.

Not assessed, and thus likely hidden in the data, is that the relationship, while important in all therapy, is not equally important in all cases. Clients exist on a continuum from people with relatively circumscribed problems and good resources both internal and external and a generally comedic/redemptive life story, to people with multiple problems, few resources, and a tragic life story. When a client is more toward the good resources end, the therapeutic bond is the foundation for change, but techniques of change become more useful and important. When a client presents more toward the multi-problem, few-resource end, the relationship becomes the major driver of change. This is graphically illustrated in Figure 10.1, where on the right (multi-problem) side the therapy is almost all related to the relationship. Note that even on the far left side (health), the area for relationship (while much smaller) does not decrease to zero. This is because relationship is foundational in any therapy.

In psychotherapy the therapist plays an essential role as witness to the telling of one's life story. It is easy to downplay just how essential the witness is. In fact, there is no story without a witness. Even stories that we never reveal to another human are witnessed by a part of ourselves; we always tell stories *to* someone. The act of witnessing is itself healing, especially if the witness is caring, listening, and able to become involved in the story. It is the witnessing that makes the act of telling a story healing.

The witness is an audience, and thus an essential part of the context of a story. As we will see in the next chapter, changing the context of a story; or changing the context within which the story gets told, changes the story.

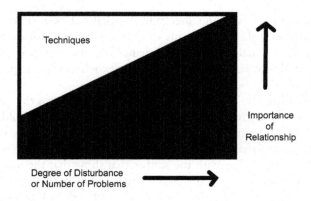

Figure 10.1 Relationship of Therapeutic Relationship and Severity of Problems

A story with a different context is a different story. Over time the psychotherapist often also becomes integrated as a character in a person's life story, a resource character who can bring wisdom and calmness to bear on events.

Memory Reconsolidation: It was the late 1990s, and the basic theory of how memory works had not changed since the 1800s. Sure, we had more particulars. We now posited different types/domains of memory—procedural, semantic, emotional, episodic, etc. And we knew more specifics about the biology of memory: how memory is a neuronal pathway, how the synthesis of proteins plays a role in bridging particular synapses, or gaps, between neurons. But the basic theory was unchanged, and it went like this. You've got some friends over to watch the game, and someone says "let's order pizza!" Now you generally try to eat more healthy, but, hey, you're the host, so you say you will order. You do not exactly have the local pizza shop on speed dial, but Bill does. He calls out the number, and you dial. Now let's say a couple of minutes later Sue calls out "I hope you got anchovies on at least part of that pizza. It's the whole reason I eat it!" Uh-oh. You're going to need to call the pizza place back. Without hitting re-dial, would you remember the number?

If you're like most of us, the answer is "no." Yet if I asked you to recall the telephone number of the house where you lived the longest as a child, odds are you could do it. Why the difference? The reason, as you doubtless recall from undergraduate psychology, is that the childhood number was very important to you, unlike the pizza parlor. And you repeated that childhood number hundreds of times. With repetition and valence over time it was thought the memory trace becomes almost indelible, entering long term memory. The process of moving from the erasable whiteboard of the moment to long-term storage is called "consolidation." Once the memory had consolidated, barring extreme neurological damage, that memory was there to stay. I could ask you for the childhood phone number, then distract you before you replied, then ask again, and you would still easily remember it (not so for the pizza parlor). I could subject you to an electric shock, and you would still be able to recall it. Even if you developed dementia, those overlearned facts and skills are among the last to go. And that was the essence of how memory was thought to work for a hundred years.

Enter Karim Nader (Nader & Hardt, 2009). Nader was a post-doctoral fellow in the NYU lab of Joseph LeDoux where they studied, among other things, fear memory in rats. While researching the history of memory theory, Nader came across some long-ago articles that postulated that long-term consolidated memories could be changed. Being counter to the dominant theory (the "normal science," in Thomas Kuhn's (1962) terms), the articles did not get much press and were soon forgotten. Nader approached LeDoux with the idea of testing the hypothesis. LeDoux noted that the lab only had so many resources, and it would be a waste to spend time testing a long-established hypothesis. Undeterred, Nader opted for forgiveness rather than permission and began running his experiments on his own time when the lab was closed. Here is how he set up the experiment.

Fear conditioning in rats is easy (as in many animals) and requires only one trial, after which the rat remembers it for life. You place the rat in a cage with either an electric grid in the floor or an electric collar on the rat's foot, and a buzzer that can sound a particular tone. You then ring the buzzer and shock the rat. The rat will stiffen and go into a traumatic freeze. The freeze is easily observable, so no complicated measures of heart rate, cortisol levels, etc. are required. If you ever place the rat back in that cage, or play that same tone in its presence, it will once again go into a freeze.

The fear memory is consolidated in a limbic structure called the "amygdala" (Latin for "almond" due to its shape). It is possible to inject a chemical directly into the rat's amygdala that temporarily prevents protein synthesis. You recall that protein synthesis is an important mechanism in memory consolidation. Thus, if you place the rat in the cage with the grid and buzzer, ring the buzzer and shock the rat, then inject the rat's amygdala with the protein blocker, the rat can be returned to the shock cage, or exposed to the sound of the buzzer, all without freezing. The rat's consolidation of the fear memory has been disrupted and the rat does not associate fear with the buzzer or cage—all as predicted by the old theory of memory.

Further, you can take a rat that learned to fear the buzzer several days previously and inject it with the protein blocker. When you then sound the buzzer, that rat will freeze, because the memory has already been consolidated. The chemical does not disrupt old proteins, it just keeps new ones from being formed. All as expected.

Nader's creative leap was to take a rat that had already been conditioned to fear a tone and then sound that tone. The rat, reminded of the fear, would freeze. Nader removed the rat to a neutral cage and waited. After a wait as short as ten minutes (or as long as several hours in other trials) Nader would inject the rat with the protein synthesis blocker. He then placed the rat back into the shock cage. No response. He then sounded the buzzer. Again, no response. The rat had "forgotten" the fear associated with the buzzer. The procedure did not affect other memories, and the old memory did not return with stress or with the passage of time (Hartley & Phelps, 2010). Nader had shown that consolidation was not a one-way, linear process. After being reminded of the fear response, the memory became vulnerable to change, even elimination. To become a stable memory, it had to be *re*-consolidated all over again. It is as if memory were a word processing program with no "save as" function. You begin typing the draft of a report and click on "save." Now, as you look it over, you realize you need to make some changes. You make the changes, then click on "save" again. Where is that initial draft, the one before the changes? Nowhere; it no longer exists. You have modified it and re-saved.

It makes sense that memory would be capable of being updated; otherwise, if the saber-toothed tiger once frightened you near the berry patch, you could never approach the berries again. Your world would become unnecessarily smaller and smaller. Now if the only way to accomplish this were to have a probe in your amygdala through which a systemically harmful drug was administered, our forefathers and foremothers would not have been able to update their memory. Fortunately, this is not necessary. The memory, once cued, only needs to be disrupted by stress, distracted by other learning, or changed directly.[1]

Realizing that long-term memory can be updated explains numerous phenomena that dwelled just at the edge of understanding. Examples include the notorious fallibility of eyewitness reports, an observation confirmed by numerous experiments. A witness describes a traffic accident he observed. The next day he reads a report in the paper that notes a red car was approaching the intersection at high speed. When the police ask him to give a second statement, he now mentions a red car—a detail omitted in his first report. It's not that the witness is lying; he now truly remembers the red car, for his memory has been updated—reconsolidated—to include the red car. And so it is, perhaps, with some of the controversial false memory syndrome (Centonze et al., 2005).

Re-consolidation also explains the degradation of memory over time. A long-held memory begins to have different details from the first telling. Perhaps its immediacy also fades; it is as if you remember remembering the incident. Each time the memory is recalled, it is vulnerable to change, and minor details are added or omitted, often related to the teller's current circumstances. Over tens of re-tellings the memory has changed, just like the folk songs and nursery rhymes mentioned earlier.

Everything changes. We change. I have a picture taken of me when I was about a year old. It's not just that I am larger and have less hair than this young fellow; almost everything about me is qualitatively different. The vast majority of my cells are different—with the exception of our cortex, eye lens, and women's egg cells, almost all cells in our body are replaced. The rate of replacement varies: skin and stomach lining cells turn over every few days, while a 75-year-old has about half the heart she had at birth. Due to epigenetics, even the expression of my genes has changed. Why would memory be different?

Since Nader's initial seminal work, hundreds of experiments have confirmed his hypothesis, showing that not only does memory re-consolidation occur in rats, but also in mice, fish, crabs, snails, nematodes, honey bees, chickens—and humans (Nader & Hardt, 2009).

Take a moment and ponder the implications. It is at once disturbing and exhilarating. Long-term memories can be changed. In fact, none of our long-term memories are stable, and it is unlikely that any of them exist in the form in which they were laid down. They are constantly re-made in the context of who and where we are at each moment of remembering. Alfred Adler anticipated this in the first half of the 20th century when he had new clients tell him their earliest recollections. At the close of therapy, he would once again have clients tell him their earliest recollections. Oftentimes the memories would be completely different; but in any case, the later telling would thematically include the gains the client had made in therapy. Adler may not have known the neurological mechanism, but he was clearly aware of the process.

The original re-consolidation research was done on fear memory, which has its correlates in PTSD and anxiety disorders in general. As we will see in Chapter 18, trauma is a causative factor, an associated link, and/or a consequence in virtually every mental illness. What if clients could change those memories of trauma in some way? They may choose not to change the memory of the events, but what if they could change the emotional impact? Or the takeaway lesson from the experience?

The implications go even further than trauma. In humans, re-consolidation can change or eliminate both procedural and episodic (event) memory in addition to emotional memories (Hupbach et al., 2007). An association between two or more representations is fundamental to psychological problems. A depressed person associates evidence of personal shortcomings or personal responsibility to situations that are not objectively evidence of either her defect or of her responsibility. A person with delusional disorder can see instances of deceit or danger in situations where none exists (Centonze et al., 2005). And a drug abuser makes a connection between environmental or physiological cues and the desire for the drug (Zhao et al., 2009). What if the memory for those associations could be disrupted? In fact, Zhao and colleagues showed that stress disrupted memory reconsolidation of drug-related memory in heroin addicts (Zhao et al., 2009).

Let's review the basic paradigm for changing or blocking the reconsolidation of a problematic memory. First, the problematic memory has to be cued or recalled. Remember that with the fear response of rats this was done by sounding the tone that had been associated with the shock. Fortunately, Hupbach et al. (2007) showed that the reminder necessary for reconsolidation in humans does not have to be a re-experiencing of the original memory, but can be a more subtle reminder. Thus, in an instance of trauma, the person does not have to re-experience details of the trauma, they just need to be reminded of the experience. This reminder opens a window of time during which the memory becomes vulnerable to change or erasure. The window is between ten minutes and three to four hours (by six hours it has begun to reconsolidate). With the memory open, the client can change the memory, have a separate learning task, or be exposed to stress—all of which will disrupt the original memory. In six hours to two days, a memory different from the original will be consolidated. The effect is more enhanced for narrative memory and for memory of events long past (Scully et al., 2017).

We will see a number of ways to consciously use this natural reconsolidation process designed to update our memory in service of psychotherapeutic change.

Resourcing: Harriet 10.1 had graduated to coming to therapy every few weeks after having divorced her alcoholic husband and reconnecting with her grown children. She recently bought a condo and a dog. She began the session with the good news. "I just got back from Nashville where I addressed the nursing association with a colleague of mine. It was very well received!"

She went on to explain that she had a lifelong fear of public speaking; this was one of only two occasions where she gave a successful public talk without undue anxiety.

Then Harriet told me the bad news. She had had cervical problems, and her doctor ordered a new MRI. Her cervix was unchanged; but the scan showed she had developed a brain tumor. Harriet began to cry.

I felt so badly for this woman who had already been through so much. I told her so as I, too, began to tear.

When her crying calmed, I asked what she most feared. "I've not had any symptoms. The doctor said I could develop severe headaches, personality changes, and seizures. It's silly, I know, but if I have a seizure, I will lose my license to drive until I am medically cleared, which is a minimum of six months. How will I get to work? I'll have to Uber, and I'm already stretched pretty thin with my new mortgage. I may go bankrupt!"

When clients are faced with death, asking about their fear often reveals the unexpected. It is rarely what you expect: those in life threatening situations often fear seemingly small consequences or the impact of comparatively benign symptoms (Harriet feared seizures more than personality change, and the loss of her car license more than death itself). Perhaps it is too overwhelming to conceive of annihilation, so we fear the imagined aspect that we can grasp. Helping clients with those smaller fears often has a profound effect on their outlook.

"Let's return for a moment to what you said about that speech in Nashville. You said you had a lifelong fear of public speaking. How, specifically, did you overcome it? Let's walk through it. What did you do differently this time?" Here I am looking for what Michael White termed a "story exception."

"Well, I did it with a colleague who has long experience and who I really trust. I prepared well, but I didn't over-prepare. One speaker told me she spent 20 hours on a half-hour talk. I knew that was crazy, even though that kind of perfectionism is what I might have done in the past."

"Let me see if I can get this down." The use of notecards to write important insights for a client is a technique pioneered by Bruce Ecker (Ecker & Hulley, 1996; Ecker et al., 2012). Ecker uses it to record the deep reason for the symptom, but it can be used to keep any number of insights from melting away, or to highlight a summary or an interpretation. It makes the insight visual as well as verbal, and the client can be asked to review it multiple times in between sessions. By enlisting the client as co-author of the card, her ownership is also ensured. I keep a notecard pad with carbon paper between the cards so that I have a copy as well.

I handed Harriet the list. "Yes," she said. "That's it."

> "Anything else we should add?" I asked.
> "No, I don't think so. Can I keep the card?"
> "Of course. But let me have it back first to see if I can add the title that works."
> I wrote "Overcoming Fear" at the top and handed the card back. The title relates to the theme of the story, and thus it is an opportunity to help make the story thematically redemptive. Harriet burst into tears. "That's the story of my whole life! When I was a child, my mother wouldn't even throw out ragged clothes in case we got into a situation where we needed them."

"Now, are you OK with some homework?" Harriet nodded expectantly. "I'd like you to read the card each day before next time and think about how to apply it to your fear of the brain tumor."

Harriet smiled. Her adaptive unconscious (Damasio, 2010) had already anticipated this and begun working. "I think I'll name the tumor 'Carl,' because I hate the name Carl." She chuckled. "I'll probably have a seizure when I'm out somewhere with my dog."

"On your way to work in the Uber," I added.

Resourcing begins with the optimistic idea that clients already have the resources to change or to accept their difficulties; the task is to find that resource and help the client apply it. This is different from helping a client develop a list of general strengths. Resourcing is helping the client find the particular aspect that can impact a problem. This aspect can range from creating or applying another character to one's story to, as in the example above, finding and applying a different foundational story. We will look more closely at using the characters in one's story as resources in Chapter 12.

Positive Trauma and Ritual: A ritual, according to Campbell (2004), is an enacted myth. By enacting a story, we connect it more concretely to the everyday world. Often rituals contain what in other contexts would be traumatic events, but because of the context and the moral, even painful events are not traumatic. They may cement the changes the ritual is meant to convey, but they do not create the symptoms of trauma. This difference in moral and in perceived context is why many people survive horrendously painful experiences without becoming traumatized. Trauma is largely about perception.

Rituals are a time-honored way for changing identity stories. Applied especially at major life turning points—joining the community as an adult, becoming a journeyman in a craft, marriage, birth, and death—they often include trials and hardship. It is back to Freytag's (1895/2012) story arc (Exposition, Complication, Climax, Falling Action, and Catastrophe), or Campbell's (1949) Separation, Initiation, Return.

Despite the disconnection and mobility of our society, ritual change naturally emerges. For example, many workplaces have an informal ritual initiation for new employees. Our schooling and graduations can be viewed in this light as a ritual identity change. People endure a grueling application process, then often move to a new location, giving up family, friends, and possessions. There they endure hard academic work, much of which is either irrelevant, or will soon be outdated. Finally, they go through a ritual ceremony culminating in a change of name at the doctoral level. One does not just know a lot about medicine or psychology or anthropology—one *becomes* a medical doctor, a psychologist, or an anthropologist.

Note that this ritual has all the elements of a story: Separation (spending less time with friends and family, or moving); the road of trials, including turning points and reversals with a midpoint or climax; and the return, which has trials equal in scope to the first part of the ritual.

When a client has an insight or breakthrough, it is often helpful to brainstorm with them what kind of ritual would help them cement that insight and bring it into action in their lives.

> Nathan 10.1, for example, came to the insight that he had tried mightily over the years to never let on that he struggled with chronic depression; and the effort at cover-up drained his energy and increased his shame and depression. Nathan was a member of a very small and close-knit church. After his insight, he invited fellow congregants to his home, explaining he had something personal he wanted to share. He was surprised by having 20 people, almost half of the church, show up. For the first time he acknowledged his long-term struggle with depression to a band of loving witnesses.

A ritual need not be as large or public as Nathan's. Sometimes just finding a picture or small trinket that can represent the insight provides the ritual. We will see later that sandtray is an excellent source of ritual.

Dialectical Change

Dialectical change grows out of the conflict between thesis and antithesis. Because it is the source of change in story itself (see Chapter 2), it is one of the most common sources of change for various therapies. Michael White (2007), for example, in narrative family therapy, helps the client to label the symptom cluster as the antithesis. Questions such as "how will you respond when Depression tries to return" makes Depression out to be the villain, a villain to be resisted or sidestepped by finding and expanding a story where Depression was less powerful.

In brief, taking a storied, dialectical perspective might lead to additional questions in narrative therapy such as, "now that you have more energy and feel more optimistic, what helpful role could Depression still play?" Or, "what often seems like pessimism in Depression is actually the ability to view things from a realistic perspective. I wonder if Depression could consult with you in future decisions so you don't get taken advantage of."

Both Jungian and ego state therapies remain truer to the complete dialectical form of stories. The process of individuation for Jungians is a stepwise progression of dialectics, where each achieved synthesis becomes the thesis for a new dialectic. One of the early tasks in Jungian therapy is to face the rejected and disowned parts of the self known as the Shadow (except where such recognition would be too destabilizing). The integration of the Shadow is an early and primary task (Johnson, 1986).

While the idea of personality integration such that the person no longer has various parts or ego states is rarely seen as a possible or even desirable goal any more in most ego state therapies, there is a smaller synthesis that is important to most ego state therapies. Schwartz (1995) speaks of "Exiles"—often child ego states that contain painful memories and have been imprisoned or banished in the psyche. Their memories and the associated emotions are actively compartmentalized; the Exiles have become the antagonists. The process of therapy is to move from a guard/prisoner relationship with Exiles to a nurturing parent relationship that allows what happened to them to be synthesized.

There is a final way in which a dialectical process is part of most therapies. The process of therapy is itself a journey story, and as such, a dialectic. Clients must first trust enough to heed the calling to the journey. Having thus begun, they identify their antagonist and begin the road of trials as they struggle with the adversary heartened by the therapist as witness and helper; or they struggle with the therapist herself, who, in this case, acts as proxy for the projected antagonist. Having met the enemy and recognized, along with Pogo, that the enemy is also ourselves, the return road of integration begins.

The road back is every bit as difficult. The client is changed, having now integrated what seemed wholly other; however, others in her life may not have changed.

The changed person is but the thesis in a new journey, facing different challenges, perhaps with the techniques and internalized support of the previous therapeutic journey. Separation, Journey, Return. Thesis, antithesis, synthesis. This is the process of narrative growth where the synthesis becomes the thesis in a new story.

Note

1. There has, of course, been great effort extended to find drugs that can disrupt consolidation/reconsolidation that are not dangerous and that do not have to be injected near the site of the memory. Propanalol, a beta blocker, shows great promise. However, reconsolidation of a problematic memory can be changed in a more nuanced manner through psychotherapy without the use of any medication.

References

Campbell, J. (1949). *The Hero With a Thousand Faces*. New York, NY: Pantheon Books, © Bollingen Foundation.

Campbell, J. (2004). *Pathways to Bliss: Mythology and Personal Transformation*. Novato, CA: New World Library.

Centonze, D., Siracusan, A., Calabresi, P., & Bernardi, G. (2005). Removing pathogenic memories: A neurobiology of psychotherapy. *Molecular Neurobiology*, 32(2), pp. 123–132.

Damasio, A. (2010). *Self Comes to Mind: Constructing the Conscious Brain*. New York, NY: Pantheon Books.

Ecker, B., & Hulley, L. (1996). *Depth Oriented Brief Psychotherapy, or How to Be Deep If You Were Trained to Be Brief, and Vice-Versa*. San Francisco, CA: Jossey-Bass.

Ecker, B., Tick, R., & Hulley, L. (2012). *Unlocking the Emotional Brain: Eliminating Symptoms at Their Roots Using Memory Reconsolidation*. New York, NY: Routledge.

Flückiger, C., Wampold, B. E., Del Re, A. C., & Horvath, A. O. (2018). The alliance in adult psychotherapy: A meta-analytic synthesis. *Psychotherapy*, 55(4), pp. 316–340.

Freytag, G. (2012; orig. pub. 1895). *Technique of the Drama: An Exposition of Dramatic Composition and Art*. London: Forgotten Books.

Hartley, C. A., & Phelps, E. A. (2010). Changing fear: The neurocircuitry of emotion regulation. *Neuropsychopharmacology Reviews*, 35, pp. 136–146.

Hupbach, A., Hardt, O., Gomez, R., & Nadel, L. (2007). The dynamics of memory: Context dependent updating. *Learning & Memory*, 15(8), pp. 574–579.

Johnson, R. (1986). *Inner Work: Using Dreams and Active Imagination for Personal Growth*. New York, NY: Harper & Row.

Kuhn, T. S. (1962). *The Structure of Scientific Revolutions: A Brilliant, Original Analysis of the Nature, Causes, and Consequences of Revolutions in Basic Scientific Concepts*. Chicago, IL: University of Chicago Press.

Nader, K., & Hardt, O. (2009). A single standard for memory: The case for reconsolidation. *Nature Reviews Neuroscience*, 10(March), pp. 224–234.

Schwartz, R. C. (1995). *Internal Family Systems Therapy*. New York, NY: Guilford Press.

Scully, D., Napper, L. E., & Hupbach, A. (2017). Does reactivation trigger episodic memory change? A meta-analysis. *Neurobiology of Learning and Memory*, 142, pp. 99–107.

White, M. K. (2007). *Maps of Narrative Practice*. New York, NY: W. W. Norton.

Zhao, L., Zhang, X., Shi, J., Epstein, D., & Lu, L. (2009). Psychosocial stress after reactivation of drug-related memory impairs later recall in abstinent heroin addicts. *Psychopharmacology*, 203, pp. 599–608.

Chapter 11

Changing Context
Story Receiving and Storytelling

All story memories have three contexts. The first context is that of the narrator's life at the time the story took place—the life context. If this is a childhood story, where did the family live? What was their ethnicity, their religion, their socioeconomic position? What was the client's situation in the family? Where was she in the birth order? What larger events may have been taking place in the family at the time of the story?

With a storied understanding, one can begin to experiment and even play with helping a client change the life context of his story. Just because there may be fewer modalities that focus on the narrator's life circumstance behind a story, this context need not limit us. "If that argument with your wife had not occurred at her mother's house, but, instead, had occurred at a crowded restaurant, I wonder what it might have been like. Imagine for the moment that that's the case and walk me through step by step how it unfolds in the restaurant."

A second context is the narrated context of the story itself, which is often introduced and set up in the first line. "Long ago in a galaxy far, far away . . ." is a different narrated context with a different tone and different time than "Call me Ishmael." As you no doubt remember from earlier in the book, this is what has traditionally been called the "exposition" of the story.

Finally, the third context is the context within which the story is told—a kind of meta-context. When Igor Stravinsky's great ballet "Rite of Spring" was first performed in Paris in 1913, it caused near riots. Far from being thrilled, or even accepting, the witnessing audience was enraged at the innovative atonal qualities. Subsequent audiences appreciated it, and it has come to be known as one of the great masterworks. The context within which a story or musical piece is performed has great ramifications. As psychotherapists, that context usually refers to the consulting room and the therapeutic relationship. The context in which a story is told, the witnessing of the story, is the context which may be most easily influenced by the therapist. Since changing any aspect of a story alters the story, changing the meta-context within which it is told can also alter the story.

Story Receiving: Time

Time is a fascinating aspect of story context. To begin with, stories are set in the past, present, or future, and, in our Western culture, the plot tends to flow linearly toward the future. Phillip Zimbardo (yes, I know his name is familiar; this is the same Phillip Zimbardo who designed the famous Stanford prison experiment decades ago) and his colleagues Rosemary and Richard Sword (2012) think of most problems as resulting from a person's being stuck in the past or the future instead of the continuing present. Thus, for example, much anxiety is about being hyper-focused on the future. The therapy is about helping a person to gradually change his major experience of where he dwells in time.

Neurolinguistic programming therapists (Grinder & Bandler, 1976; Hoobyar & Dotz, 2013) contend that we each map our experience of time onto our personal space. Take a moment to see if this is true for you. What did you have for dinner last night? As you think of that, where is it? Behind you? To your left or right? Now think of something you plan to do tomorrow. Where is that? How does time flow for you? From where to where? Is it linear?

There is an old story, more of a joke in our culture, that goes like this: "It was a dark and stormy night. Three men sat around a flickering and hissing campfire. Two of the men looked expectantly at the third. One spoke up. 'Tell us the story, Abdul.' Abdul gazed into the fire for a long moment, then cleared his throat and began. 'It was a dark and stormy night. Three men sat around a flickering and hissing campfire . . .'"

A linear flowing of time from past to future is the way we often conceive of our life narrative. However, as with the campfire story, this is not the case in all cultures and has definitely not been the case for all time. In some quarters time is circular, much as the phases of moon and the seasons and young women's menstrual cycles. In a context where time is mostly conceived as linear, flowing inexorably from the past to the future, circular stories stand out and can have a particular power. Think, for example, of the movie *Groundhog Day*.

Problematic stories, on the other hand, *do* tend to be circular with the basic plot, theme, and characters repeating over and over. Freud anticipated this with his concept of repetition compulsion. We are all familiar with the woman who consults us in the midst of her third abusive relationship; or the man who, despite his resolution to the contrary, has just married his second alcoholic spouse.

The role of witness is often co-opted to place the therapist in another, more familiar role in the client's story; this is the essential nature of what has been called "transference." Placing the therapist in another role is understandable, given the rarity of having a concerned, non-judgmental person witnessing what is most important. This is especially true for many of those who seek help for symptoms caused by a background of abuse, neglect, and/or betrayal.

In listening to a client's stories, it is extremely helpful to be able to recognize when the therapist is no longer seen as the concerned witness, but has assumed another role, or has become identified as a character in the person's life story. The use of Malan's triangle of transference (Smith, 2003) is a way of listening that allows the therapist to sense the moments when the client can no longer tolerate a concerned witness and must place the therapist in a more familiar role.

The triangle is a way of listening based on the concept that powerful and problematic stories recur in time, and so are independent of past, present, and future. Think of a triangle with one angle referring to the past, one angle referring to the present circumstances in the client's life, and one angle referring to the present relationship with the therapist. Any story, indeed, any comment by the client, can be seen as if it is thematically simultaneously applied to all three angles. The primary roles in a problematic story can be fulfilled by any number of different people—including the therapist. So a story set in the client's current life may be similar to one occurring in the client's past; or in the immediate present with the therapist (see Chapter 6 on Understanding Foundational Stories).

Let's listen as Nathan describes a brief current story. "So I went to the movies last night with Trevor and Mary. I'd looked forward to it all day. The movie got good reviews online, and I like Mary and Trevor. I guess it started in the ticket line when Mary and Trevor started talking about sailing. Now I've taken a sailing course, but I felt as though whatever I said didn't matter, like they were talking together and I was a third wheel. The theater was crowded, and we couldn't get seats together, so of course they got seats together and I was in another part of the auditorium altogether."

Applied to the past, one might reflect, were there important foundational stories where Nathan felt left out in a group of three? With his parents? Did he have two siblings?

Applied to the immediate present with the therapist, to what extent does Nathan feel not listened to now? To what extent is the therapist experienced as too far apart from him; or in a different space altogether? Why does he mention this now? What was the conversation immediately before? Could Nathan have experienced it as a micro-rejection that triggered the issue of being left out? These are questions for the therapist to first ask herself.

A vignette about the past would be similarly reflected on to see if it might also apply to the client's current life; or to the present circumstance with the therapist. A direct statement to the therapist (less common, as any direct communication about one's current relationship is more anxiety provoking) would be examined to see if it also applied to the client's current life and to his past. Listening via Malan's triangle does not mean the client *necessarily* lives the same story in all three time contexts; it merely raises the possibility so that the therapist can look for confirmation of a similar plot and theme.

Story Receiving: Thematic Witnessing

Since all stories require a witness, the quality of the therapist's witnessing is a crucial part of any change. Listening in a concerned but safe and objective manner with as few preconceptions as possible creates a context that the Jungians call the *temenos*, or holding environment/sacred space.

> Nathan 11.1 was a man who surely fit into the severe, multi-problem, far right of the graph in Chapter 10. Nathan was a large, rotund fellow who explained his size thusly: he had the misfortune to be born with three stomachs. It thus took both three times as long to digest his food as it did ordinary humans, and he was able to derive three times the calories from a given portion. While few of us share his belief, many of us can identify with the sense of how much easier it is to gain weight than to lose it, and with the unfairness that a half hour on the treadmill is barely equivalent to one chocolate bar.
>
> Now, Nathan had a couple of habits that made him a difficult tenant at his apartment building. For one thing, he liked to play the bagpipes, and he was pretty good with the pipes; he would march in the annual St. Patrick's Day parade. Unfortunately, his favorite time to practice was at 2:00 in the morning. This, however, was not the only—or even the main—thing that was a roadblock to his tenancy. Nathan was convinced that the superintendent in his building wanted, indeed was planning, to kill him. And Nathan knew the method of murder. The super was planning to gas him by releasing poison gas under the door and through the vents. On one evening when the odor of gas was particularly strong, Nathan stuffed towels and rags under the door and in the vents. He then proceeded to stop all the drains in the sink, the basin, and the toilet and turn on all the water and flush the toilet. He later explained that the particular gas the superintendent was using would dissolve in water. The resulting flood caused the ceiling in the apartment below to fall.
>
> When Nathan appeared at his group the next day, he was even more disheveled and agitated than usual. With encouragement from his compatriots, he finally told the above story. The group members listened quietly, and when he had finished, one man commented, "you really haven't felt safe in your own home." Nathan visibly relaxed.
>
> A woman added, "I don't know if your super wants to kill you or not, but I do know he has said some poisonous things. Remember that day when you came home in your band uniform and he called you a fat elf?"

Rather than commenting on the illogic of Nathan's actions, or the dire consequences, of which he was already painfully aware, the group instead reflected on the theme of his story. Even if Nathan could not feel safe in his apartment, he could at least have a home in the group.

I call the kind of witnessing that the group had been trained in "thematic witnessing" (or "thematic listening"). Thematic witnessing involves attending to and reflecting the themes in the client's stories. Hearing the themes in what one relates becomes a deep and profound listening that quickly lets the person know she has been heard. We do not often recognize our own themes, so that kind of reflection is at once new and familiar.

Carl Jung once commented that when approaching a new patient, he made an effort to forget everything he knew about psychotherapy. Admittedly that must have been a prodigious undertaking for Jung—not so much for the rest of us. But the sentiment is clear. We would do well to be anthropologists before being psychotherapists. Anthropologists are not trained in "microskills" (Ivey et al., 1968); instead they are trained to acknowledge, then forget, their assumptions and to hone their curiosity. They do not assume even common word meanings. This means, as psychotherapists, when a client says he is "anxious" or has been diagnosed "bipolar" that we do not profess to know what he means. This entails learning to live with our own anxiety about not knowing, about not being the expert on the client's experience.

Early in my career I had an experience which brought this home to me. I was working in community mental health, which at the time was a far cry from the underfunded and buffeted programs of today. It was a time of excitement about applying psychodynamic and behavioral skills to the full range of the populace, and about preventive mental health care which could operate by empowering communities. With what today would seem like almost surplus funding, staffs were comprised of seasoned psychiatrists and innovative researchers and psychoanalysts, and the untrained and inexperienced alike (and everything in between).

As a rookie therapist, I was supervised by a psychoanalyst who I knew as "Bill Masterson." The only problem was, I despised him. He would make these pronouncements and interpretations from on high. One day he told me, "you'll know you've made it as a psychotherapist when you can let a patient commit suicide." That was proof, I thought, of the ineptitude of the man and his methods.

I got my satisfaction shortly afterwards when the mental health center began a drive toward bureaucracy that in subsequent decades would drown it. They began by checking staff references (incredible as it seems now that references were rarely checked on hiring). When they called Masterson's references, one had a disconnected number and the other stated that he had never heard of Bill Masterson.

This prompted a call to his analytic institute and to his graduate school. Neither had any record of his matriculation. About this time Masterson stopped showing up at work, so the Center sent two staff to his apartment. The apartment had been cleaned out and the landlady informed them that Masterson had left the previous week.

It took me years to acknowledge that Masterson was right. I still like to think that he was just being provocative and did not really understand the wisdom in what he had said. As I hear it now, it is not a literal pronouncement that one would not stand in front of the window to prevent a client's jumping, or even that one would not assess and hospitalize someone if the need arose. Rather, it is about an atmosphere that the client can be whoever she is, living whatever story, no matter how tragic; and she and I will try to witness and understand it together.

Telling Stories

Witnessing as a relationship is not only about the atmosphere of receiving stories, but is about telling stories, as well. Not only telling one's story to a concerned witness, but hearing stories in return that resonate with who one is and what one is trying to communicate can be an important confirmation of being heard, and it can be a powerful teaching tool. It took me years to feel free enough to tell stories in therapy. Now, at last, I am also free to tell stories as well as to deeply hear them.

An important caveat in telling stories in therapy is to ask oneself, "who am I telling this story for?" If the answer is "myself," or anyone other than the client, then best to hold off. This is a place for the client to be witnessed. You will undoubtedly be witnessed at some point, as well, but that is not the goal. A second, related question is "why am I telling this story at this particular time? Is this the best way to affirm the client, or to help her feel or understand her story differently?" The proper story told at the proper time can be a most powerful intervention.

Over time, as one encounters similar situations, one will develop a stable of stories that help with certain difficulties. But often the most helpful is a story remembered or made up on the spot. Choosing a story is not best logically determined, but rather intuitively out of the current relationship with the client. It both mirrors the client's recognized and unrecognized story while opening possibilities. A couple of examples follow; you will find your own.

(Told to a woman who, since her divorce, has filled her life with activities and meetings and extra work assignments.)

> When I was a boy, I grew up in a river town. There was a broad, quiet river that went through the city, almost like a long lake. And every fall the town would host a speedboat regatta. People would line the banks for miles to watch these roaring boats as they raced one another, speeding down one side of the river, then back up by the other bank. And the highlight of the regatta, always placed at the end, was the huge, super-fast jet boats. Unlike most of the speed boats, which would push off from beside a pier and tool out to where the race began, these boats would start their engines on land, then launch off a special ramp at the

end of Main Street so that when they hit the water they would already be going at good clip. The reason they had to launch the jet boats that way was because those boats didn't float unless they were moving. And if they ever had engine trouble during a race, they would sink.

(Told to a man, a baseball fan, who had grown up as the only child—and possibly a surprise, as his step-siblings were many years older and grown. His parents had both been strivers, rarely at home; they had all but moved on with their lives by the time of his birth. He prided himself on his independence and ability to do things on his own.)

> One of my daughters had this gift early on where she would say things that weren't quite right. But in not being quite right, they made so much more sense. Kind of like Yogi Berra—you know, "this place is so crowded that no one comes here any more." Well one day my daughter comes in from playing outside and she says, "Daddy, I feel sorry for Meg." Now Meg was this girl in the neighborhood who seemed perfectly fine; we knew her parents. And so I said, "why do you feel sorry for Meg?" And my daughter said, "I feel sorry for Meg because she doesn't have any sisters, and she doesn't have any brothers. She's what they call a 'lonely child.'"

Taking time outside of work to read folktales is an especially good method for priming your own story pump. Doing your own Foundational Story Questionnaire may also be a way of priming stories from your own life. Telling stories is not something to prepare; rather it is something to allow out of the connection with your client.

Thus, changing the witnessing context within which a story is told creates change. Witnessing the story in an honest and concerned manner, whether through thematic listening or through telling resonant stories, changes the context within which a story is told. By definition, this creates a change in the story.

References

Grinder, J., & Bandler, R. (1976). *The Structure of Magic II*. Palo Alto, CA: Science and Behavior Books.

Hoobyar, T., & Dotz, T. (2013). *NLP: The Essential Guide to Neuro-linguistic Programming*. New York, NY: HarperCollins.

Ivey, A. E., Normington, C. J., Miller, C. D., Morrill, W. H., & Haase, R. F. (1968). Microcounseling and attending behavior: An approach to prepracticum counselor training. *Journal of Counseling Psychology, 15*(5, Pt. 2), pp. 1–12.

Smith, J. D. (2003). Transference, triangles, and trajectories. *Psychodynamic Practice, 9*(4), pp. 439–462.

Zimbardo, P. G., Sword, R. M., & Sword, R. K. M. (2012). *The Time Cure: Overcoming PTSD With the New Psychology of Time Perspective Therapy*. San Francisco, CA: Jossey-Bass.

Chapter 12

Helping Transform Characters

Characters are one of the elements essential to the formation of a story (minimally, the others are external and internal context, including a witness to the story; and a plot, minimally consisting of a problem or desire followed by an action and a reaction). There are always at least two characters in a story, a protagonist and an antagonist; and the protagonist is almost always personified. As mentioned earlier, the antagonist may be another person or another aspect of the self, but it can also be a force of nature or society. Since, as adults, we all have a life story that explains who we are, where we have been, and what we seek, then it is both logical and intuitive that we all have internal characters. As the Jungian Robert Johnson (1986, p. 45) observes, "We are all made up of many personalities or inner 'persons,' coexisting within one mind and one body. We think of ourselves as one individual, with one single viewpoint on life, but actually, if we pay attention, we have to admit that it feels as though there were several people living somewhere deep inside, each pulling in a different direction."

The stable of internal characters comes mostly from three sources. The first is from how we have repetitively inhabited the recurrent roles we have played (see Chapter 8). The second is from emotional or even traumatic experiences we have lived. The third source comes from adopting or modeling the important characters and roles we have encountered, especially in our early years. The psychoanalytic term for this third source has been widely adopted far beyond its use in analytic circles, and with good reason, as it is very descriptive. The term is "introject," and it comes from the Latin meaning "to throw inside." Introjects may be problematic, or they may be resources. We will return to working with problematic introjects.

The view that what we think of as a unitary psyche actually consists of two, three, or numerous parts sometimes conflicting, sometimes cooperating, is as old as modern psychotherapy. The characters in a foundational story have variously been called "ego states," "parts," "sub-personalities," "voices," "sides," "self-states," and "complexes." Pierre Janet (1907/2012) noted that a collection of ideas could become separated from a person's main personality, and could exist as an unconscious, separate personality. Later, Freud famously talked about the id, the ego, and the superego. Although for Freud these were more explanatory rather than elements to be directly accessed, because he was Freud, the view of the multi-part psyche took root in numerous subsequent therapists. Eric Berne (1964), before he published the concept of script (rigid life story), became known for his popularization of "Parent," "Adult," and "Child."

Connected, but parallel to Freud, Jung developed his concept of "complexes" out of his own experimental studies on the word association test (Jung, 1973). There he noted that the psyche is actually composed of clusters of thought, each of which is united by an affect. These clusters he termed "complexes." He later noted that some of these complexes were not just personal, but universal. We each express them in a personal manner, but it is our personal expression of a universal theme. This, of course, was the basis of the "archetype." Even Alfred Adler, who famously declared the psyche as unitary, managed to borrow Jung's idea of the complex in writing about the "Inferiority Complex."

Frederick ("Fritz") Perls (1993) saw "Top Dog" and "Under Dog" as common psychic divisions. Top Dog is related to the idea of superego, and Under Dog has id elements. Adapting some of J. L. Moreno's psychodrama techniques, Perls developed creative ways of working with the two dogs—methods that have influenced a variety of subsequent psychotherapists.

Also influenced by Freud, the husband and wife hypnotherapist team of Helen and John Watkins (1997) worked directly with what they called "ego states," which were the part and full personalities that make up the psyche. Psychodynamically oriented, John was the theoretician who explained their work in rather psychoanalytic terms, and Helen was the incredibly gifted and creative psychotherapist.

In a somewhat separate track was the work of another husband and wife duo, Hal and Sidra Stone (1989). They developed what they called the "voice dialogue" method for working with "subpersonalities."

What I hope to convey is that there has been an undercurrent, sometimes practical and sometimes theoretical, going back even before Freud, of the notion of a divided psyche containing differing characters. The divided psyche moved center stage in the mid-1990s, with the work of the Watkins' hypnotherapist protégées Maggie Phillips and Claire Frederick (1995); and that of the family therapist turned individual ego state therapist, Richard Schwartz (also 1995). From there the acceptance and use of psychic parts in therapy has mushroomed. The recognition that many clients easily relate through their own experience of having different sides, or differing voices in their minds, and that accepting this and delving into the parts and their relationships rather than engaging in an all-too-often vain struggle to deny, eliminate, or unify voices in service of the notion of a unitary personality, can be freeing for therapist and client alike.

What few seem to have recognized is that these characters are part of one's life story; "parts" are also characters in the larger dance of one's story. This understanding opens possibilities and flexibility. As a therapist, one can begin with characters (parts, ego states, sub-personalities) and allow them to lead to story; one can also begin with story and use that to access and work with characters. Many ego state therapists, perhaps influenced by Schwartz, begin by introducing the client to the concept of a multi-mind, then help the client find and work with his parts. This can be extremely useful, all the more so if the therapist has an eye to these parts and roles being characters and roles in the client's life story. In work with characters, it is helpful to have the flexibility to approach the work by beginning either with characters or by beginning with story. This enables the therapist to better individualize the treatment.

It is not the focus of this work to survey the plethora of psychotherapies using parts, ego states, or related concepts. Rather, in taking a storied view of the psyche, I will touch on theories and techniques that may especially help the reader elucidate and work with the characters in a life story.

Working with Characters (General):

Nathan 12.1, a government scientist, returned to therapy after a resurgence of depression and anxiety. His agency had been under extreme political pressure because their scientific studies ran contrary to the administration's views on climate change. There had already been one failed attempt to shutter the office; now the politicians were looking to relocate the office to the hinterlands in hopes that none of the staff would transfer. In that climate, Nathan found that he had submitted a report with a minor statistical error. Although the error in no way changed the conclusions and could only be found by re-analyzing the data, it set off a cascade of self-recrimination for Nathan. Nathan felt that, in the past, he had been able to temporarily "feed" his self-castigating part as a result of his previous therapy, and that had given him sometimes lengthy periods of relief.

I asked Nathan if he would be willing to contact and better understand the self-critical part. Nathan agreed, and I helped him calm, then used a modified focusing procedure by asking him to hold the self-critical part in mind while he got a bodily sense of "all of that." I then asked what words or images emerged. Nathan immediately said that an image of a young man pulling a large rock by a rope came to mind. As it was near the end of the session, I helped him re-orient to the current place and time with the suggestion that he could remember all that he had experienced while retaining the calm that he had felt. As homework, I asked Nathan if over the ensuing week he would be willing to reflect on the image he had encountered. Nathan readily agreed.

I knew the image was important; I did not know what part of Nathan the young man represented, nor what the rock denoted; nor how, specifically, it related to self-castigation. Also, we had a scene, but no story yet. I could generate speculations, but that might make me less open to whatever Nathan's experience proved to be. Patience is a bitch.

When he returned, Nathan had indeed been reflecting. He noted that it occurred to him that the young man in the image was in his late twenties or early thirties. This was a time in his own life when he went to graduate school and when he got married. It was also a time when his depression was quite severe, and he feared that others could read his thoughts and would ostracize him for them. Nathan easily returned to the image, this time as his current self. When he approached the young man, the young man attempted to hand the rope to his current self. Nathan refused and backed away; he did not want to hold the rock for fear he would be tethered to it in his current life. Now we had a story. Once again, I asked Nathan to reflect on what he had experienced.

When Nathan returned, he said he had realized that the young man had not been trying to give up the rope and the rock, as he had no concept other than that pulling the rock was his fate. The young man had merely wanted current Nathan to understand, to experience the burden that he carried, to be a witness.

It would have been far too easy to make assumptions, like that the young man wanted to give over his burden. It is so important to follow the client until there is a complete story; and it will always be a story you had not imagined. Now we had the story of a tethered young man who assumes that the future will be like the present; who has surrendered to what he considered his fate; and who wants only to have someone understand. Now we could co-create a different story.

I asked Nathan to return to the image and listen as the young man recounts his experience of dragging a rock that others cannot see. Then I asked Nathan to explain that he was from the young man's future, and to tell him what was going to happen: that Nathan would complete graduate school, and would become a respected government scientist; that the marriage the young man was contemplating would be a lasting support for all these years; and that he would have two children, a boy and a girl, who would grow up to find their own way.

At this, the real-life Nathan burst into tears. Between sobs, he said that his younger self never imagined that this was possible. He said the younger man was now sprawled on his back, looking up at the sky, and as relaxed as he had ever been.

When Nathan returned, he stated that he had told his wife and a good friend of his imagery experience, and they both immediately understood, leaving him even more validation. Also, a researcher from another agency had not responded to several emails about a joint project. Nathan found himself in an old loop, thinking he must have done something wrong and the guy must be angry at him. He tried exercising, which often helped him calm, but to no avail. He noted he was headed for a miserable weekend of spiraling self-recrimination and depression. Then he remembered "I do not have to take the young man's rope; and the young man can remember that it will work out well." Instantly the anxiety, depression, and self-castigation ceased. Nathan stated it was like flipping a switch (and indeed it was, a switching to a changed story).

He had recently read an article touting the instantaneous cure of depression that some people experienced as a result of taking hallucinogens. Nathan had thought at the time that the article was a bit overblown. He said, "I realize now that sometimes depression can be turned off, and without the use of a drug experience."

The example of Nathan 12.1, above, is an example of beginning with character work and using that to lead to story. The story in that case was one not remembered, but created by the client using a modification of a procedure first identified by Carl Jung called "active imagination." It makes no difference whether the story is remembered or created, as long as it is consonant with the template of the client's life story. As we saw in Part 2, memories are themselves creations to a greater or lesser degree.

Accessing Characters

For those therapists who do not have a background in ego state or parts work, helping a client access internal characters can feel daunting. Rest assured that for many clients this will feel much more natural than it does initially for you as therapist. After all, they are expressing how they naturally organize the world; you are re-training.

Although some who work with ego states begin therapy by introducing the client to the idea of the divided psyche (Schwartz' book *An Introduction to the Internal Family Systems Model* (2001) is a very accessible introduction for clients interested in learning about the multiplicity of mind), I find it most useful for such work to emerge organically. Not every client is able or willing to work in this manner, so I do not set up the expectation that this will be the modality. Instead, I listen for possible entries. One easy entry is when the client says something to the effect of "part of me wants to take that job, but part of me is reluctant." The client already has some sense that she is of at least two minds, so this is easy to build upon. The therapist can respond with "tell me about the part that is reluctant." I try to begin with the side that is likely more emotionally powerful, the "Under Dog" in Fritz Perls' therapy.

In response to "tell me about the part that . . ." the client is likely to respond with reasons for not changing jobs rather than directly answering the request to tell about that part of herself. "Well, I've got seniority, and though I don't particularly like my boss, she's not the worst and I generally know what she wants . . ." It is then helpful to bring the client back imagistically to a part of herself. "I wonder if you would take a moment and go inside to let an image emerge of that part of you that needs the familiar and the safe? Just allow whatever picture or story or feeling comes."

If the client responds with an image or a feeling, help her expand on it. "It's strange, but when you asked me to go inside, I felt this warm, damp place in my chest."

"Good. Now let yourself focus on that warm, damp place. How big is it?" (then how heavy or light? What kind of texture does it have? What color is it? Does it make any sound? Does it have a gender? Etc.). After helping the client expand the image, you can ask for the image to give a name: "now ask that warm damp place what it would like to be called. Just wait and see what word or phrase emerges."

The naming is literally a characterization. That feeling or image will undoubtedly be connected to foundational memory stories in which that character is the protagonist. Those stories may or may not have been previously accessible. You can ask the client directly for the associated stories. "How old is 'Warm Feeling?' Ask her to tell you the story of how she came into your life." Or, "ask 'Warm Feeling' what her job is, what role she plays in your life."

> "She says Protector (common)."
> "Ask her to tell you a story of a time when she needed to be the protector."

You are, in effect, using characters, parts or ego states to access foundational stories. The example given above begins with the client expressing ambivalence about an upcoming decision. It could just as well have begun with an expressed affect, as Robert Johnson (1986) and Jay Noricks (2018) show. For example, a client who complains "I've been feeling down in the dumps lately" can be asked if they have access to that feeling now (it is very likely they do, as this is the source of their bringing it up). They are then asked to let that feeling give them an image, story, or sensation, and you can proceed as above.

When the client complains that no image comes, Richard Schwartz (1995) asks the client to go inside and see if there is some other part that is preventing an image. He then works to access *that* part. It is a way of seeing defense as protection and accessing the character who is protecting.

Jay Noricks (2018) uses a delightful guided imagery when no image is forthcoming, and this is often useful prior to Schwartz' method of finding the blocking character. After getting permission to proceed, he has the client take several calming breaths, then imagine they are walking along the seashore. He helps them expand the sensations of the ocean sounds, the sand under their feet, the salty smell, so that they are in the scene. He then asks them to notice two old fishermen dressed in their yellow rain slickers and walking toward the client. As they get closer, the client can notice that they hold a net between them. It is a magic net that can pass harmlessly through anything and anyone, but it is able to catch and hold that part (that does not want to change jobs; that is depressed; etc. whatever the character is that you are trying to help the client access). The fishermen pass on either side of the client, and as they do so, the mesh passes harmlessly through her, netting the hidden part. The fishermen stop, and she can look into the net. What does she see?

Noricks is in effect creating a story that assists the client in accessing the repeating characters in their own story. In the rather rare event that neither Noricks' nor Schwartz's technique is effective, accessing and working directly with characters may not fit for the client at this time.

The above are methods for identifying emerging persistent characters in a person's foundational and life stories. The Character Map (see Chapter 9) can also help to identify the stable of characters in a person's life story.

Once having helped the client identify and contact internal characters, one of the issues becomes that of the role of the therapist. Helen Watkins (1997) spoke directly to the person's characters, as if the person had brought in a group of people for therapy. Fritz Perls (1993), on the other hand, believed that having the therapist directly in the dialogue could introduce transference projections onto the therapist by different characters, and could make for an unnecessary complication. I have tended to heed Perls' warning, and find it helpful to have the person dialogue with his own characters. This way, too, the person learns directly to work with her own characters, and the dialogue becomes an integral part of any change or agreement. The client cannot say it results solely from the therapist's intervention.

Working With Characters, General

Through the development of active imagination, Jung was one of the first therapists to identify and dialogue with the characters in a person's story. Active imagination is the often-unacknowledged technique that enables either the client or the therapist in every ego state therapy to engage in a conversation with various parts; a conversation that, just like the dialogues with our friends, is unpredictable. It is called "active" because the person actively engages with the images.

The technique of active imagination as Jung practiced it involves beginning with an image or a character from a dream. Hold that character in mind until there is some change in the image. Step into the image and speak to the figure, listening to what it has to say (Pascal, 1992). The inner figure will take on a life of its own, and will often say or do surprising things. Pascal recommends writing during the dialogue, or doing a summary immediately thereafter. When done with a client, you can record the highlights and give the notes to the client.

Robert Johnson expands on the technique in his excellent book *Inner Work* (1986). He speaks of four entries into active imagination. These include having the client become aware of her daydreams and actively stepping into them, dialoguing with the characters. We choose our daydreams because they resonate with our story, and this turns a passive fantasy into an active, agentic activity. A second entry is that of dreams. A third entry is what Johnson terms "personification," as he is helping the client personify her problem. Here you encourage the client to turn inward and say "I'd like to speak to the one who is anxious (depressed, cannot manage the finances, keeps checking the locks, etc.)." This becomes similar to Richard Schwartz' "inner dialogue."[1]

In the fourth entry into the work, Johnson helps the client enter active imagination by going to a particular place in fantasy and seeing who you meet there. Mark Lawrence (2009, Personal Communication) used an imagery exercise for this task. He would help the client calm, then imagine entering a long hallway with doors on either side. He would have the client first observe and listen at each door, then choose a door to knock upon and enter to see who or what he may encounter. He then goes to each room in turn, or to as many as time allows. Behind each door the person encounters a different self character. A helpful variation on the technique is to have each character tell a story. These are treated as foundational stories.

The spontaneous use of place to engage characters in active imagination is illustrated in the case of Harriet 12.1.

> One day Harriet, with a sheepish look, confessed, "I think I'm in love." Harriet was usually neither shy nor sheepish. I tried to contain my shock as I asked, "so tell me more." Harriet, a very bright and creative woman in her mid-30s, had given up a promising career to become the sole caregiver for her special-needs son. Her husband's job entailed often travelling away from home for weeks at a time. The marriage had been strained, in part by the husband's attitude that his son should suck it up and act normal. Harriet and her husband had not been in love in years, and I could not imagine that Harriet had either the time or the energy for an affair.
>
> "Well," said Harriet, "I think I'm in love with a Viking." She went on to describe how she had begun watching Viking movies on TV. It had turned into something of an obsession, inhabiting her daydreams and her nighttime dreams. She had begun to image one particular Viking.
>
> "Have you spoken with him?" I asked.
>
> "Oh, God, no!" She responded with the awe and fright of a smitten schoolgirl.
>
> "I wonder if you might consider speaking with him here?"
>
> Harriet was quiet for a long moment. "I'd be too embarrassed, you know, with you watching, and all."

"I can turn my back." I swiveled my desk chair until I faced away. Harriet turned inward and began what became a years-long collaboration with Thor the Viking. At odd moments—after her son had retired in the evenings, while waiting in the doctor's office during her son's treatments, even while waiting in line, Harriet would travel to a particular wharf where various long boats and a Viking ship were docked. Eventually Thor would meet her. Sometimes he would take her sailing on the Viking ship to a different adventure each time. Every adventure had a lesson, something neither she nor I would have anticipated, but always something that fit. On this first meeting he told her, "you need to take the helm of your own ship."

Working With Characters, Interactive

Since many of our internal characters are derived from the stories we have lived and heard interacting with others, it comes as no surprise that there are often alliances and conflicts among our internal characters, just as in our family of origin. I remember some years ago seeing a cartoon in *The New Yorker*. It showed a huge auditorium with a speaker behind the dais on stage in the front. He was looking out over a vast sea of empty seats. The caption was "The First Annual Meeting of the Non-dysfunctional Family Society."

The pattern of those interactions can become not only problematic, but solidified. Helping a client to change the interactions among her internal family opens and changes her life story. Very often two characters become polarized in issue or outlook (Stone & Stone, 1989). These represent a personification of two opposing internal viewpoints that buffet the client back and forth (rarely can a person be simultaneously cognizant and accepting of both). In those moments the therapist may become the family therapist or the management consultant helping the warring parties to air their differences.

One common and helpful technique to aid in this is that of the internal conference room (Pace, 2007; Schmidt, 2009; Mark Lawrence, Personal Communication, 2012; Tinnin & Gantt, 2013). I use a guided imagery with hypnotic elements to guide the client down steps in a comfortable building. At the bottom of the steps is a nicely appointed conference room with relaxing chairs looking out on a garden. I have the client invite the polarized characters, plus any resource character who can be supportive but neutral. The client is encouraged to ask if there is anyone else who should be there but is not. The object is to fully understand both parties and how they came to their positions—not to come to any agreement or decision unless one spontaneously emerges. The client is encouraged to show and demand respect throughout. At the end, the participants can each go to wherever they feel most comfortable. The client is taken back up the steps, back to the current time and place with a sense of comfort and a memory for all that transpired.

Some clients like this technique so much that they commence regular "family meetings" on their own in the internal conference room. This is not only an occasion to examine all reactions and ideas to a current situation; but it begins to change the life story by changing the story tone to one of self-acceptance. Note that once again a dialectical story has been used to change the client's story. By fully hearing both sides, a story stuck in the conflict between thesis and antithesis can allow a synthesis to emerge.

Working With Character Emotion

The characters in our story all have back stories (which are often foundational stories), desires, and emotions. Schwartz (1995) finds that negative and chronic emotions are often carried as burdens by one or more characters; indeed, sometimes it is that character's job, like the Sin Eater in English folk tradition,[2] to absorb and carry the negativity for the whole system.

There are two especially helpful methods for releasing unwanted emotion, both once again creating new stories to deal with an old story. The first, a guided imagery called the "silent abreaction," was designed by Helen Watkins (Watkins & Watkins, 1997). In imagery, she has the client accompany her on a path through a pleasant wood. They round a turn and find a large boulder blocking the path. Nearby is a stout wooden cudgel. The therapist encourages the client to pick up the staff and strike the boulder. She tells her that the boulder represents whatever has blocked her path, and emboldens the client to strike it repeatedly until she is exhausted. They are then transported to a lovely meadow where the therapist requests the client to say something positive about herself. This allows the client to safely release frustration and rage without recrimination from herself or others.

The second technique is one designed by Jay Noricks (2011). In it the therapist asks if the client is ready to release whatever unpleasant feeling she has been carrying. If the client responds in the affirmative, the therapist asks her whether she would like to release it to fire, air, or water. Whichever the client picks the therapist assists her in designing an image that completely dissolves the unwanted emotion. For example, if the client picks air to dissolve her shame, she might imagine herself standing in the desert in a strong wind that blows through her and catches and scatters the droplets of shame into ever smaller particles ever further away. If the client states she is not ready to release the negative emotion, then her need to hold on to it becomes the focus.

Resourcing

It is at the level of characters that one of the basic change methodologies, that of resourcing, is most specific. See Chapter 13 on changing plot for an example of how bringing in a particular resource character can change the plot.

Changing the Story Character Perspective

We tend to see ourselves as protagonist in our story, the "I" to other characters' "it." When a client can succinctly describe a current dilemma, describing that dilemma in a detailed manner from the vantage point of a minor supporting character or an uninvolved friend can change the client's understanding. It is often too difficult at first to describe the story from the vantage point of the one considered the antagonist (the mean boss, the hurtful spouse), but seeing it from a third-party perspective lends distance and priority.

Working With Problematic Introjects

Many ego state and parts theorists have noted that some parts are modeled upon the parents or other early significant others of the client. Therapists have suggested that clients have taken inside, or "introjected" their early conception of their parents. Many theorists distinguish these introjects from actual parts or characters of the client, as they are taken from without rather than being a true division of the psyche by repetition or trauma. While it is commonly understood that parts, as divisions of the psyche, may at times be subsumed or integrated, they cannot be expelled, any more than one could expel an arm. With introjects, however, Gordon Emmerson (2007) tells them to leave with reported success.

The confusion may be at least partly resolved if introjects are seen to be roles as opposed to characters. A role can be shed. Noricks (2011) has an elegant way of doing this. He has the client observe what seems to be the often large and frightening part. As they observe, they are to notice a zipper. They are to pull the zipper, causing the character to shed its costume and revealing what is often a scared child beneath.

Creating a Character:

> Nathan 12.3 was a bright and affable man, the sort of fellow who makes fast friends and whom both men and women enjoy being around. He had a college degree, but worked installing cable for a cable company. Nathan was a hard worker, and his boss was a big fan; it seemed as if he could easily rise in the company if he wanted. Nathan had many friends, a job that he did well and that paid sufficiently for a bachelor, and a dedicated girlfriend. He seemed satisfied with his life, so much so that I was not clear why he sought psychotherapy.
>
> And then he just disappeared. He had always been early to work and never one to take time off. So when he didn't show or call his boss, the boss at first thought it strange, then became concerned. Nathan's girlfriend could not reach him, either. Frantic, she contacted his boss and together they went to his apartment.

The apartment was tidy and retained all his possessions; it was as if he had left for work. The two filed a missing persons report, but to no avail. Days became weeks. The company filled his job and his distraught girlfriend tried to get on with her life. His possessions were auctioned and his apartment rented.

Several months had passed when I got a call from Nathan. Could he come in and see me? He had just gotten a job with another company and was in the process of re-building his life. I agreed to see him.

Finally Nathan told me his story. It was a tragic story in the classic Greek sense of the well-respected hero who has everything, but retains a tragic flaw (the vulnerability of Achilles where his mother held him by the heel when she dipped him into the protective waters of the River Styx, or the oracle's prophecy for Oedipus such that by trying to avoid the predicted fate he actually invites it). This was not the first time that Nathan had disappeared. In fact, every year or so when Nathan had a job and friends and a lover and, by his own account, felt happy, he would walk away. He knew that the leaving time was approaching when he begun saving cash and stashing it in his apartment. When the day came, he would abandon all his responsibilities, relationships, and possessions and take a bus to a small rural town in another state. There he would take a room in a cheap motel and stay until his cash was exhausted. Then he would make his way to a metropolitan area, often, but not always, the same city, and begin his life afresh. His own protagonist was caught in a cycle of building a life, then throwing it away, then re-building and repeating like a perverse scene from the movie *Groundhog Day*. On even those rare occasions (usually upon his return from exile) when he had acknowledged the cycle to a therapist and had even been medicated for supposed depressive episodes, the circle would claim him again and he would stop medications and drop out once more.

The tragic repetitive story was impervious; Nathan needed a new story.

One of the most effective routes to building a new story is through the creation of a new character. The first theorist of which I am aware of describing the building of a new character was George Kelly (1963). Writing in the 1950s, Kelly is often lumped into the category of behavioral theorists, but no category of therapy is a fit for the iconoclastic Kelly. Inventor of the Rep Grid, Kelly was at least as cognitive and constructivist as he was behavioral. Kelly thought of the individual as a budding scientist who continually attempted to see what worked in his/her own circumstances to make a successful life. Kelly believed we experience the world via bipolar categories he called "constructs."

One of Kelly's many innovative therapy techniques was to have the person choose someone (real or fantasied) s/he would like to be more like. He would then have the client write a long character sketch of that person, then begin to role play the person, first in the office, then in situations in the client's life.

> Accordingly, I asked Nathan what his long-range vision was of what he would like to do in his life. Nathan responded that "it may sound silly, but I've always wanted to own a winery and vineyard." Nathan and I began to develop a character sketch of the vintner. Of course, to be a successful vintner, one must be incredibly patient and consistent, as the grapes will not even bear fruit for years. And there are few vacations, let alone disappearances, for the successful vintner. Nathan began to practice summoning the vintner into his everyday life.
>
> I last heard from Nathan several years later. He did not own a winery; but he was a successful manager at a telecom company, and he had called on the occasion of his marriage. He had not had any further disappearances.

Although I was not aware of it at the time, Kelly's method of helping a person create a new story through developing a new character is similar to a child psychotherapy technique pioneered by, of all people, Arnold Lazarus. Lazarus, you may recall, was the developer of multimodal behavior therapy. Somewhat apart from his behavior therapy thrust, Lazarus wrote a very useful book on the use of imagery in psychotherapy called *In the Mind's Eye* (Lazarus, 1977). In the book he describes a technique which he calls "emotive imagery" for children. The procedure involves finding a child's hero or heroine, then creating a story that allows the child to overcome her problems by becoming the assistant to the hero in a new story.

Characters and the Self: A Brief Treatise

As you are no doubt aware, many whole books have been written on the nature and existence of the self, and I certainly will not do the topic justice here. I can only point to the range of conceptions and my own evolving understanding as it relates to story. The topic especially emerges in character work, as once you realize that the psyche is not unitary, you begin to wonder just who is doing the realizing.

Schwartz (1995) believes in an almost transpersonal Self who ultimately takes charge of all the characters in a successful therapy. Indeed, so important is this to Schwartz that he labels his website "Selfleadership.org," and a good part of his therapy is in shoring up the skills of Self and various characters' acceptance of a Self. However, when he writes about Self, he notes it is characterized by a host of "C" words: Courage, Calm, Commitment, etc., which seems to make it merely an idealized resource ego state.

Perhaps equally effective is Maggie Phillips and Claire Frederick's (1995) having the client access "the wisest part of yourself," which is clearly a resource state with no transpersonal overtones.

Similar to Schwartz is the Jungian Jeffrey Raff, who, in his book *The Practice of Ally Work* (2006) uses active imagination techniques to access transpersonal allies. Jung himself saw the Self as the whole of the interconnected psyche. In this view, consciousness is a small bottle afloat on a vast ancient unconscious ocean with the wisdom and resources of humankind and of the planet. Jung himself had a transpersonal ally whom he called "Philamon."

On the opposite pole, Mark Lawrence (Personal Communication, 2009) believed in the psyche as composed of ego states formed through repetition or through trauma. He never spoke of an overriding Self. In a sense, this is akin to the Buddhist doctrine of "no self," the concept that we, like the rest of the universe, are in constant change with no separate, enduring and over-arching self.

William James (1988), father of American psychology, as always, offers some wisdom on the nature of the self. He asserted that there are two forms of self: the "I" and the "me." The "I" is a protagonist/author who is of active voice, and the "me" is a protagonist/actor recipient of action. McAdams and others have built on this, coming to conceive of the self as story, or perhaps as author/story synergy.

Summary: I have only here skimmed the surface of the works related to ego state therapy in an attempt to help the reader make a useful literature even more so by interpreting it in light of its application to character and to story. We have examined briefly the changing of foundational and life story through the use of the characters involved; accessing characters using variations on active imagination; working with the conflicts and polarizations among characters in a life story; working with negative or overwhelming emotion; changing stories by changing character perspective; using characters as resources to change story; and reflecting briefly on the self as it relates to author, narrator, and protagonist. In our next section we will focus on the changing of plot in foundational and life stories.

Notes

1. Schwartz uses either an inner dialogue, or an external dialogue. The external dialogue is similar to Fritz Perls' two-chair technique, except Schwartz interacts directly with the characters. Schwartz says little about when he might use one or the other technique. In general, I find it depends upon the client, and I usually offer them a choice. My observation is that the internal dialoguing fits for more introverted people, and the external dialoguing for more extraverted.
2. For a few shillings the Sin Eater would eat bread that had been placed on the breast of a corpse, symbolically taking on the sin of the departed one so that his/her ghost

would not have to wander. As he plied his trade, the Sin Eater would become more and more of a pariah in the village, becoming increasingly identified with the sins he had absorbed.

References

Berne, E. (1964). *Games People Play: The Psychology of Human Relationships*. New York, NY: Grove Press.
Emmerson, G. (2007). *Ego State Therapy*. Carmarthen, Wales: Crown House Publishing.
James, W. (Reprint 1988). *The Principles of Psychology*. Chicago, IL: Encyclopaedia Britannica.
Janet, P. (1907/2012). *The Major Symptoms of Hysteria: Fifteen Lectures Given in the Medical School of Harvard University*. London: Forgotten Books.
Johnson, R. (1986). *Inner Work: Using Dreams and Active Imagination for Personal Growth*. New York, NY: Harper & Row.
Jung, C. G. (1973). *The Collected Works of C. G. Jung: Volume 2: Experimental Studies*. Princeton, NJ: Princeton University Press.
Kelly, G. A. (1963). *A Theory of Personality: The Psychology of Personal Constructs*. New York, NY: W. W. Norton.
Lazarus, A. (1977). *In the Minds Eye: The Power of Imagery for Personal Enrichment*. New York, NY: Guilford Press.
Noricks, J. (2011). *Parts Psychology: A Trauma-Based, Self-State Therapy for Emotional Healing*. Los Angeles, CA: New University Press.
Noricks, J. (2018). *Healing Amelia: How Parts and Memory Therapy Heals Rage PMS, PMDD, Postpartum Depression, and Failure in Mother-Daughter Bonding*. Los Angeles, CA: New University Press.
Pace, P. (2007). *Lifespan Integration: Connecting Ego States Through Time*. Roslyn, WA: Lifespan Integration, LLC.
Pascal, E. (1992). *Jung to Live By: A Guide to the Practical Application of Jungian Principles for Everyday Life*. New York, NY: Warner Books.
Perls, F. S. (1993). *Gestalt Therapy Verbatim*. Gouldsboro, ME: Gestalt Journal Press.
Phillips, M., & Frederick, C. (1995). *Healing the Divided Self: Clinical and Ericksonian Hypnotherapy for Post-Traumatic and Dissociative Conditions*. New York, NY: W. W. Norton.
Raff, J. (2006). *The Practice of Ally Work: Meeting and Partnering With Your Spirit Guide in the Imaginal World*. Berwick, ME: Nicholas-Hays.
Schmidt, S. J. (2009). *The Developmental Needs Meeting Strategy: An Ego State Therapy for Healing Adults With Childhood Trauma and Attachment Wounds*. San Antonio, TX: DNMS Institute.
Schwartz, R. C. (1995). *Internal Family Systems Therapy*. New York, NY: Guilford Press.
Schwartz, R. C. (2001). *Introduction to the Internal Family Systems Model*. Eugene, OR: Trailheads Publishing.
Stone, H., & Stone, S. L. (1989). *Embracing Ourselves: The Voice Dialogue Manual*. Novato, CA: New World Library.
Tinnin, L., & Gantt, L. (2013). *The Instinctual Trauma Response and Dual Brain Dynamics: A Guide for Trauma Therapy*. Morgantown, WV: Gargoyle Press.
Watkins, J. G., & Watkins, H. H. (1997). *Ego States: Theory and Therapy*. New York, NY: W. W. Norton.

Chapter 13

Changing Plot

> The Plot, then, is the first principle, and, as it were, the soul of a tragedy.
> —Aristotle (Butcher, S. H., trans.) (2013), *Poetics, Book VI*, The Project Gutenberg eBook of *Poetics*, Project Gutenberg #1974

As Aristotle notes, the plot is the essential bones of a story. The plot is the movement through time of the protagonist(s) as she pursues her goal or approaches her problem. It is altered by changes to any other part of a story: if the tale takes place in a different context, or a story is narrated from a different character's point of view, the plot is changed. Change the ending or alter the tone or theme of the story, and you change the plot.

Many therapeutic approaches indirectly change plot by altering the context in which the story is told (humanistic therapists and interpersonal therapists); or by working with the characters to alter their emotions or interactions (ego state therapists); or by changing the theme (Young's schema-focused therapy or Mann's brief dynamic therapy); or by enlarging the life story (Jungians). By far the most common way of indirectly altering plot is by altering the perceptions or cognitions of the protagonist or narrator. Both cognitive behaviorists and psychodynamic therapists focus here, albeit with different methods. By and large the CBT therapists directly target the illogical cognitions of the narrator/protagonist. Psychoanalysts interpret the problematic ways in which the person relates to the analyst as a way of eliciting an emotional experience of the here-and-now example of how the person relates to important others in both the present and the past. Certainly, virtually all of these approaches also impact other aspects of the client's life story—fair enough. I have tried to encapsulate here what I see as the primary emphasis of these theorists, the parts of story they each think most important to change. My point is that only a few theorists work directly with plot.

Two of these approaches are the Core Conflictual Relationship Theme (CCRT) of Lester Luborsky (1984; and Luborsky, L. & Crits-Cristoph, P., 1990) and the imagery theory of Mark Lawrence (Personal Communication, multiple dates in 2009).

Lester Luborsky

Lester Luborsky (1920–2009) was a prolific psychodynamically oriented researcher who penned some nine books and over 400 articles in a long career. He developed the CCRT to understand the central theme that a client is concerned about, but the CCRT is actually a way of summarizing the narrative plot of a person's life story.

The CCRT can be very easy to use and very helpful in evaluating recurrent plots. Although it has been used in much research by examining written transcripts, it can be easy to use in the course of therapy. It involves listening to interpersonal stories from the client, which Luborsky calls "relationship episodes." Luborsky makes the point that most stories in therapy are interpersonal in nature.

One then formulates the story plot in terms of three components. The three components are: Wish, Response from Others (RO), and Response from Self (RS). The wish includes the protagonist's needs, hopes, intentions, and desires, as well as wishes. The responses from others and from the self can be in the form of behavior, emotion, or thoughts. Luborsky rates the most frequent occurring wish, RO, and RS. He finds the same frequent CCRT occurring across the relationship with the therapist, current relationships in the client's life, and past important relationships. In other words, he has summarized an important plot in one's life story.

All plots begin with a problem or desire. The protagonist is propelled to solve the problem or seek what is desired (hope or desire can be conceived as a common type of story problem; then the problem is the perceived lack of what is desired). When seen in light of plot, Luborsky's "wish" is the desire that propels the protagonist to solve the problem. The Response from Others is the frequent scene one of the story, or occasionally scene two (where Response from Self is scene one). The Response from Self is either scene two (the protagonist's response to other characters' response) or, sometimes, scene one (the protagonist's response to her own wish). Thus Luborsky's CCRT is Motivation—Scene One—Scene Two. This forms a handy summary of most of the plot.

For research purposes, Luborsky has lists of 34 common wishes and 30 responses from others and 30 responses from self, making for the possibility of over 30,000 plotlines. These were developed by his colleagues Crits-Christoph and Demorest from the literature (e.g., Murray's needs); and from judges' rating of CCRTs with clients (Barber et al., 1990). Sample Wishes are: To be understood, to be accepted, to accept others, to be close (or distant) to others, to help or be helped, to hurt or be hurt, to avoid conflict, to be like others, to be independent, to assert, etc. In the Responses from Others, the list includes that others: are/are not understanding, do/do not respect me, are helpful/unhelpful, oppose me, are controlling, give me independence, are cooperative, are angry, are loving, etc. The Responses from Self include: understanding, liking/disliking others, independence, self-control, confidence, anger, feeling loved/unloved, jealous, anxious,

150   Changing Foundational and Life Stories

ashamed, happy, etc. Thus, Responses from Others seem to include more behaviors, and Responses from Self more affect. The above examples give a sense of the level of generality that Luborsky uses. Reviewing these categories shows that the wishes and responses are those either directly expressed by the client or generalized from them in a manner that is no more than moderately inferential. It is instructive to peruse these, but in a clinical setting one need not be confined by looking for particular wishes or responses.

Let us look at a foundational story from an earlier chapter to determine the CCRT.

The story is reprinted here. I would encourage you to think to yourself what the Wishes, Responses from Others, and Responses from Self are, then see the list I have developed below the story (Table 13.1). Responses in parentheses are those that include a rater's generalization or assumption. The most important CCRT would be the one that recurs most frequently across multiple stories.

> I was three, because we had just moved to the house where I grew up and I was three at the time we moved. I had just met the little girl "Cathy" who lived behind us, and she had come over to play. There was a pile of old bricks in the back of our yard, and Cathy was helping me stack the bricks to make a filling station. The brick filling station got to be almost as tall as I was. I put one more brick on top, and all the bricks fell down. One of them hit me on the back of the hand. It must have cut a vein, because the blood poured out. It did not hurt badly, but when I saw all the blood, I got scared and began to cry. I got up and ran toward the house. Mother came out and wrapped my hand in towels, then put me in the back of our old black Plymouth and drove me to the doctor's house. The pediatrician did not believe in stitches, so he closed the wound with a butterfly bandage; consequently, I had the scar for decades. It seems afterward that my father told me you had to stack bricks flat so they would be less likely to fall. It was a bit disappointing, because that meant I couldn't build as high.
>
> Feeling: Excitement, then fear.
>
> Part that stands out: Running toward the house with blood pouring from my hand.
>
> Feeling: Frightened.

Table 13.1 Foundational Story CCRT Example

Wishes	Responses from Others	Responses from Self
To create, build high	Join, assist, cooperate	(Not aware of limits)
(To seek help, comfort)	Aid, rescue, (provides aid inadequately in order to avoid hurting)	Frightened
	Advise	Disappointment; (acceptance and enactment of advice)

Note that while the CCRT places the spotlight on the interpersonal aspects of a story, there are necessarily potentially important elements that may be omitted. In the above foundational story, the setting among change and newness comes to mind. Also, in the above story, there is a difference in how the protagonist experiences peers and authorities. Further, there is a difference in how female and male authorities respond. Females are "all in," whereas males either hold back or remain at a distance and advise. None of this is obvious from just the CCRT.

In psychotherapy, Luborsky first listens to the client's communications and stories. He figures the most frequent CCRTs, and/or the ones related to the presenting problem. He notes both the part(s) of the CCRT most related to the client's problem or suffering, and any conflicts within the CCRT. He then uses the CCRT to inform treatment focus. His treatment utilizes interpretations based upon the CCRT, noting that the entire CCRT need not be invoked in every interpretation. He uses the part of the CCRT that the client seems most responsive to, keeping in mind the classic psychodynamic guidelines for the timing of an interpretation: 1. It is based on something the client has recently experienced; 2. It is a theme near to awareness; and 3. The issue is impeding treatment, especially as it characterizes the transference. Luborsky then listens to how the client responds to the interpretation so that he can better tailor subsequent comments (Luborsky, 1990).

One does not have to be psychodynamic in orientation to make use of the CCRT. It can be helpful in fleshing out the interpersonal aspects of a client's difficulty, and in helping to inform the focus of treatment regardless of the methods one uses. A brief survey of published academic articles using the CCRT found 592 references in Italian, Spanish, German, and Japanese journals, as well as American. The CCRT has been used to study a host of topics, including the client-therapist relationship (Wiseman & Tishby, 2017); counter-transference (Johnson, 2016); and populations including adult offenders (Hackett et al., 2013), persons diagnosed with borderline personality disorder (Drapeau et al., 2010; Bourke & Grenyer, 2010), chronic fatigue (Vandenbergen et al., 2009), and alexithymia (Vanheule et al., 2007). It has been used to analyze novels written by authors who suffered from anorexia (Stirn et al., 2005), and both childhood trauma's impact on adult functioning (Drapeau & Perry, 2004) and child molesters (Drapeau et al., 2004). In several studies, it has even been used to study the relationship between God and people in the Bible (Popp, Luborsky, Andrusyna et al., 2002; Popp, Luborsky, Descôteaux et al., 2003).

Over time there have been a number of methods of synthesizing plot and theme, but none as simple to use nor as well researched as the CCRT. I encourage you to experiment with it. When you are taking session notes, write at the top of the page:

Wish   Response from Others   Response from Self

When you listen to a client story—and most clients tell 4.1 stories per session (Luborsky & Crits-Christoph, 1990), try to fill in the three categories. If you are unsure about one or more of the categories, ask the client ("What were you hoping for there?" Or "I'm not sure just what you needed." Or "how did you respond inside and outside to that?). See what pattern repeats for this person and how that plot skeleton relates to and expands on the person's presenting problem.

Mark Lawrence

Mark Lawrence (1940–2011) was a Harvard-trained psychiatrist who was, of necessity, steeped in psychodynamic theory and the burgeoning and lucrative practice of medicinal treatment for psychiatric disorders. He worked at NIMH, then as director of a community mental health center. Despite this more traditional background, Dr. Lawrence studied Eriksonian hypnosis and Gestalt therapy, then developed his own imagery-based therapy which he practiced and taught to a small number of journeyman psychotherapists through his organization, The Center for Healing and Imagery (CHI). He had begun writing a book about his approach when he died suddenly and tragically. As a result, he left few writings other than workshop notes and some basic web-based articles.

Although Dr. Lawrence considered himself an imagery and ego state therapist, he is included here under techniques for changing plot because his basic intervention involved finding the relevant foundational story and changing the plot.

In order to do this, Lawrence relied on the affect bridge (see Chapter 5 for a description of the technique). The affect or sensation bridge helps the client travel from a symptom to the associated foundational story. Lawrence then has the client relate the recalled story. Sometimes the story is traumatic and the client begins to become dysregulated, either dissociative or with great affect. When that occurs, or when the therapist anticipates that that may be the case, Lawrence invented the helpful technique of giving the client a "special remote." This is an imaginary remote control that the client can use to pause the action; to fast forward (in which case any sounds become high pitched and chipmunk like); to slow the action; or to rewind so that the actors move in reverse and speak backwards. In addition, Lawrence gives the magical remote a special volume button such that the volume controls not the sound volume, but the volume of the emotional intensity. When the volume is turned up, the intensity becomes greater, but the picture becomes blurrier. When the volume is turned down, the intensity is reduced, but the picture becomes sharper.

When the client has related the story and has been able to identify with the protagonist, Lawrence would ask: "Now what needs to happen for little Nathan (the protagonist) to feel OK?" Some clients know immediately; others need suggestions. For the latter group, Lawrence would suggest: "feel free to let go of historical reality. You can alter the events, or you could bring in anything or anyone. You could bring in a hammer or a microphone, or Superman or Lassie." What Lawrence is searching for here is either a direct alteration of the plot, or a resource character or state that the client can use to change the plot. If a resource tool or character, it also might prove useful in other situations.

When the client identifies the resource, Lawrence encourages them to bring that character or state into the story. "So you can let go of historical reality and let your grandmother come into the story. What happens next? What happens then?" After the story is related with the resource integrated or the plot changed, Lawrence asks the client how she feels. This provides a comparison with the original, probably dysphoric, mood. The client is then asked to relate any subsequent stories that (see Pace, 2007) come to mind with that same affect, bringing the resource into that story as well.

In the following case excerpted and adapted from notes from Mark Lawrence (Personal Communication, 2009), note how Lawrence helps the client find and integrate a resource character.

> Nathan 14.2, a 55-year-old man, entered therapy because of recurring anxiety following heart bypass surgery. Fearing he might suffer another heart attack, Nathan refused to travel, even locally. Gradually, his life became smaller, until even going to work became a battle. Any heartburn or digestive discomfort was a cause for panic.
>
> Lawrence asked for any memories of the surgery. "I remember being wheeled to the operating table on the gurney," said Nathan. "I felt incredibly cold. I began to shake uncontrollably. Even so, I bantered with the nurses and the resident. I asked if they couldn't do a tummy tuck while they were at it."
>
> "What do you make of the bantering?"
>
> "I guess it was sort of 'whistling past the graveyard.'"
>
> "What does 'whistling past the graveyard' make you think of?"
>
> "Funny, but it reminds me of my grandmother. I remember she once told me the story of how when she was a girl she and some friends snuck into the old churchyard. The other girls ran away, but my grandmother opened a family crypt and saw the body of a young woman through a glass topped coffin."
>
> "Even as a young girl, your grandmother was brave."
>
> "One of the bravest people I ever knew."
>
> "What would your grandmother say about your current situation?"
>
> "She'd probably say, 'would you rather wilt, or live your life?'"
>
> "Now I wonder if you could re-tell the story of your surgery, only this time let your grandmother be there with you (Nathan does so)."
>
> "The next time you have occasion to go out of the house, I wonder if you could take your grandmother with you?"

Lawrence has changed the story by helping the client, as protagonist, find a brave companion, thereby accessing his own courage. The resourcing would have been unlikely to work had Lawrence requested Nathan to, for example, draw up a list of his positive traits. Courage would not likely have made the list; and if it had, the idea of courage is so general that it is hard to apply in a specific situation. Finding a specific characterization of courage that can be applied to a problematic story becomes far more helpful.

From a story perspective, what Lawrence has done is to access the earliest foundational story most closely related to the symptom. He then helps the client create or access a resource character which is then integrated into the plot, changing the nature of the plot. The primary change mechanisms would seem to be resourcing and memory reconsolidation (see Chapter 10). Because memory is "filed" by affect, it is likely that the relevant foundational story is cued as soon as the affect bridge is begun. As long as the memory is available for ten minutes prior to integrating the resource part into the plot, that foundational story memory is within the reconsolidation window and thus vulnerable to change.

We turn next to an aspect of story which is more frequently the focus of change—that of theme.

References

Aristotle. (Butcher, S. H., trans.). (2013). *Poetics by Aristotle*. The Project Gutenberg E-book of Poetics [E-book #1974].

Barber, J. P., Crits-Christoph, P., & Luborsky, L. (1990). A guide to the CCRT standard categories and their classification. In Luborsky, L., & Crits-Christoph, P. (ed.), *Understanding Transference: The CCRT Method*. New York, NY: Basic Books.

Bourke, M. E., & Grenyer, B. F. (2010). Psychotherapists' response to borderline personality disorder: A Core Conflictual Relationship Theme analysis. *Psychotherapy Research*, 20(6), pp. 680–691.

Drapeau, M., de Roten, Y., & Körner, A. C. (2004). An exploratory study of child molesters' relationship patterns using the Core Conflictual Relationship Theme method. *Journal of Interpersonal Violence*, 19(2), pp. 264–275.

Drapeau, M., & Perry, J. C. (2004). Childhood trauma and adult interpersonal functioning: A study using the Core Conflictual Relationship Theme method (CCRT). *Child Abuse & Neglect*, 28(10), pp. 1049–1066.

Drapeau, M., Perry, J. C., & Körner, A. (2010). Interpersonal behaviours and BPD. Are specific interpersonal behaviours related to borderline personality disorder? An empirical study using the Core Conflictual Relationship Theme standard categories. *Archives of Psychiatry & Psychotherapy*, 12(3), pp. 5–10.

Hackett, S. S., Porter, J., & Taylor, J. L. (2013). The Core Conflictual Relationship Theme (CCRT) method: Testing with adult offenders who have intellectual and developmental disabilities. *Advances in Mental Health & Intellectual Disabilities*, 7(5), pp. 263–271.

Johnson, M. C. (2016). Using the Core Conflictual Relationship Themes (CCRT) method as a countertransference coding technique. *Dissertation Abstracts International: Section B: The Sciences and Engineering*, 77(3-B, E).

Luborsky, L. (1984). *Principles of Psychoanalytic Psychotherapy: A Manual for Supportive-Expressive Treatment.* New York, NY: Basic Books.

Luborsky, L., & Crits-Christoph, P. (1990). *Understanding Transference: The CCRT Method.* New York, NY: Basic Books.

Pace, P. (2007). *Lifespan Integration: Connecting Ego States Through Time.* Roslyn, WA: Lifespan Integration, LLC.

Popp, C. A., Luborsky, L., Andrusyna, T. P., Cotsonis, G., & Seligman, D. (2002). Relationships between God and people in the *Bible*: A Core Conflictual Relationship Theme study of the *Pentateuch/Torah*. *Psychiatry: Interpersonal and Biological Processes, 65*(3), pp. 179–196.

Popp, C. A., Luborsky, L., Descôteaux, J., Diguer, L., Andrusyna, T. P., Kirk, D., & Cotsonis, G. (2003). Relationships between God and people in the *Bible*, Part II: The *New Testament*, with comparisons with the *Torah*. *Psychiatry: Interpersonal & Biological Processes, 66*(4), pp. 285–307.

Stirn, A., Overbeck, G., & Pokorny, D. (2005). The Core Conflictual Relationship Theme (CCRT) applied to literary works: An analysis of two novels written by authors suffering from anorexia nervosa. *International Journal of Eating Disorders, 38*(2), pp. 147–156.

Vandenbergen, J., Vanheule, S., Rosseel, Y., Desmet, M., & Verhaeghe, P. (2009). Unexplained chronic fatigue and Core Conflictual Relationship Themes: A study in a chronically fatigued population. *Psychology & Psychotherapy: Theory, Research & Practice, 82*(1), pp. 31–40.

Vanheule, S., Vandenbergen, J., Desmet, M., Rosseel, Y., & Insleghers, R. (2007). Alexithymia and Core Conflictual Relationship Themes: A study in a chronically fatigued primary care population. *International Journal of Psychiatry in Medicine, 37*(1), pp. 87–98.

Wiseman, H., & Tishby, O. (2017). Applying relationship anecdotes paradigm interviews to study client therapist relationship narratives: Core Conflictual Relationship Theme analysis. *Psychotherapy Research, 27*(3), pp. 283–299.

Chapter 14
Thematic Change

Jeffrey Young

One of the most comprehensive understandings of problematic narrative themes is that of Jeffrey Young. Although Young takes a cognitive behavioral approach for addressing themes, his insights apply to problematic foundational stories and life narratives. He defines what he terms as "early maladaptive schemas," which he thinks of as the deepest level of cognition. He defines early maladaptive schemas as "extremely stable and enduring themes which develop during childhood and are elaborated upon throughout an individual's lifetime" (Young, 1990, p. 9). The schemas are implicit and were originally thought of as unconditional. He later identified five schemas as conditional and therefore secondary to an unconditional schema (Young et al., 2003).

Young originally noted 15 problematic themes which he grouped into four categories re-organized here from likely earliest to later developmentally: Connectedness, Autonomy, Limits and Standards, and Worthiness (Young, 1990). In a popular book format, he and Janet Klosko selected 11 of the 15 themes to expand (Young & Klosko, 1994). He later revised the categories and added three additional themes for his major work (Young et al., 2003).

Let us look at each of these categories and the problematic story themes (schemas) that can result from each.

An infant's first task is bonding with the mother or nurturing parent. It is this attachment and the style of attachment developed that will follow her throughout life. Problematic themes that the infant can take from a failure in Connectiveness are: Abandonment, Mistrust and Abuse, and Emotional Deprivation. Because these themes occur so early, before the advent of language, when present, they are integrated into a person's life story in a visceral way as deep emotional tones and bodily expectations.

The second in my delineation of Young's categories is that of Autonomy. The schemas, or problematic life story themes, that are part of this category are: Dependence, Vulnerability, and Defectiveness. Having made a connection, the toddler begins to explore the world. According to Erik Erikson (1980), this budding autonomy is vulnerable, and it is here that the emotion of shame can result. Shame is about one's view of himself as damaged and therefore unworthy to be included in the family or tribe. This is about who one is, and is more basic than guilt, which, at the next phase, is about what one has done or not done. As the child, now an older toddler, experiments, the thrill of newfound autonomy makes the world her oyster.

This is an age when limits from adults are crucial, and the way those limits are set deeply affects the child's view of himself and his ability to set firm but kindly limits on himself and others. "No!" becomes the most important of words, and the young child uses it in abundance as both an expression of budding autonomy and as a step toward internalizing the limits set by adults in his life. I recall sitting on a wide, sandy, deserted beach with our son when he was about two. It was not an ocean beach, but a beach on the sound side of the Carolina barrier islands. The sounds are large, calm, shallow expanses of water between the barrier islands and the coast, so the beach sloped so gradually that 50 yards out you would not be waist deep. There was no trouble to be had save for an old, rusted, half-buried barbed wire fence 25 yards away. With his unsteady gait, our son toddled right toward the barbed wire. As he wobbled forward, he repeated out loud, "No. No. No. No."

When the limits are too rigid and excessive, the theme that may result is that of Unrelenting Standards. On the opposing pole is the absence of limits. A child raised in this environment (one that Alfred Adler referred to as being "coddled") can leave the child feeling overly entitled (the schema or life story theme is that of Entitlement).

The general category of worthiness is solidified as the young child enters primary school. These days, with the modification of kindergarten to be more about academics than about socialization and the fun of learning, worthiness is at issue even in kindergarten. This is Erikson's "Industry vs. Inferiority." Possible problematic life themes include Failure and reinforcement of Unrelenting Standards.

School is also the environment where one has to interact with peers apart from one's siblings. In earlier years children do not interact reciprocally with peers; it has been said they engage in "parallel play" where they are immersed in their own games in the presence of other children. With school comes actual interaction that is not just parallel, nor functional (one child takes another's toy), but occasionally even cooperative. With dawning interaction, how one is accepted by one's peers becomes important, and one is vulnerable to the problematic life themes of Social Exclusion and Failure.

See Table 14.1 for a developmental organization of Young's themes. I have used the schema categories which he presents in his popular press *Lifetraps* book, as these categories better lend themselves to a developmental interpretation than his later categories. The developmental categories, together with the life story themes placed in approximate developmental order, is presented in Table 14.1.

Note that a single asterisk by a theme denotes what Young calls "conditional" themes. These are themes which are secondary, in the sense of being

158   Changing Foundational and Life Stories

Table 14.1 Life Story Themes Derived from Jeffrey Young's Schema Therapy

Category of Life Story Theme (Schema for Young)	Problematic Life Story Theme
Connectedness	Abandonment
	Mistrust & Abuse
	Emotional Deprivation
Autonomy	Dependence
	Vulnerability
	Enmeshment/Undeveloped Self
	Defectiveness
	Subjugation*
	Self-Sacrifice*
	Emotional Inhibition*
Limits & Standards	Entitlement
	Insufficient Self-Control/Self-Discipline
	Punitiveness
	Unrelenting Standards/Hypercriticalness*
Worthiness	Failure
	Approval Seeking*
	Social Exclusion
	Emotional Inhibition*
	Negativity/Pessimism**

* Conditional Schema
** Negativity/Pessimism seems more tone than theme

ways of coping with (dare we say defenses?!) the primary themes. Thus, a person with an Emotional Inhibition theme in their problematic story may quietly stay on the periphery of a group and experience social anxiety as a way of avoiding feared Social Exclusion. In this example, the primary theme is Social Exclusion; the Emotional Inhibition is manner in which the person copes with feared Social Exclusion.

In Table 14.1, Negativity/Pessimism has two asterisks. This is because when applied to a life story, negativity seems to better define the overall tone of the story protagonist than it does a story theme, which relates to a summary plotline.

Read through Young's list of themes and think about each as a possible theme of a problematic life story. While not an exhaustive list, the list seems quite helpful in explicating the range of problematic themes with which clients present.

In Young's therapy, he works with the client to identify their primary schemas by using questionnaires, discussion, and some interesting imagery techniques. In most of the imagery techniques, he has the client first develop a Safe Place. As mentioned in the chapter on trauma, I much prefer to use the title "Calm Place," for many traumatized clients will create a "Fortified Place" in response to "Safe Place" without ever feeling the inner relaxation one might hope would emerge from the exercise. Thus, I have modified Young's instructions to refer to "Calm Place."

Having helped the client create a calm internal space, Young instructs them to close their eyes and "let an image float to the top of (your) mind (Young et al., 2003)." He instructs them that it is like watching a movie in your mind, but he wants them to not only watch, but experience the movie. He then asks questions about the sensory experience ("what are you seeing? What are you hearing?"). He then asks about all the characters in the imagery, what each is thinking and feeling. The imagery session is ended back at the calm place.

In subsequent sessions following this free-form imagery, Young follows up with more structured imagery sessions of: 1. Any upsetting childhood image; 2. An upsetting image of each parent; and 3. Upsetting images of any other persons (e.g. siblings, peers, other adults) where the interaction "*may have contributed to the formation of a schema.*" Note that without directly stating it, Young is aware of how foundational stories contribute to problematic life themes.

The final imagery session (number four) is quite interesting in that it links the past to the present by switching to a current image that retains the same feeling as one of the childhood imageries. This ties the foundational story to the present. It also moves in the opposite direction as the affect or somatic bridge, a very useful technique covered in Chapter 5. Throughout the imagery sessions Young is listening for the story themes (schemas). He also makes the point that the imagery helps the therapist become empathetic to the feelings of the client.

Young's imagery is very evocative and a useful assessment as well as entrée into therapy. However, I believe there are some crucial caveats to keep in mind before using these techniques—caveats that Young does not delineate. First, many victims of trauma and many psychotic patients (even people with so-called "compensated" or "incipient" schizophrenia where the psychosis is not that obvious) can become quite dysregulated upon closing their eyes. Given this, it is always preferable to give an imagery client the choice as to when and whether he will close his eyes. A second crucial caution is that experiencing the imagery movie may be equivalent to re-experiencing the trauma for a trauma survivor. As noted in the chapters on trauma, there is no need to have a survivor directly re-experience a trauma story in order for healing (let alone assessment) to take place. There are many techniques for letting the person tell the story without re-experiencing it.

Young notes that there are basically three coping responses to a schema: overcompensation, avoidance, and surrender, which he relates to fight, flight, and freeze. Thus, a person with a Dependency theme who copes with it by overcompensation may present with what psychoanalysts termed "counter-dependency." This is different than true independence; it is "too much." This is the person who refuses to rely on anyone for anything, priding themselves on their "independence." Common in adolescence, the kid who rebels and does the opposite of what the adults in his life require is still controlled by those same adults, just in a reverse manner. In adolescence this may be a steppingstone to true interdependence in later life. If the theme occurs in a 30-year-old woman, however, it may make for a much more problematic life story.

While he does not explain this, by combining the three coping styles with the life story themes, Young has come up with common problematic plotlines. The theme defines the nature of the story while the coping style delineates the plot.

> Harriet 14.1 works some 50 hours a week as a physician. Her husband, a former administrator in a large company, took an optional early retirement. He spends his days watching television, driving his late-model sports car, or playing online poker. He regularly loses an amount equal to his retirement, and so relies on his wife for the bills and house payment. After a long day at the office, Harriet returns home and fixes dinner. If she is later than usual, she will find her husband sullen and hungry, not having eaten.

Harriet's overcompensation style defines the nature of the plot she lives. Her story theme is in the worthiness category; she constantly fears being a failure.

After the assessment phase, Young and the client prioritize which schemas are most troubling and begin to work on changing those. Having identified the schema, or story theme, Young's therapy uses a variety of approaches to help the client change. As might be expected, he uses CBT techniques of helping the client dispute the logic of her themes (schemas). He also relies on what a psychoanalyst supervisor I had many years ago called being "loaded for bear." That meant keeping the problematic pattern in front of the client, keeping it in awareness, and interpreting difficulties that arose for the client in terms of that same problematic theme. It is a procedure not unrelated to narrative therapist Michael White's technique of externalizing the problem, then working to recognize and combat it at every turn. Finally, interestingly enough, Young uses dialogues with what he calls "modes." These modes are really what others call parts or ego states; they are the characters in a person's life story. Chapter 12 is an introduction to working with characters as explicated by a variety of theorists, so we will not expand here.

James Mann

James Mann's short-term dynamic therapy ("Time-limited Therapy") is another instance of focusing upon theme (Mann, 1973). Mann attempts to uncover the focal conflictual theme behind the symptom, then, using the finiteness of time as an ally, makes that theme the object of most every therapist statement (again, being "loaded for bear"). Indeed, by formulating this theme and presenting it to the client, Omer (1993) credits Mann with "the invention of the instant psychobiography."

For Mann, the granddaddy theme that gives rise to all problematic themes is separation-individuation. Writing before the popularization of John Bowlby and the attachment theorists, Mann cites Margaret Mahler and Melanie Klein (Klein analyzed Bowlby) on the importance of the infant's connection to the mother and of the infant's separation from the mother as a template for later life themes. Therapy follows this template of attachment and separation for Mann. Thus, it recapitulates, triggers, and re-works early attachment followed by separation and individuation.

Mann accomplishes this by making time his co-therapist. The therapy is exactly 12 sessions long. Even in instances where further treatment is indicated, Mann does not hold this out as a possibility until the last session. In effect, the therapy has the client re-experiencing the early trauma of problematic attachment and loss in a different, consistent relationship and with verbal awareness.

Of course, no one enters therapy saying, "at root my difficulty is a problematic attachment and difficult separation from my mother when I was an infant, and I hope to re-work this." It is an age-old difficulty with many, especially dynamic therapies, that the therapist believes she has some secret pre-determined understanding into which the client will be inducted over the course of treatment. It heightens the already one-sided power dynamic (if recognized at all, this is seen as helpful, for it more accurately recapitulates the child's position vis-á-vis the parents). To the extent that the client can re-define her problem in the therapist's terms, she is more likely to improve. She has already changed the problem by re-defining it.

For Mann, the separation-individuation dynamic gives rise to four themes which underlie most psychological disturbance. They represent the range of ways that humans cope with the existential reality of one's own death, the ultimate separation. The problematic themes that for Mann have their roots in early separation experiences are:

Dependence-Independence: This is viewed as an internal conflict that is often expressed outwardly. One can rely solely on others, feeling incapable of voicing one's own desires; or one can assume the opposing stance of refusing to rely on anyone else for even the smallest need. Caught in between these poles and buffeted by ambivalence is the person who feels guilty when he expresses his own views and desires, yet confined and trapped when he conforms to or seeks help from others.

Activity-Passivity: Related to the dependency conflict is the polarized theme of active-passive. The passive person struggles to marshal energy to make decisions or take even needed action. Often the fear is that he will displease others and they will subsequently reject him. It can lead to an external locus of control that one is the constant victim of circumstances or of other's actions. The opposing pole of avoiding any semblance of passivity becomes an over-reliance on control. To relinquish control, or to be temporarily quiet as opposed to frenetic, is to invite (like the speedboat example earlier in the book) sinking into a bottomless void.

Adequate vs. Diminished Self-Esteem: Diminished self-esteem relates to one's own sense of worth. One of the ways that problems continue down through generations is that we are often inclined to treat ourselves as we feel we were treated. The child who feels unwanted can have great difficulty wanting himself or feeling worthwhile.

Unresolved or Delayed Grief: In one of his most enlightened little books, Freud, in *Mourning and Melancholia* (1917), relates depression to incomplete grieving. While we know that some depression may have a biological genesis—or at least a biological correlate—Freud's concept is well worth keeping in mind when you encounter stories of depression. Freud also makes the cogent point that grieving a loss, say the loss of a person, or the loss of health, is not just about coming to terms with the absence of that person or that state. It is about coming to terms with the myriad of little griefs—the clothes the person left behind, the way he whistled when he cooked, the way the pillow smelled, the quirks, even those that were frustrating in their time.

One may or may not accept Mann's thesis that all problems ultimately stem from difficulty in attachment or separation; or that there are four, and only four problematic thematic ways of dealing life. Regardless, one can see that Independence/Dependence, Activity/Passivity, Diminished Self-esteem, and Unresolved Grief are important life story themes that frequently emerge. By being aware of Mann's, and of Young's, lists of themes, we can be more attuned to the possible themes in both foundational and in life stories.

References

Erikson, E. (1980). *Identity and the Life Cycle.* New York, NY: W. W. Norton.

Freud, S. (Strachey, J., trans.). (1917). Mourning and melancholia. In *The Standard Edition of the Complete Psychological Works of Sigmund Freud: Volume XIV (1914–1916): On the History of the Psycho-Analytic Movement, Papers on Metapsychology and Other Works,* 237–258. London: Hogarth Press.

Mann, J. (1973). *Time-Limited Psychotherapy.* Cambridge, MA: Harvard University Press.

Omer, H. (1993). Short-term psychotherapy and the rise of the life-sketch. *Psychotherapy: Theory Research & Practice, 30*(4), pp. 668–673.

Young, J. E. (1990). *Cognitive Therapy for Personality Disorders: A Schema-Focused Approach.* Sarasota, FL: Professional Resource Exchange.

Young, J. E., & Klosko, J. S. (1994). *Reinventing Your Life: How to Break Free from Negative Life Patterns and Feel Good Again.* New York, NY: Plume.

Young, J. E., Klosko, J. S., & Weishaar, M. E. (2003). *Schema Therapy: A Practitioner's Guide.* New York, NY: Guilford Press.

Chapter 15

Transforming the Moral and the Whole Story I

In this chapter I will introduce you to two theorists who work with identifying and helping the client to change her problematic life story. You may be familiar with one or even both, but I hope here to help you view them through a storied lens and to present them in a way that gives practical ideas which you can integrate into your own work.

Bruce Ecker

Perhaps one of the most elegant theories to focus on changing the whole problematic story is that by the constructivist therapist Bruce Ecker (Ecker & Hulley, 1996; Ecker et al., 2012). Although he does not speak of a narrative understanding, his work is easily viewed through a narrative lens. Ecker believes that symptoms, as painful as they may be, are implicitly necessary either to avoid some feared catastrophe, or as unintended consequences of that avoidance. That feared catastrophe can be seen as an implicit problematic story. Ecker contends that the problem or symptom of the client, no matter how painful, is necessary. Giving up the problem would lead to the fear of far greater existential pain.

The part of the story that makes the symptom necessary (the pro-symptom position, or PSP) is usually implicit; the client is only aware of the symptom, its tenacity, and its painful ramifications. Because of this, the client enters therapy in order to lessen or eliminate the symptom without understanding how the symptom is also necessary.

The therapist's job is first to empathize with the pain of the symptom without lingering in an anti-symptom position (ASP). The therapist then attempts to determine what makes the symptom necessary and help the client emotionally "bump into" this wisdom, as insight alone is fleeting and insufficient. To help the client do this, the therapist uses a variety of techniques. One of these is a repetitive verbal sentence completion, where the client is instructed to fill in the sentence blank with the first response coming to his mind. For example:

"If I am not depressed, then _____."
"If I am not depressed, then _____."
"If I am not depressed, then _____."

The sentence with its blank is repeated three to five times for the client's response, or until no further insight is forthcoming.

Another question uses the so-called "miracle question" of Insoo Kim Berg (Berg & Reuss, 1998), actually also used by Alfred Adler. However, Ecker's use is different than that of either Berg or of Adler. The question goes like this: If, unbeknownst to you, a miracle occurred in the night such that when you awoke in the morning, your (depression, urge to drink, social anxiety, other problem) had vanished, what would be the first thing you would notice? What would happen next? And next?

Whereas Berg is trying to find an exception to the problem or symptom of the client that can be reinforced and expanded, Ecker is looking for the first subtle sign of trouble where being without the symptom is a problem. For Ecker, this may be an example of why the symptom is necessary.

Not allying with the Anti-Symptom Position is crucial, as trying to eliminate the symptom is doomed and only strengthens the Pro-Symptom Position. This requires tenacity and patience, as it flies in the face both of what most therapies are about and what the client originally wants. And it involves doing so initially without knowledge of why the symptom is necessary to have, only retaining the conviction that this is so. Of course, once the Pro-Symptom Position is uncovered, the wisdom of the symptom and its doggedness become abundantly clear.

Having recognized the wisdom of the symptom and having helped the client to recognize it is only the first phase of therapy. Insights are ephemeral and Ecker next works to keep the recognition of the Pro-Symptom Position in the client's awareness. One of his methods for doing this is by writing the insight on a three by five card and giving it to the client to carry with him and read several times a day, especially when he notices the emergence of his symptoms.

Often, of course, the necessity for the symptom emerged in childhood as a compromise solution to an otherwise emotionally devastating circumstance. The solution is that crafted by a young—often pre-operational—child. For this reason, the card is written in simple language that a child could understand, and in an emotionally evocative manner. It begins with empathy for the pain caused by the symptom and concludes with the necessity for maintaining the symptom. For example:

"Even though I feel terribly lonely and overwhelmingly tired such that the least task is an effort, I MUST remain depressed so that Mommy and Daddy will worry about me and stop fighting."

Often carrying and reading the card, and thereby living with the deep purpose of the problem, is sufficient to alter the client's symptoms. When it is not, Ecker helps the client find an exception, frequently a foundational story vignette. For example, Nathan 17.1 is very brusque with the women at work, and avoids most encounters with women in his home life. His presenting problem was not ever sustaining a romantic relationship. His Pro-Symptom Position was "all women are stingy and untrustworthy like my sister." He had been involved in a minor car accident on a holiday weekend when all his friends were away, and subsequently stranded in an unfamiliar area. His car had been towed, and his phone lost in the accident. A woman passerby lent him her phone, then gave him a ride clear across town to his apartment. Ecker's technique is to have the client hold both images or experiences in mind simultaneously. Since they both cannot be true (all women cannot be stingy AND a woman stranger go out of her way for him), the task, like a Zen koan (meditating on the sound of one hand clapping, for example), is impossible; holding that impossibility in mind leads to a kind of emotional dissonance and subsequent re-organizing.

Ecker would say, convincingly, that the operant change process is memory re-consolidation. In fact, he has reviewed much of the reconsolidation literature and believes that it is the experiential mismatch that initiates reconsolidation. He shows that even in experimental studies where reconsolidation is less than effective, the problem is not the reconsolidation process *per se*, but rather a failure to provide an initiatory mismatch. A study by Pedreira et al. (2004) agrees.

By giving voice to the deep implicit meaning of the symptom, the person has storied the symptom, which is a change in what was a behavioral and feeling tone memory. The memory has gone from purely implicit to also being an explicit memory, and becomes re-consolidated in that more robust form. When the deeper symptom story is held in mind with the exception story, this is a cognitive and emotional dissonance; both cannot simultaneously be true. This dissonance is also a kind of disruption in a long-term memory that corresponds to some of the disruptions used in memory re-consolidation studies. Thus, that older symptom meaning is transformed.

In effect, Ecker is saying that most clients enter therapy with the major part of the problematic life story buried. The early task of the therapist is to find the part of the story that makes the symptom necessary and understandable. In some cases, this may be a joint discovery with the client; in others, the therapist finds it first and verifies it by the client's reaction upon being helped to encounter the missing part of the narrative. Thus, Ecker finds and helps change the whole problematic story.

One change aspect that Ecker demonstrates in his interviews but does not elaborate extensively in his writings is that of relationship. It is clear that he is following the client intently and that whatever s/he may say is accepted unconditionally. The connection is enhanced by Ecker taking frequent pauses, introducing them with statements like "let me take a moment and reflect on what you've just said." The implied message of "what you experience and say is important," and "I don't have the answer, but I'm confident that we can find our way through this together" pervades his interviews.

The difficult aspect for the therapist is in not helping the client counter the symptom. Many of us—most especially those trained in cognitive behavioral therapy—have been trained that countering the symptom *is* the therapy. The difficulty is compounded by the client's desire for symptom relief. Most clients enter with the concept that they just want this anxiety or this anger or this shyness excised with no impact on the rest of their lives or stories. Of course, this is often impossible, because the anger or shyness has a function; it is a part of who they are, of their story, and of how they relate to others. We have all experienced a client making changes in his life, only to find that his new story no longer fits with that of his spouse. If the spouse is unwilling to change, the marriage becomes either unhappy or severed.

Ecker employs some novel techniques. Outside of Ecker, I have not encountered the use of notecards except in Cognitive Analytic Therapy (Corbridge et al., 2018). It is a very useful tool, both as Ecker uses it to remind the client of the implicit story that makes the symptom necessary, and as a session summary, or as a reminder of insights gained, or of homework assigned. I will sometimes have a client record his/her brief summary of the session highlights at the end of a meeting, then we can discuss. I ask the client to review the card daily, preferably including before going to sleep. With couples, it is often fascinating to see and discuss the differences in what each recorded about what was important in the meeting.

So that you gain an understanding of how Ecker finds and changes the whole problematic story, I'll relate a personal example. The book you are now reading was written over the course of ten or 15 years—in my head. I had notes in various notebooks, but had not been able to actually begin writing the book, much less approach a publisher. I had received support, ideas, and encouragement from family, colleagues, friends, and supervisors, but had written little.

I attended an advanced two-day workshop with Ecker for clinicians already familiar with the method. After doing a demonstration, Ecker asked us each to choose a personal issue and divided us into small groups where we were to take turns being client, clinician, and observer. My issue was how to put pen to paper on this book. With my partners' help I realized that the book was the synthesis and culmination of an entire clinical career. An understanding of story was the tapestry that wove it together. The book was the only item on my bucket list; it was something I had to write before I died. The deeper implicit meaning became "when I write the book, my life will be over and I will die." No wonder I put it off! Emotionally, I was seeing the book as an end, not as the beginning of a new, even more satisfying turn in my career. Emotionally realizing this was freeing. Since I had already written the book in my head, I often have the sense that I am transcribing it rather than writing it. It is still difficult to find the vast amount of time writing a book entails, but the problem is logistical, no longer emotional.

Ecker's therapy, besides being unique and often quite powerful, is a reminder that much of both a client's problem story and her life story is implicit. We are presented with the visible iceberg and must surmise and impact that which lies beneath.

Kim Schneiderman

The final therapy to be explained here is one that works very directly with the entire life story, recognizing the story aspects of context, character, and plot. Kim Schneiderman uses therapeutic writing in both her workshops and in her individual treatment to help clients divide their lives into chapters and explore and integrate their life stories (Schneiderman, 2015). James Pennebaker and others have shown the value of expressive narrative writing in decreasing the impact of a host of problems, from trauma to unemployment (Pennebaker & Seagal, 1999; Pennebaker & Smyth, 2016). However, unlike Pennebaker's free form writing, Schneiderman uses structured writing exercises based on the classic story aspects and arc (context, character, plot, theme) delineated in Chapter 2.

To enable clients to gain perspective on their story, Schneiderman has them write in the third person (see Tinnin & Gantt, 2013). She notes that the third-person author has a wider view than from first-person authors (see Zimbardo et al., 2012 regarding how just changing one's view to encompass a distant future or simply a wider perspective puts the current difficulty in another context, one that carries less anxiety).

Schneiderman has clients reflect on how they tell the story, which is a kind of meta factor. She gives the example of telling *The Wizard of Oz* as a tragedy, then as what she calls a "triumph" (originally called "comedy"—which did not have to do with a funny story; in the literature this is now called a "redemptive story").

In Schneiderman's workshops, participants begin with what they determine is the current chapter. By approaching the life story with only one chapter, she notes, it becomes more manageable. Although Schneiderman does not mention it, there is a wisdom in opening with an understanding of the current chapter, as we interpret all of our memories and stories through the lens of our current situation and current ways of understanding the world (Mahoney, 2003). She helps the client draw out the story aspects of his most recent life chapter with questions to guide his writing.

The essential dynamic for Schneiderman is that of conflict between the protagonist in one's life story and the antagonist. She notes that the conflict, and thus the antagonist, can be one or a combination of four types: man (woman) vs. man (woman); man (woman) vs. nature; man (woman) vs. society, corporation, etc.; and man (woman) vs. self. It is this dynamic that powers the story. Thus, Schneiderman's theory is dialectical in its essentials: the conflict between opposing forces leads to a synthesis. Writers are encouraged to welcome this synthesis by inquiring, "what does this antagonist have to teach me?" I am reminded of the Japanese martial art of Aikido where one's opponent is viewed as one's teacher. This dialectic appears to be the major kind of change that her approach relies upon. There is also a certain amount of ritual in the writing exercises which solidifies the gains, but the gains are largely the result of the dialectic. When you think of how common the story form of protagonist against antagonist is, it is easy to see how many life stories can be framed in this manner (see Part 2).

For clients interested in writing, Schneiderman's book is a handbook for life story writing therapy. Her workshops are helpful in gaining a narrative perspective for clients and therapists alike that have access to them (they are largely based in New York City). Otherwise, with some adaptation, the approach can be a very helpful way of taking a client's history, one that simultaneously introduces the client to a storied perspective on their lives. I will describe briefly one way of approaching this and give an example. The questions listed are both adaptations of those that Schneiderman uses and those that I have added.

It is helpful to have a white board and markers available. One might begin by saying something like: "I'd like us to spend the next meeting or two understanding what you have lived, your life story. It can help us both to understand patterns and ways forward that fit. To begin, imagine your life as if it were a novel or movie. Let's think about what the different chapters would be. Five chapters seem to fit for most, but feel free to have as many or as few chapters as you wish. What would be the first chapter? From what age to what age? (Write, or have client write it on the board.) The second chapter? What is the next chapter, etc. to the current chapter? If you had to guess, what would the next (future) chapter be?"

The white board can contain a summary of the chapters. Begin with the chapter numbers and the age of the client in each. As the client continues to expand the narrative, beginning with the first chapter, you can add headings that will be used throughout. Table 15.1 shows a suggested outline.

Table 15.1 Life Story Chapter Outline

Chapter	Age From ___ to ___	Title	Moral
1.			
2.			
:			
:			

Approaching it in this way allows the client to determine what defines the chapters without being confined to arbitrary age ranges. Having outlined the number and ages in different life chapters, return to the first chapter. "Now let's return to the first chapter and Little Harriet (the client or protagonist). Tell me about that chapter." Here your questions are presented like a funnel, with more open questions in the beginning, becoming increasingly specific as either the client needs increased structure, or as more details are needed. This insures that to the extent possible, the client structures the response so that it reflects her approach to the world. Possible follow-up questions include:

Theme: What would you title this first chapter?

Setting: Tell me about the setting of this first chapter. Where was it? Who else was in the story? What was the emotional climate in this first chapter?

Protagonist: What kind of person is little Harriet in this chapter? If she were a superhero, what would her special powers be? What vulnerabilities does she have? What are the healed and the open wounds that she has? Who and what does she care about?

Roles: List the roles little Harriet plays in this first chapter. What was her primary role in the family? In chapters where there are multiple roles, have the client rank order them by importance, keeping in mind Karpman's distinction between identity roles and action roles (Chapter 8). What gifts and demands are a part of each? What is little Harriet's favorite role? Are there roles which are problematic for her?

Problem/Goal: What was her major problem or struggle in this chapter? What is her primary desire or dream? Does she have a secret dream or desire? What does she really need, and does this differ from what she wants? If so, how? What does she have to lose if the obstacles thwart her? If she does not act, what does she have to lose?

Antagonist: What gets in the way of little Harriet's desires? Think of both external and internal obstacles. What circumstances or people did she struggle against?

Supporting Characters: Who is in her corner? Who or what supports or helps her?

Plot: How does the action unfold in this first chapter? What is the turning point or crisis? How does it end?

Moral: What is the lesson or moral that Little Harriet (the protagonist) takes from this chapter? Looking back on it from your more mature vantage point, what might be the moral that she should or could have taken, one that could have made a positive difference?

Re-write: If you were to re-write this chapter for little Harriet, what if any changes would you make? What supports or helpers would you add?

Foundational Story from This Chapter: From this chapter, what is one strong memory, a particular time or incident, that has stuck with you? What part of the story stands out for you? What was the feeling? Why has that incident been so powerful and lasting?

After the client has completed discussing all the chapters, you can help her look at her story as a whole. What were the major turning points? What is your favorite chapter? Your most difficult? In what chapter did your symptoms start? What was your proudest moment? Is there an overall theme? How do the chapters connect? Are some parallel? Do some things build across chapters? Remember Powers and Griffith's (1987) method of understanding multiple stories by looking at sequence, similarity (multiple chapters with similar antagonists, plots, or themes), and symmetry (some chapters may show contrasting or polarized sides of the same issue).

Integration and Summary

Each of the theorists in this chapter works with two related life stories for each client. It is those two together that make the complete life story for a person. Kim Schneiderman briefly discusses the External Story and the Internal Story. The external story relates to the people and events in the client's outer world, while the Internal Story consists of internal voices, plots, and dreams. We all live in both worlds, and, although Schneiderman does not talk about the relationship between the two, they often parallel one another. Characters and other elements from our outer lives often are carried inward to populate our inner worlds. This is the process of *introjection*. Likewise, we see our outer worlds through the lens of our inner world. This is the process of *projection*. And, when we act in a way to ensure the outer world mimics our inner world (as opposed to merely viewing the outer as like the inner), that is *projective identification*.

There are also two stories for Ecker: an explicit story and an implicit story. The explicit story is what he terms the "anti-symptom position." It is a story in which life would be relatively good but for this anxiety, sexual compulsion, drinking problem, or whatever the symptom is. In this story the symptom needs to be eliminated, and the person fights against it, avoids it, or capitulates to it. The implicit story is what he terms the "pro-symptom position." That is the story in which the symptom not only makes sense, but is necessary to have either in order to avoid some greater existential pain, or as an unintended consequence of avoiding that greater pain. Thus, the implicit story both provides the larger context for the anti-symptom explicit story, and complements it.

The concept of two connected life stories was also an important part of the transactional analysis theory of Eric Berne (1972) and Claude Steiner (1974), delineated in the first chapter. The problematic story is called the "script,"

Table 15.2 Relationship Between Stories in Theories with Two Stories

Relationship Between the Two Stories	Story #1	Story #2	Theorist
Parallel	Outer	Inner	Schneiderman
Contrasting	Problem (Script)	Ideal (Counter-script)	Steiner
Complementary/ Completing	Explicit (Anti-Symptom Position)	Implicit (Pro-Symptom Position)	Ecker

which is the rigid, repetitive tragic program for living one's life that begun with parental messages in childhood. The "counterscript" is the opposite story, more idealized and communicated more explicitly. It comes from the overt message from the parent. Of course, the covert, emotional message is more powerful. Thus, a mother's admonition "Don't be a lush like your father" is a double message. On the surface it is a benign wish for the child's good health. Covertly, it reads, "Don't be a lush like your father (and I'm attracted to and married a lush, so if you love me and someday want to marry a woman like me, become a lush)." Students of hypnosis know that in the concrete world of trance, like in early childhood, "no" does not exist. "Don't be a lush" brings up the possibility of becoming an alcoholic.

Thus, each of these theories delineates two simultaneous life stories with the two stories differing from each other in various ways. We can summarize these differing ways of conceiving of two life stories as summarized in Table 15.2.

By being aware that there are often two life stories with one only partly, if at all, within the client's awareness, the therapist is able to understand life stories with a broader and more helpful lens.

References

Berg, I. K., & Reuss, N. H. (1998). *Solutions Step By Step: A Substance Abuse Treatment Manual*. New York, NY: W. W. Norton.

Berne, E. (1972). *What Do You Say After You Say Hello? The Psychology of Human Destiny*. New York, NY: Grove Press.

Corbridge, C., Brummer, L., & Coid, P. (2018). *Cognitive Analytic Therapy: Distinctive Features*. New York, NY: Routledge.

Ecker, B., & Hulley, L. (1996). *Depth Oriented Brief Psychotherapy, or How to Be Deep If You Were Trained to Be Brief, and Vice-Versa*. San Francisco, CA: Jossey-Bass.

Ecker, B., Tick, R., & Hulley, L. (2012). *Unlocking the Emotional Brain: Eliminating Symptoms at Their Roots Using Memory Reconsolidation*. New York, NY: Routledge.

Mahoney, M. J. (2003). *Constructive Psychotherapy: A Practical Guide*. New York, NY: Guilford Press.

Pedreira, M. E., Pérez-Cuesta, L. M., & Maldonado, H. (2004). Mismatch between what is expected and what actually occurs triggers memory reconsolidation or extinction. *Learning and Memory, 11*(5), pp. 579–585.

Pennebaker, J. W., & Seagal, J. D. (1999). Forming a story: The health benefits of narrative. *Journal of Clinical Psychology, 55*(10), pp. 1243–1254.

Pennebaker, J. W., & Smyth, J. M. (2016). *Opening up By Writing Down*. New York, NY: Guilford Press.

Powers, R. L., & Griffith, J. (1987). *Understanding Life-Style: The Psycho-clarity Process*. Chicago, IL: The America's Institute of Adlerian Studies, Ltd.

Schneiderman, K. (2015). *Step out of Your Story: Writing Exercises to Reframe and Transform Your Life*. Novato, CA: New World Library.

Steiner, C. M. (1974). *Scripts People Live: Transactional Analysis of Life Scripts*. New York, NY: Bantam Books.

Tinnin, L., & Gantt, L. (2013). *The Instinctual Trauma Response and Dual Brain Dynamics: A Guide for Trauma Therapy*. Morgantown, WV: Gargoyle Press.

Zimbardo, P. G., Sword, R. M., & Sword, R. K. M. (2012). *The Time Cure: Overcoming PTSD With the New Psychology of Time Perspective Therapy*. San Francisco, CA: Jossey-Bass.

Chapter 16

Transforming the Moral and the Whole Story II

Foundational Storyboarding

In the course of reading this book, you have met with numerous approaches to changing foundational and life stories. One method for integrating many aspects of these approaches is what I call "Foundational Storyboarding." It builds especially on Linda Gantt's Graphic Narrative (Tinnin & Gantt, 2013; see Chapter 19), as well as the research on memory reconsolidation (Chapter 10), the use of storytelling in therapy, and the importance of ritual to sustained change (Chapter 10). The significance of an event or of a story is a function of how the person perceives it, what moral or life lesson they take from it. Thus, helping transform that life lesson directly is an efficient pathway to change.

Foundational Storyboarding is a way of working directly with a foundational story, drawing it scene by scene in much the same manner as a movie director might work with a script, drawing and writing it scene by scene. Actually drawing the memory scenes has advantages over imagery in that both the client and the therapist can see the story; the action is, in effect, stopped so that the client can also become a witness and can reflect upon the narrative; and any missing scenes become apparent.

Because the storyboarding involves recalling the story memory for more than ten minutes and less than four hours, it is well within the reconsolidation window for modifying a memory (see Chapter 10). I still keep a ten-minute hourglass on my desk, but this is unnecessary, as the process always takes longer than ten minutes. The changes to the story make for the discontinuity that Ecker (Chapter 15) sees as crucial to the reconsolidation process (Ecker et al., 2012).

For the procedure I ask the client in advance if she might be willing to work with a particular foundational story. I have at the ready a table, a set of markers, and a stack of plain 8.5"x11" copy paper. If the incident was potentially traumatic, I also have a photo of the client's calm place sandtray (see Part 5) where she can see it. I then explain that I will be asking her to draw the story scene by scene, in much the same manner that a director storyboards a movie. I ask her to begin with a scene right before the story takes place.

Occasionally clients will complain that they cannot draw. I explain that, just as in the movies, the task is not to make beautiful images, but just to get the gist and flow of the story. If the client still expresses reluctance (rare), I tell her that she is welcome to describe each scene in writing (doing so, of course, brings to mind the internal images of the story).

The client then proceeds to storyboard the incident, one page per scene, beginning just before the occurrence and ending with a scene in which the story has ended. The client is asked to draw herself in each of the scenes, which puts her in the position of witness as well as narrator. After drawing each scene, I ask the client about it and make my own notes so that I can remember her description. I keep alert for any missing scene or break in the narrative. When these occur, I have the client add a scene. If the client does not recall a missing scene, I ask her to draw what might have logically occurred.

When the client finishes, she has already begun to change the story by elaboration, by adding missing scenes, and by providing an ending. I then ask, "looking back on this story from your vantage point now, what might you have learned instead that might have been helpful in your life?" Most clients have an immediate idea. Not that they necessarily would have chosen to endure the described event, but having endured it, something valuable could emerge.

If the client cannot think of a different moral, there are two possibilities for proceeding. One is for the clinician to intuit what the client could have gained from the story, and incorporate that into the next phase of the procedure. This, of course, depends on the clinician's intuition skills and on her connection with the client. It does risk being off the mark and thereby less helpful.

The other possibility is to ask the client how she would change the story if she could. You can let her know that it is the story about the event that she is imagining, rather than the real life sequence of events (which cannot be known with certainty), and she is free to bring in any real or fanciful character or alter it in any way she wishes. She is then requested to draw scenes showing the altered story, and those altered or added scenes are used to replace the original scenes on the table. You can then ask what the lesson or moral might be from the altered story.

Figures 16.1 to 16.8 show the storyboarding images for the foundational story described in Chapter 13. Each scene is drawn on a separate sheet of paper. In Figure 16.1, the client and his friend are building the brick filling station in the backyard. The bricks tumble down, and the midpoint finds our protagonist shocked with blood streaming from his hand. In the return phase of the story, he runs to the house. His mother wraps his hand in towels and his parents drive him to the doctor in the black Plymouth. The kindly doctor stems the bleeding with compression and butterfly bandages; his father advises him to lay the bricks flat. Figure 16.8 contains an added scene

Figures 16.1–16.8 Foundational Storyboarding Example

Figure 16.2

Figure 16.3

Figure 16.4

Figure 16.5

Figure 16.6

Figure 16.7

Figure 16.8

for a changed moral. Here our little fellow and his friend are building a new filling station. They have taken his father's advice and are laying the bricks flat for safety, but they are also using boards so they can build just as high.

The next phase of the procedure involves telling the story back to the client (see Tinnin & Gantt, 2013). It is incredibly captivating to be told one's own story. In preparation for the retelling, display the client's pictures on the wall and stand where you can point to them in turn. Explain to the client that she is free to interrupt with additions or corrections. Begin with a title that captures the revised moral or lesson. For example, "this is how little Nathan learned to build his dreams safely." After explaining the last picture, which is at the end or after the story, finish with "the end."

Resume your seat, and, just like after some of the guided imagery explained in earlier chapters, remain quiet and allow the client to speak first. Being told a story, particularly one's own story, elicits a mild trance, and the client may need a few moments to gather his thoughts and re-orient. In the discussion, it is helpful to ask what other life stories might have been affected by the change in this story.

Following the discussion, when you have a sense that the client has integrated the changed perception, discuss with him what kind of activity or ritual might remind him of the new outlook over the next several weeks. This can range from telling important people of his new insight to posting a phrase or one of the pictures where he will see it frequently. The sandtray is a valuable source of ritual. You can have the client create a scene that represents what he gained from the experience, then take a picture to reflect on daily until he returns to therapy. For the above story, the client found a small plastic brick from a building set his daughter had tired of. He glued a chip of wood to the flat side of the brick, then put both into a small sandwich bag which he carried with him.

The steps of Foundational Storyboarding are:

1. Secure the client's willingness and permission to work with a particular foundational story.
2. Have the client draw the story scene by scene while telling the story.
3. Help the client fill any gaps by including what may logically have occurred.
4. Be sure the client provides an ending scene demarcating that the incident is finished.
5. Ask the client what helpful lesson she might have gained from the occurrence.
6. Display the pictures and tell the story back to the client scene by scene with a title that evokes the lesson that could have been gained. When finished, say "the end."
7. Wait for the client to speak, then discuss.
8. Design a ritual with the client to remind her of the changed story and the insight gained.

Expect foundational storyboarding to take a couple of hours. If you cannot schedule a longer session, tell the client about ten or 15 minutes prior to the end of the session that "we only have a few minutes left, so we will have to continue this process next time." When the client completes the current picture that she is drawing, have her skip over to the last (ending) picture and draw that before the session's end. This makes for an ending to the material so that the client can more easily put it aside until the next meeting, whereas leaving a story in the middle engenders a sense of incompleteness and can contribute to difficulty in putting it aside over the following days.

This method of eliciting and altering essential aspects of a foundational story draws upon both the understandings of story and many of the change processes described earlier. We next turn our attention to a particular and ubiquitous kind of foundational and life story: that of trauma.

References

Ecker, B., Tick, R., & Hulley, L. (2012). *Unlocking the Emotional Brain: Eliminating Symptoms at Their Roots Using Memory Reconsolidation*. New York, NY: Routledge.

Tinnin, L., & Gantt, L. (2013). *The Instinctual Trauma Response and Dual Brain Dynamics: A Guide for Trauma Therapy*. Morgantown, WV: Gargoyle Press.

Part 5

Trauma and the Life Story

Chapter 17

From Fat Farm to Child Abuse

In the mid-1990s, the big health conglomerate Kaiser Permanente was looking for cost-cutting measures. Managed care had begun in earnest, and any big insurer had not only to pay medical staff, facilities and equipment costs, but now the health dollar had to cover more administrative expenses, executive salaries, and shareholder profits, as well. A review of their expenses showed that, by far, the costliest medical problems were chronic illnesses: diabetes, coronary artery and heart disease, hypertension, etc. These all led to expensive tests and ongoing care, plus periodic hospitalizations and emergency visits. The reviewers searched the literature to see what factor(s) these illnesses might have in common. It did not take long to see that a major contributing factor to all these chronic and debilitating illnesses was obesity. If they could lower obesity rates in their insured, they could substantially decrease health care costs, and, at the same time, improve the quality of life for subscribers. A win-win!

Accordingly, Kaiser set about developing a state-of-the-art obesity clinic, one that could be replicated in every major area where Kaiser had a foothold. They brought in experts in all phases of the physical and emotional aspects of obesity to design a premiere clinic which would provide service free of charge to Kaiser subscribers.

The designers knew that a major drawback of obesity clinics in the past had been the high drop-out rate. They no doubt hoped that with the combination of state-of-the-art programming and no cost, this perennial problem could be mitigated. The model clinic began operation, but to the company's dismay, it was soon evident that the drop-out rate was almost as high as for other obesity clinics. The dream of lower health costs was as ephemeral as ever.

To their great credit, they did not stop at the apparent failure. Dr. Vince Felitti and his team began by reviewing the records of those who had dropped out. To their surprise, almost every person who left the program dropped out at the same point in their treatment. What was the point in treatment where people stopped coming? It was precisely at the point when they began to lose weight.

The team located every person they could who had dropped out and subjected them to in-depth interviews about their lives, comparing them to the smaller number who had continued in the program. What they found astounded the researchers. Almost every person who had discontinued treatment had a childhood history of abuse or neglect.

The researchers realized they were on to something potentially game-changing, and they contacted the Centers for Disease Control in Atlanta. Together with the CDC, the Kaiser team devised a large-scale study to understand the effect of trauma in childhood on subsequent health in adulthood. Ideally for science, of course, they would have randomly assigned two equal groups of children randomly to either be abused or not (control), then followed them well into adulthood. But things are never ideal—institutional review boards, professional ethics, etc. can get in the way of perfect science. So, the authors designed the study as best they could, given the limitations. What they could do was to use a large sample size (they used a cohort of over 17,000); they could carry the study over many years; and they could design both a retrospective part (i.e., see what if any illnesses people had who had been abused or neglected as children and how that varied with having experienced more or fewer types of abuse) and a prospective part (predicting incidence of future disease based upon the extent of a person's childhood history of abuse or neglect). After all, the participants were Kaiser members, so their health records were available to researchers.

The results and patterns began to emerge. If the researchers had been surprised first by when people dropped out of obesity treatment (when they began to lose weight), then by the drop-outs having experienced childhood abuse, they must have been astounded by the initial results. To begin with, more than half of the participants acknowledged having experienced at least one type of abuse as a child (Felitti, 2002). By and large these were middle-class Californians, people who had jobs or family support such that they could afford Kaiser healthcare. Then there was the range of types of illness, physical and emotional, associated with childhood abuse and neglect: ischemic heart disease, certain types of cancer, smoking and COPD (emphysema and related maladies), diabetes, hypertension, sexually transmitted disease, depression, suicide, alcoholism, drug abuse, and numerous other illnesses, including, of course, obesity. A third surprise was the pattern. There was a linear relationship between the number of types of abuse experienced and the incidence of chronic disease—the more types of abuse, the greater the incidence of disease. In public health, as in psychology, the patterns between things tend to be complex and the effect size small; a simple linear relationship with a large effect size is rare.

In the prospective part of the study where people were followed over the course of years to see what if any health problems emerged, the same pattern continued: the more types of trauma and neglect a person experienced as a child, the greater the likelihood a person would contract one or more of the illnesses enumerated above. And persons who had experienced four or more types of abuse or neglect on average died 20 years earlier!

The Adverse Childhood Experiences, or ACE study, as it has been termed, has been replicated numerous times, not only in different states, but in different countries and cultures—and the essential findings have consistently held up. For example, a retrospective Irish study of over 8,000 participants nationally representative of the Irish population age 50 and older was conducted which included corrections for current socioeconomic status and for memory loss (using a word learning and recall task). The authors concluded "a clear dose-response relationship was evident across the majority of the different disease types examined in the present study and the experience of *two or more* adverse events during childhood was associated with significantly increased risk of cardiovascular disease, lung disease, asthma, arthritis, ulcers, and any emotional, nervous, or psychiatric disorder in the full multivariate adjusted models [italics added]" (McCrory et al., 2015, p. 4).

A 2012 meta-analysis of 124 studies concluded, "this overview of the evidence suggests a *causal*[1] relationship between non-sexual child maltreatment on a range of mental disorders, drug use, suicide attempts, sexually transmitted infections, and risky sexual behavior. There is also emerging evidence that neglect in childhood may be as harmful as physical and emotional abuse [italics added]" (Norman et al., 2012, p. 21).

The proliferation of studies has continued since Norman's work, many of them trying to tease out pathways from child trauma to adult consequences, or evaluating particular links in more detail, or looking at more possible adult health consequences of childhood trauma. For example, higher ACE scores have been associated with a greater incidence of cancer (Ports et al., 2019), irritable bowel syndrome (Park et al., 2016), asthma (Wing et al., 2015), metabolic syndrome (Jakubowski et al., 2018), and psychosis (Roper et al., 2015). Studies have been performed in countries as diverse as India (Damodaran & Paul, 2017), Japan (Matsuura et al., 2013), and Romania (Meinck et al., 2017).

Monnat and Chandler of Penn State (2015) examined self-report surveys of some 52,000 respondents across 14 states looking at the ACE factors (minus neglect) and the factors' individual contribution to functional limitation, diabetes, heart attack, and self-rated overall health. They found some differences in impact of the ACE factors. For example, childhood physical abuse is associated with all four negative adult health outcomes, whereas witnessing parental domestic violence is associated only with adult onset diabetes. They note that a higher childhood ACE score likely depresses adult socio-economic status (SES) status *irrespective* of childhood SES.

The latter conclusion was shown in a recent equation modeling study (read regression and pathway analysis) with a cohort of over 14,000 participants from Washington state (Jones et al., 2018). Jones and her colleagues looked at the pathways from childhood adversity to adult mental health problems. While they showed that childhood trauma and abuse can directly lead to adult mental illness, there are also indirect pathways, the most notable of which is via poverty. By disrupting a child's school performance, trauma leads to lower educational and career attainment, increasing the risk for depression and anxiety in adulthood. The other pathways that proved significant, although not as robust as that of income, were via adult trauma (childhood trauma increases the likelihood of adult trauma—more on the traumatic breeding of vulnerability later) and via lessened social supports.

Conclusion: Childhood abuse and childhood neglect are bad. Really bad. Worse even than you thought, because of their ability to increase the risk for virtually all mental illness and many chronic, debilitating, and deadly physical ills *decades* after its occurrence. In the next chapter we will look at the impact of trauma on stories, and some possible pathways for mitigation.

Mental illness forms a synergistic tapestry with trauma. Shown in the ACE study is how many mental illnesses (including substance abuse) and chronic physical illnesses have their roots in childhood abuse and neglect. Add to that the disorders like PTSD, Brief Psychotic Episode, and the Adjustment Disorders that are a direct result of childhood or adult trauma. Add again the mental illnesses, like schizophrenia, whose course becomes problematic because of trauma (traditionally the acute psychotic symptoms like hallucinations, pressured speech, and loose associations emerge in late adolescence only after an experience of separation traumatic to the individual, such as leaving the childhood home or having a traumatic drug experience). Add again the traumas that occur as a *result* of mental illness or a result of attempts to cope with mental illness. The conclusion is that virtually all mental illness results from, is exacerbated by, or leads to trauma.

As the ACE study demonstrates, many incidents of depression and suicide are associated with childhood trauma. Preventing child abuse and neglect not only becomes a public health priority, but mitigating the impact of childhood trauma now becomes a personal mental and physical health priority for the millions of adults who have grown up in abuse and neglect. A storied lens on that mitigation is the subject of our next chapter.

Note

1. In situations where double blind studies are not feasible, the evidence for causality can be estimated using what has been called the Bradford Hill Framework, which combines criteria such as the strength and consistency of the association, evidence of a linear relationship, strength of the temporal relationship (e.g., evidence from both retrospective and prospective studies), plausibility of results, and possible alternatives.

References

Damodaran, D. K., & Paul, V. K. (2017). Patterning/clustering of adverse childhood experiences (ACEs): The Indian scenario. *Psychological Studies*, *62*(1), pp. 75–84.

Felitti, V. J. (2002). The relation between adverse childhood experiences and adult health: Turning gold into lead. *Permanente Journal, 6*(1), pp. 41–47.

Jakubowski, K. P., Cundiff, J. M., & Matthews, K. A. (2018). Cumulative childhood adversity and adult cardiometabolic disease: A meta-analysis. *Health Psychology, 37*(8), pp. 701–715.

Jones, T. M., Nurius, P., Song, C., & Fleming, C. M. (2018). Modeling life course pathways from adverse childhood experiences to adult mental health. *Child Abuse and Neglect, 80*, pp. 32–40.

Matsuura, N., Hashimoto, T., & Toichi, M. (2013). Associations among adverse childhood experiences, aggression, depression, and self-esteem in serious female juvenile offenders in Japan. *Journal of Forensic Psychiatry & Psychology, 24*(1), pp. 111–127.

McCrory, C., Dooley, C., Layte, R., & Kenny, R. A. (2015). The lasting legacy of childhood adversity for disease risk in later life. *Health Psychology, 34*(7), pp. 687–696.

Meinck, F., Cosma, A. P., Mikton, C., & Baban, A. (2017). Psychometric properties of the Adverse Childhood Experiences Abuse Short Form (ACE-ASF) among Romanian high school students. *Child Abuse & Neglect, 72*, pp. 326–337.

Monnat, S. M., & Chandler, R. F. (2015). Long-term physical health consequences of adverse childhood experiences. *Sociological Quarterly, 56*(4), pp. 723–752.

Norman, R. E., Byambaa, M., De, R., Butchart, A., Scott, J., & Vos, T. (2012). The long-term health consequences of child physical abuse, emotional abuse, and neglect: a systematic review and meta-analysis. *PLoS Medicine, 9*(11), pp. 1–31.

Park, S. H., Videlock, E. J., Shih, W., Presson, A. P., Mayer, E. A., & Chang, L. (2016). Adverse childhood experiences are associated with irritable bowel syndrome and gastrointestinal symptom severity. *Neurogastroenterology & Motility, 28*(8), pp. 1252–1260.

Ports, K. A., Holman, D. M., Guinn, A. S., Pampati, S., Dyer, K. E., Merrick, M. T., Lunsford, N. B., & Metzler, M. (2019). Adverse childhood experiences and the presence of cancer risk factors in adulthood: A scoping review of the literature from 2005 to 2015. *Journal of Pediatric Nursing, 44*, pp. 81–96.

Roper, L. J., Purdon, S. E., & Roper, L. J. (2015). Childhood and later life stressors and psychosis. *Clinical Neuropsychiatry: Journal of Treatment Evaluation, 12*(6), pp. 148–156.

Wing, R., Gjelsvik, A., Nocera, M., & McQuaid, E. L. (2015). Association between adverse childhood experiences in the home and pediatric asthma. *Asthma & Immunology, 114*(5), pp. 379–384.

Chapter 18

The Trauma Story
Holes, Shards, and Morals

The potential impact of trauma has been known for centuries. Let us listen as Kate, Hotspur's wife, bemoans the state of her husband in Shakespeare's *Henry IV Part 1*:

> O, my good lord, why are you thus alone?
> For what offence have I this fortnight been
> A banish'd woman from my Harry's bed?
> Tell me, sweet lord, what is't that takes from thee
> Thy stomach, pleasure and thy golden sleep?
> Why dost thou bend thine eyes upon the earth,
> And start so often when thou sit'st alone?
> Why hast thou lost the fresh blood in thy cheeks;
> And given my treasures and my rights of thee
> To thick-eyed musing and curst melancholy?
> In thy faint slumbers I by thee have watch'd,
> And heard thee murmur tales of iron wars;
> Speak terms of manage [horsemanship] to thy bounding steed;
> Cry 'Courage! to the field!' And thou hast talk'd
> Of sallies and retires, of trenches, tents,
> Of palisades, frontiers, parapets,
> Of basilisks, of cannon, culverin,
> Of prisoners' ransom and of soldiers slain,
> And all the currents of a heady fight.
> Thy spirit within thee hath been so at war,
> And thus hath so bestirr'd thee in thy sleep,
> That beads of sweat have stood upon thy brow
> Like bubbles in a late-disturbed stream;
> And in thy face strange motions have appear'd,
> Such as we see when men restrain their breath
> On some great sudden hest. O, what portents are these?
> Some heavy business hath my lord in hand,
> And I must know it, else he loves me not.
>
> (Shakespeare, 1936 [*Henry IV Part 1*, Scene III])

We have a shutting down of sexual response, gastro-intestinal problems, anhedonia, sleep disorder with nightmares, exaggerated startle, dissociation, depressed mood, and flashbacks. The DSM and the ICD are barely as complete and not nearly so poetic. "Thy spirit within thee hath been so at war."

We can see that Kate is quite worried for her husband. Most concerning to her is that Hotspur is unavailable. He lives in a haunted world of his own, and Kate is not a part of it: "Why dost thou bend thine eyes upon the earth," and "thick-eyed musing." Of all the ills affecting Hotspur, the granddaddy is that of dissociation. The internal disconnection becomes an externalized disconnection with the world around him, including his wife.

The barriers separating various mental aspects (between thoughts and feelings; between imagination and experience; between past and present; and between the experience of various characters in one's story) exists on a continuum ranging from impermeable through semi-permeable to permeable. In order to function effectively, our barriers are mostly semi-permeable, allowing some aspects of mental and emotional life to pass but not others, and allowing some aspects of the external world to pass within, but not others. Thus, for example, we have access to and awareness of our feelings. We are neither totally unaware of our feelings, nor are we completely buffeted by them.

Trauma disrupts those barriers such that they swing between the two extremes of too impermeable to too permeable. For example, when the barrier between memory and current experience is too permeable, we experience nightmares and flashbacks, like Hotspur. When that barrier is too impermeable, we may have no verbal memory of even an important incident. A more impermeable barrier is referred to as "dissociation."

Dissociation is a natural and useful process. How many times have you taken a long drive and been lost in thought or music remembering nothing of the trip? Dissociation makes for the "trance" in hypnosis. It is also the natural protection of the storied self in the face of potential trauma.

> Nathan 18.1 called in a panic. Fortunately, I was between appointments and picked up the phone. "Dr. Marr," he cried, "I don't know where I am! I'm lost!" When asked about his circumstances, he said, "I'm driving and there're cornfields all around." I encouraged him to look for a wide shoulder and pull off the road.
>
> "Now, Nathan, what do you remember about when you left and where you planned to go?"
>
> "That's just it. Nothing—it's like I just woke up and I was here, driving."
>
> "Look around; what do you see?"
>
> "Just corn everywhere, here and across the road."
>
> "What color is the corn—is it more green or brown? How tall is it?" I wanted him calmer and firmly rooted in his present circumstances and identity.

"It's green and not too high, maybe as high as the car."

"Nathan, in a minute I'm going to have you carefully get out of the car, but first I want you to look around and tell me what other cars and trucks are coming."

"There's no traffic. Oh, God, I'm all alone!"

"Nathan, it's going to be alright. Make sure there is no traffic, then get out of the car and stand close by the door. What do you see now?"

"There's a road sign, you know, an arrow, 'Curve Ahead.' It's got shotgun holes in it. Oh, my God! There's all these dents and scratches on my car. How did they get here?! Wait. Further up the road. There's like a billboard. It says 'Acme Tool and Die—One Mile.'"

"Good. Now wait just a minute while I look that up. Nathan, you're on the Eastern Shore of Maryland. How do you feel? Do you think you can safely drive?"

Nathan was able to drive to the tool and die plant where he got directions to return some 50 miles back to Washington, D.C.

Nathan had dissociative identity disorder; some of his characters (alters) did not even know of the existence of others. Here the dissociative barrier between characters is impermeable.

Because dissociation is the natural protection of one's self narrative, virtually all stories of traumatic incidents contain elements of dissociation. In the extreme, there is no verbal memory of traumatic incident(s) at all. The story memory resides only in bodily sensations and movements. More frequently, the story of a traumatic incident will have gaps—holes in the flow of the narrative, missing scenes where the author and the narrator went off line (Sewell & Williams, 2002). These holes fragment the story. Dissociated story bits or dissociated sensations become disconnected memory fragments. These shards can be subtly triggered by external events or internal musings; then, like scripts or small recordings, they play, and the person experiences a flashback—a sensation or a bit of story that is not just remembered, but relived.

My wife used to run the art and activities therapy department at Walter Reed Army Medical Center. She recalls that every day at sunset they would lower the colors (take down the flag) to the backdrop of ceremonial gunshots. She would find hospitalized soldiers *under* their beds. These men were re-living disconnected shards of traumatic firefights. Because the flashbacks were severed from context and had no complete story or ending, they played over and over, echoes of horror.[1]

This points to the importance of getting the entire story of a traumatic incident, with context, with no missing scenes, and with an ending. Frequently clients will be able to see there are missing scenes, once it is pointed out. A common response is "I know there is a part missing, but I don't remember it." I respond by encouraging the client to put in what would logically have occurred. Trauma is not the result of historical truth, but of narrative truth (see Spence, 1982, on historical and narrative truth).

Trauma affects foundational stories in yet another way. In 2012 Philip Zimbardo (yes, the same Zimbardo famous for designing the Stanford prison experiment where students were randomly assigned to be jailers or prisoners) wrote *The Time Cure* with Richard and Rosemary Sword (Zimbardo et al., 2012; see Chapter 11). The authors' premise was that each of us has a primary time perspective, which is a variant of past, present or future. Trauma victims live in the negative past, and the therapy involves helping the person balance her time perspective to include positive past, present, and future.[2] I believe the major contribution of Zimbardo and the Swords here is recognizing that trauma causes a disorder of time perspective. I would word it differently than they do. Rather than thinking of trauma as causing a *person* to live in the negative past, I think of the trauma *story* as existing in the continuing present with no end. The problem is that the story is *not* in the past where it belongs. It is a matter of what is emphasized: do you help change the person or the story?

Trauma stories that exist in the continuing present can undoubtedly shift the time perspective of the person to emphasize the negative past. That is a change in one's life story, and is one of the insidious ways that traumatic foundational stories alter one's life story.

Traumatic foundational stories alter one's life story in yet other ways. They can change the role of the protagonist in one's life story from hero to victim (or, better, survivor). And traumatic foundational stories can change the theme and the moral (life lesson) of a person's life story. As Judith Herman (1997) famously put it, trauma leaves one feeling like a damaged person in a dangerous world. Any complete trauma therapy must address both the foundational story of the trauma, and the impact on the individual's life story.

Thus, any trauma, but especially childhood trauma, affects stories in at least two broad ways. First, the trauma itself becomes an unfinished, affect-ridden foundational story, one with gaps and an incomplete ending so that the trauma story continues in the present. Second, trauma alters the time perspective, the protagonist, and the theme of one's larger life story. Trauma therapy must address the impact both on the foundational story of the trauma itself, and the impact on the larger life story.

In sum, a traumatic story differs from other foundational stories in at least four ways. The story itself has more gaps, more missing scenes, and it lacks an ending so that it exists in the continuing present—it is something that *is happening* rather than something that *happened*. It carries intense, negative affect, and its theme and moral is a variant of the notion that "I am damaged" and "the world is unsafe," existentially dangerous. It is, quite literally, a living nightmare. In the next chapter we will look at universal phases in helping a person overcome the impact of such a story.

Notes

1. Paula complained to the hospital administration and the practice was stopped. It begs the question of why the practice was instituted to begin with in a treatment center for trauma—much of which was the result of gunshot.
2. Zimbardo is one of too few theorists to recognize the importance of one's perspective on time. Hypnotherapists recognize this, as did Frederick Melges (1982), a psychodynamic theorist who saw differing mental illnesses as differing disorders in one's perception of time.

References

Herman, J. L. (1997). *Trauma and Recovery: The Aftermath of Violence-From Domestic Abuse to Political Terror*. New York, NY: Basic Books.

Melges, F. T. (1982). *Time and the Inner Future: A Temporal Approach to Psychiatric Disorders*. New York, NY: John Wiley & Sons.

Sewell, K. W., & Williams, A. M. (2002). Broken narratives: Trauma, metaconstructive gaps, and the audience of psychotherapy. *Journal of Constructivist Psychotherapy*, 15, pp. 205–218.

Shakespeare, W., in Kittredge, G. L., ed. (1936). *The Complete Works of Shakespeare*. New York, NY: Ginn and Company.

Spence, D. P. (1982). *Narrative Truth and Historical Truth: Meaning and Interpretation in Psychoanalysis*. New York, NY: W. W. Norton.

Zimbardo, P. G., Sword, R. M., & Sword, R. K. M. (2012). *The Time Cure: Overcoming PTSD With the New Psychology of Time Perspective Therapy*. San Francisco, CA: Jossey-Bass.

Chapter 19

A Trauma Treatment Primer
Phases of Trauma Treatment

If one looks across the plethora of therapies that have been adapted or created to address trauma, it becomes apparent that there are fundamental aspects that all have in common, whether it is the more well known like EMDR or exposure therapy, or the more marginally known like brainspotting or emotional freedom technique (EFT—tapping). These can be seen as phases:

1. Safety
2. Stabilization
3. Assessment
4. Trauma Therapy, including:
   a. Re-storying of the trauma incident
   b. Treating the larger life impact (mitigating the impact on the person's larger life story)

Safety

The process of treating traumatized persons always begins in safety, because, at its heart, trauma is a disintegration of a person's sense of safety. Trauma is a disorder of safety. Safety here refers to the presence of elemental existential trust. Eric Erikson rightly put "Trust vs. Mistrust" as his first developmental phase, established normally in very early childhood. This is a trust that, while it emerges in relation to others, is a trust that the world is generally a safe place. It is the damage to that existential trust that Judith Herman (1997) referred to in the second part of her observation that trauma leaves one a damaged person *in a dangerous world.*

I remember when one of my daughters was about three or four. She insisted on taking showers instead of baths, because showers were associated in her mind with being all grown up. Of course, my wife and I hovered whenever it was shower time to ensure that the water was not too hot and that she did not slip. When she completed her shower, she very proudly turned the water off all by herself. It was then that a small hand would appear from between the curtains, with the clear expectation that a towel would fall out of the Universe. And of course, with my wife and I hovering nearby, it did. This is that general existential trust that the Universe will provide what you need. It is precisely this kind of trust that is shattered in trauma.

Safety must become a part of the external context to the trauma survivor's story—i.e., the story must be told and healed in an atmosphere of safety—safety in the consulting room, safety in the therapeutic relationship. The consulting room needs to be comfortable, with no likely triggers to trauma. I recall seeing a therapist's office once where over the toilet in the bathroom hung a print of Edvard Munch's picture "The Scream." I have seen other offices that, while not as overtly potentially triggering, were very formal and expensive in a manner that reminded me of either a lawyer's office or of my grandmother's formal living room where children were not allowed to play. I try to have comfortable seats, restive watercolors on the walls, and a few intriguing knick-knacks: wooden masks from Bali and India, a small Hopi and two small Chinese statues; and the sandtray figures prominently displayed. On a table beside the chairs is a grounding stone and a basket of polished pebbles (dipping one's hand in the basket is calming and grounding).

The quality of the therapeutic relationship, including the manner of witnessing, is a crucial element to the context of safety. See Chapter 11 about managing the therapeutic relationship in a manner that promotes security and connection. An important part of managing the relationship in a safe manner is managing our own expectations. When one's very belief that there could be safety in the world has been shattered, how quickly do we expect that person to trust a stranger?

A safe therapeutic context within which a person's story is told changes the context of that story to one of greater safety, i.e., not as traumatic. In addition to ensuring the therapeutic context is one of safety, there are techniques that can facilitate clients feeling safe. Many trauma clinicians use a safe place guided imagery (Shapiro, 2010), where they assist the client in slowing his breathing, then imagine a place that is very safe and comfortable. Others use a similar art technique of having the client draw or paint a secure and comfortable place (Tinnin & Gantt, 2013). These safe places are very useful and can be elicited throughout the therapy when the client might become dysregulated or dissociative.

Especially for victims of interpersonal trauma, the notion of a "safe place" often conjures instead a "secured place" with guard dogs and riflemen or tigers. There is a part of these clients that is always on the alert, and consequently can rarely experience calm, only relative security. This is the genesis of much of their sleep problem, as they must always sleep "with one eye open."[1] To the extent possible, I want them to experience calm, not just relative security. To that end, even when using the safe place imagery or safe place picture, I refer to it as a "calm place" rather than a "safe place." The difference is subtle, but can be important.

Even more helpful than the safe or calm place imagery or picture is a technique which I call the Calm Place Sandtray. Its advantage is that it is three-dimensional and directly involves the tactile sense as well as sight. To initiate the Calm Place Sandtray, I explain to the client that I would like to help her generate a sense of calm that can be useful on its own as well as in working through trauma. With the client's permission, I introduce her to the sandtray and to the figures.

The traditional tray is rectangular, often of wood, and of precise dimensions. My own tray is round because the circle is traditionally the symbol of the self. The bottom and interior walls are painted blue so that by moving sand the client can represent water or sky if she wishes. I store it under the desk and place it on a card table to use it. I wet the sand sufficiently so that it can be molded. I run my hands through the sand as I introduce the procedure. This is tacit permission to work in a medium that often relates to enjoyable times in a sandbox or at the beach as a child, but that also can conjure embarrassment at being seen enjoying something "childish." Thus, the tacit permission is important.

I explain: "I would like you to create a calm, serene scene in the sand. Should you wish to represent water (and you don't have to), the bottom is painted blue (I move the sand aside to expose the blue bottom as I talk). You can use the sand and as many or as few of these figures as you wish (here I point to the open bookcase where the figures are displayed). It seems to work best if you don't plan or think it out too much, just let your hands create a calm scene."

I then sit back quietly and let the client grapple with the task. Virtually all clients enjoy the experience and are able to create a scene. When the person has finished, I say simply, "tell me about it." I then suggest the client make two different kinds of pictures of the scene. The first is an internal picture. I have the client imagine where in the scene she would most want to be, then describe the sights, sounds, and textures from that vantage point. I suggest she can return to that scene at any time; and that it is useful to practice going there each day until we next meet.

The second picture is a photograph, which I have the client either take on her cell phone; or use a small camera which I provide and then either send or print the picture for her. Following standard sandplay[2] protocol, I do not dismantle the scene in front of the client,[3] but let her know I will put the figures away later. Both the physical and the internal image can be useful as trauma treatment proceeds.

The need for safety heightens and diminishes throughout the therapy. While any trauma treatment must begin in safety, the phases are iterative, meaning there is not often a linear path through them. Each phase is returned to as needed over and over. Thus, it is rarely sufficient to establish a safe relationship and environment early in the treatment and never have to return to it. Equally important, the assessment phase is an ongoing process as well, becoming increasingly nuanced as the person feels increasingly safe. It is not a one-time protocol, but a process that is repeated in different ways to inform different phases. Of course, different therapies emphasize different phases, but the attention applied to each phase must be sufficient—and repeated often enough—to be healing to the individual without leading to either fleeing or re-traumatization.

Stabilization

You no doubt remember from some long-ago Intro to Psychology course that the most efficient learning takes place under conditions of moderate anxiety. Too much anxiety, and concentration and recall are disrupted; ditto too little anxiety. Psychotherapy is a learning process, and a client who is buffeted by intense affect is not an efficient learner, nor is the client who is dissociated—zoned out and existing somewhere else.

> Harriet 19.1 called from under the desk in her classroom. Between sobs and gasping breaths, she managed to explain that, while working alone at her desk in her free period, one of the male administrators had stood staring outside the door to her classroom. When she had spoken to him, he had just turned and walked away. She flashed on how her uncle used to stand outside her bedroom door and stare before entering to molest her. "And the children will be coming into the room in ten minutes!" she wailed.
>
> I asked what she could see from under the desk. "I see my shoes," she said, continuing to sob.
>
> "Describe your shoes," I asked.
>
> "They're black and worn. I wear them because they are so comfortable."
>
> "What is that comfortable feeling you get from the shoes like?"
>
> "It's kind of like a hug for my feet." The sobs were coming further apart. "What if he comes back!"
>
> "What else do you see from where you are?"
>
> "There's a cabinet where I have the children keep their work."
>
> "Tell me about it. What color is it? What size?"
>
> "It's big and square, kinda bulky. I painted it orange and red, bright colors."
>
> "What kind of work is in there now?"
>
> "The children have been working on people from the American Revolution. For the first project they each picked a famous person, read a story about them and drew his or her picture. Those pictures are in there."
>
> "What's your favorite so far?"

"One really cute little boy got an old Golden Book from his grandmother called *Ben and Me* about a church mouse that helped Ben Franklin discover electricity. The picture shows Ben riding in a kite held by Ben Franklin. I could really use some Kleenex."

"Do you have any in your room?"

"Uh-huh, on top of the desk."

"Without looking, see if you can describe the box to me."

"That's easy. It's small and square and pink. It has pictures of daisies on it; I bought it because I liked the flowers."

"Let's see if you remember accurately. Let me know when you are ready to get the box."

"I'm ready. Oh, it's a blue box, but I was right about the daisies."

"Where are you now?"

"I'm sitting at my desk."

"When you're ready, you might take two long, deep breaths."

(Quiet). "The children will get here shortly, and I've got to get their projects out for them. Thank you."

"You're welcome."

There are numerous techniques for stabilizing and grounding a person. A superb resource not only for stabilizing methods, but for all things trauma related is Glenn Schiraldi's book (2016) *The PTSD Sourcebook*. Virtually all of the techniques for helping someone ground and stabilize have in common helping the person re-orient to the physical world around them whether it is by touching and manipulating a grounding stone; or smelling a strong or pungent scent; or by naming three items above eye level, at eye level and below eye level; or by noticing how his feet feel in his shoes in contact with the floor, and how his buttocks and back contact the chair, which is rooted on the floor (literally how he is grounded).

The triggering of traumatic material can disrupt a client's emotional equilibrium in one of two polarized ways: the client can dissociate, or the client can experience overwhelming affect. In either state the person is not available for therapeutic work, and there is the danger that the work, or even the therapist and the office, can become associated with the traumatic experience.

"Dissociation" can range from a temporary glassy-eyed stare where the person has "spaced out" to an almost catatonic state where the person is difficult to arouse, or to an abrupt change in voice tone, affect, and perspective. Where dissociation presents as a spacing-out or absence, gently calling the person's name may return them to the room. When an abrupt change in presentation occurs (frequently in dissociative disorder NOS or in dissociative identity clients), it is best approached through some of the techniques you will find in Chapter 12 on "Helping Characters Transform."

When the person is overwhelmed with affect, the therapist's contrasting calm presence is especially important. Most high affect will dissipate, as the body can only sustain the state for so long. Common overwhelming affects include panic/grief (which is about abandonment and loss) (Armstrong, 2015), fear, rage, and shame (shame is the primal experience of being rejected from the group because of who you are. See Nathanson (1992) for an excellent understanding).

Sadness is often about loss or regret, a lower volume of panic/grief, and thematic listening (Chapter 11) and empathy is helpful. Anger, or rage, is often a secondary emotion, a response to the panic/grief of abandonment or betrayal. Allowing some dissipation, then connecting the rage with the likely source of abandonment is calming. After the initial dissipation an empathetic counter story is also calming (e.g., "do you remember the scene in *Forrest Gump* where Forrest accompanies Jenny, his girlfriend, to the field outside the cabin where she had been abused? Jenny picks up a rock and throws it at the cabin; then another and another. Do you remember what Forrest Gump says? 'Sometimes there are just not enough stones'"). See Chapter 12 for Helen Watkins' excellent guided imagery for dissipating rage.

When a traumatized person experiences overwhelming anxiety, the prevailing wisdom is to engage the client in deep breathing or other relaxation methods on the theory that the relaxation response is incompatible with anxiety. Have you ever tried this? How did it go? Not so easily, I venture to guess. Precisely because the relaxation response is incompatible, it is a very hard shift from anxiety to relaxation. When anxious, it is difficult to sit still; the body wants to move. Courtney Armstrong (2011) makes the point that therefore first aid for anxiety entails movement: pacing, jumping jacks, any movement. Consider accompanying the client so you can gradually lower the pace of movement. When the client has calmed somewhat, then it becomes a more gradual transition to deeper, slower breathing or other relaxation exercises, such as systematic relaxation.

Trauma Assessment

Only after a modicum of safety and stabilization are established can one help a person assess the extent and impact of her traumatic experiences. Whatever methods you choose, it is helpful to have the client's calm place sandtray picture, or calm place drawing out and within her gaze. If you used a calm place imagery exercise in the initial safety portion, take a few moments and have the client return in imagery to that calm place.

There are four overall areas needed in trauma assessment apart from a general story/psychotherapy assessment. Those areas are: the nature and extent of a client's trauma history, including the likely impact of the trauma stories themselves; the degree of dissociation the client experiences; the client's external and internal resources; and the client's readiness/willingness to work on her trauma.

Trauma History Assessment

A number of trauma approaches have the client make a list of her or his traumas. Many clinicians instruct the client to make a list of her traumas and the age at which each occurred while in the presence of the therapist. In this early step you are just naming the traumas, not expounding upon them. I remember once asking a middle-aged trauma survivor for such a list. He took fully three sessions to list the incidents of repeated trauma he had suffered; he had hundreds of items on the list. I remember feeling overwhelmed. Not so my client. When he was done, he exclaimed, "It helps to see it in writing. What a relief! It's only twelve pages long, it has a finite end. I thought it would go on forever!"

While the trauma list can serve as a goal setting template for therapeutic work to come, sometimes a free-form list *can* be overwhelming. This free-form list, because of its content and lack of structure, can be triggering, leading to de-stabilization (as discussed above), or to re-experiencing one or more traumas. Because of this, I typically use a structured list of common types of trauma for the client to check off which apply and at what age. This list is reproduced as Appendix IV. Notice that the list moves from likely milder, "little *t* traumas" (traumas less likely to cause symptoms) to those which are more severe and interpersonal in nature that are likely to be overwhelming to anyone (rape, loss of a child, torture, etc.), and thus more likely to cause symptoms.

You may notice that some of the items on Appendix IV have an asterisk. These are items that relate to the categories assessed in the ACE Study (see Chapter 17). By counting the number of starred items endorsed, one can get a rough estimate of the client's ACE score. Recall that as the score increases, the probability for severe physical and emotional illness also increases in a linear fashion. An ACE score of four or more without treatment is highly suggestive of multiple and severe health problems and shortened lifespan (Felitti, 2002).

After the person concludes the questionnaire, I inquire about his or her experience in completing it. I then review the list with him, asking him to name (but not describe—we want to approach the actual stories carefully) the events he has listed. By marking what categories a person has experienced, when, and how often, then a plan can be made for gathering the trauma stories.

Following the trauma list (free-form or structured), we then usually have sufficient information to proceed to gathering and working with the individual trauma stories. Ideally, we would begin with the earliest traumatic occurrence and proceed in time order because early traumas can exacerbate and channel the response to later traumas. Often in outpatient treatment we may not have that opportunity, so we may begin with the trauma story that is most recent, or the one that results in the most symptoms. We can then pick up earlier related traumatic foundational stories as needed.

Degree of Dissociation

Dissociation is compartmentalization of psychic processes that are usually more integrated (see also Chapter 18). Thus, one can be unaware of a foundational story; of a feeling, or of feelings in general ("alexithymia"); of the passage of time; or of whole aspects of experience. It can range from a momentary spacing out (similar to the *absence seizure* from which it is sometimes important to distinguish) to the loss of time to disorientation and loss of experiences similar to an alcoholic blackout.

I recall a woman who called the county police because her apartment had been burglarized. There was no evidence of forced entry. When the police inquired about what was taken, the woman acknowledged that none of her extensive jewelry collection had been disturbed, nor had any of the electronics or cash, which were all in plain sight. She stated only that she was missing some personal papers that it seemed unlikely anyone would have an interest in. The officers inquired as to when the theft occurred. She stated it had been in the last couple of days. When asked about her own whereabouts, she finally admitted that she had no idea where she had been.

The phenomenon of dissociation and its relation to trauma was first expounded by Pierre Janet (1907/2012), then by Josef Breur (Sandhu, 2015). Freud's concept of repression was a likely derivation. Much has been written about dissociation of late, and a review of that literature is not in the scope of the present work. For an excellent introduction to it, I recommend Shapiro's book, *The Trauma Treatment Handbook* (2010).

For our purposes, it is helpful to recognize that dissociation exists on a continuum from mild forgetfulness of events to dissociative identity disorder wherein a character with a wholly different storyline becomes narrator and protagonist with little or no knowledge of the usual narrator, protagonist, or self story.

Where on a dissociative continuum does the person generally live? Where does she typically live in regards to reality and fantasy, thoughts and feelings, experience of time (in severe dissociation people can "lose" periods of time ranging from hours to weeks; and even intense memories can be inaccessible), and the boundaries among characters?

A formal assessment is usually needed only when you suspect severe dissociation that is not apparent. If you suspect severe dissociation, the *Dissociative Experiences Scale II* can be a helpful assessment. It is available for free online. Read through the questions to get a sense of the range of dissociative experiences and what severe dissociation might entail. Even if you never use it, it is instructive to download the questionnaire and read through it; it will lend you increased understanding of dissociative phenomena.

Client Resources

The third assessment in trauma is that of resources, both external and internal. I remember an article I read in the late 1990s; I even remember the journal (*Family Process*), but I have not been able to locate it. The gist of the article was that the more disorganized and overwhelmed the family (and, by extension, individual), the more the clinician needed to focus on strengths over problems. Who and what are potential resources in the survivor's life? What internal resources can be marshaled?

Resources are of little help unless they are specific. To know a person is courageous or personable is complimentary, not therapeutic. What is a story that exemplifies their particular courage? What ritual can remind her of that courage in an ongoing manner? How internally do they summon being personable? Do they have access to a personable character? If so, how and when might the client summon him? There is more on the use of resourcing in Chapter 10 on sources of change, and in Chapter 12 on working with characters.

Readiness for Trauma Work

The fourth aspect of trauma that is important to assess is the client's readiness to work on the trauma. This is really an ongoing estimation of the pace and focus of trauma work. "Not being ready" may mean merely that the client needs to internalize more of a sense of safety before proceeding. Occasionally, the client needs more time in therapy to better absorb the safety of the therapy relationship. Alternatively, the client may be so vulnerable to destabilization that the pace must be exceedingly slow.

Tinnin and Gantt (2013) refer to what they call "trauma phobia," or a reluctance to approach the trauma story for fear of re-experiencing the traumatic event. Reassurance can help—reassurance backed up by the knowledge that you can help the person tell the story without re-experiencing the trauma, and that you can help them ground should that become necessary.[4] Again, your intuition and conversations with the client are the best guides to when to suggest proceeding, when to lay low, and when to focus therapeutically on the secondary phobia (trauma phobia).

Recognize that trauma phobia also can apply to us as clinicians, for hearing about the pain and cruelty inflicted in our world is rarely pleasant. Tune inward toward your own feelings. Is there any part of you that would avoid the client's difficulty? For whom is the reluctance, you or the client? If for the client, what are you concerned about? Consider discussing your intuition with the client.

If the reluctance is more your own, how overwhelming is it? Can you ask it to step back for now (a technique use by Richard Schwartz, 1995)? If not, you may wish to seek consultation or supervision. Often client's trauma stories may trigger our own stories. It seems to be a corollary of Murphy's Law that whatever issue or unfinished personal business you have, you will be referred a client who will trigger just that issue. Consider a therapy consult for yourself.

Recall that the trauma treatment process is iterative; that is, it can recycle on itself in any number of permutations. Sometimes as assessment proceeds, we have to return to safety; occasionally we must return to stabilization. The clinician's perceptiveness, empathy, and willingness to directly question ("We just listed some pretty heavy occurrences for you. How are you feeling? Is it OK to proceed, or do we need to discuss a break?") are crucial.

Re-storying Foundational Trauma Stories

Helping a client change both a traumatic foundational story and assisting in changing a life story filled with assumptions based on trauma is like walking along a narrow parapet: there are pitfalls on either side. If the client directly re-experiences the affect, she may become triggered and de-stabilized. This is unnecessarily painful, and may lead to re-traumatization or to fleeing the therapy all together (likely the cause of the high drop-out rate in some trauma treatments). On the other hand, if the client cannot tell her story, then many of the avenues to healing have been blocked (a downfall of some so-called "supportive treatments" that emphasize maintenance, giving no hope of healing).

The middle way involves helping the client tell her story of what happened while also helping her manage her affect. There are many avenues to this once you recognize this as the goal. Most of them involve using dissociation to help process the trauma story without either unbidden dissociation or uncontrolled affect. Two of the techniques are Mark Lawrence's (Personal Communication, 2009) use of the "magic remote" (Chapter 13), and the theatre technique from neurolinguistic programming (Hoobyar, 2013).

If telling the trauma story is likely to become very triggering, a technique borrowed from neurolinguistic programming (Hoobyar & Dotz, 2013) can help. The technique relies on a double dissociation. Have the client image that he is in a movie theatre just before showtime. The movie will be his trauma story. But now, instead of sitting in the audience, he is sitting in the projection booth where he controls the projector. Because the projector is in the way, the client cannot see the screen at all, but he can see himself from the back, sitting in the audience. He is to play the movie in such a way, with pause, rewind, and fast forward, that the client in the theatre is able to pay attention with no distress, even when he plays the movie forward at normal speed. He can then merge with the client in the audience and describe the movie scene by scene.

Both techniques make use of controlled dissociation to titrate the tolerance of the trauma story. In that way, they are similar to Tinnin's (2013) "Hidden Observer," which is described later in this chapter. The techniques may be successfully combined, for example, by having a Hidden Observer hold the Magic Remote. Both the Lawrence, the NLP, and the Tinnin techniques can also be used in working with nightmares.

Having helped the client to tell the trauma story with tolerable affect in safe environs has already changed the story. You may help the client change the story further by using the Storyboarding technique of Chapter 16; the Graphic Narrative of Gantt (see below); the Resourcing technique of Lawrence (Chapter 13); or other methods for co-altering any of the aspects of story (see Part 4). Remember in whatever method you use to help the client tell the trauma story, assist the client to fill in any dissociated scenes, and to make an ending. This latter can be done by continuing the story to the point where the client knew the trauma was over, at least for the time being.

The interested reader can note the same phases of trauma treatment (Safety, Stabilization, Assessment, Re-storying the Trauma, and Changing the Life Story) through numerous trauma therapies.

Understanding the experience of trauma forms the backbone of an innovative trauma therapy that treats the whole story of trauma (Tinnin & Gantt, 2013). In the 1980s, Louis Tinnin, a training psychiatrist at West Virginia University, noted that many of the patients seeking treatment at University Hospital were victims of trauma. Vietnam veterans presented with alcoholism, depression, rage, and other wounds of war. In addition, there were the victims of farming and mining accidents that rural states like West Virginia dispatch into hospitals by the dozens. Finding little in the literature of the time about treating trauma victims, Tinnin began sodium amytal interviews in order to learn about his patients' trauma experience—even the experiences they were unwilling to relate or unable to remember when not medicated. What Tinnin found was that most of the traumatized patients described similar phases of experience regardless of their type of trauma or of their personal background. Tinnin came to think of this as ubiquitous, even instinctual. The stages he noted were:

> *Startle*—This is the moment when the person recognizes that something is terribly awry. The truck suddenly cuts in front of you, your foot slips on the icy sidewalk, or the large man approaching you on the street unexpectedly reaches into his pocket.
>
> *Thwarted Intention*—It had been noted for many years that in crises there is an inherent reaction to fight or flee as the body is suddenly flooded with cortisol. Blood rushes to the extremities to prepare the limbs for action, and consequently away from the gut and the groin. Digestion and sexual response grinds to a halt. What Tinnin noticed in those who had been traumatized was a step further. The body prepares for

action, but at almost the same time the person realizes that *no action is available*. This sets the person up for the next phase, which is the phase that separates those who have trauma related symptoms from those who do not. That phase is the:

Freeze—You have certainly noted the freeze in nature movies. When the lion separates the impala from the herd and tackles him, the impala goes limp. The body is immobile and the pain threshold is incredibly heightened. This is a mammalian response, but Tinnin was able to distil the human experience of this. He noted that it occurs only when the person or animal is convinced there is no way to avoid or overcome the trauma (i.e., following the thwarted intention). When van der Kolk, for example, encourages sexually assaulted women to take a realistic self-defense course (2014), he is helping them experience a do-over where the fight response is not thwarted, thus the freeze never occurs.

The freeze in humans is the template of the dissociative experience. The deepest sense of oneself is disconnected or compartmentalized from the events occurring around one.

Altered State—Tinnin found that humans experience any number of sensory and perceptual distortions following or in conjunction with the freeze. Time often seems to slow. Sometimes one's position in space is altered; it is not uncommon, for example, for victims of multiple car collisions to have the experience of witnessing the crash from a position high above the moving cars rather than in the cockpit of one. Virtually any experience one can have as a result of hallucinogens can be mimicked through trauma.

Bodily Sensation—Often the altered state includes a *lack* of conscious awareness of one's body. By no means does this mean that the body does not experience sensation and pain; it can retain its own implicit memory of the experience. Hildegard, the early hypnosis researcher, showed that when subjects were hypnotically inured to severe pain (holding one's hand in ice water while hypnotized and told to feel no pain), he could access a part which he called the "hidden observer" that intensely experienced and remembered the sensation (Laurence & Campbell, 1981).

Self Repair—Once a traumatic event has ended and the person recognizes that she has at least temporarily survived, one automatically begins a kind of self checking to assess physical and experiential damage and to try to soothe the now-felt pain and anxiety.

Tinnin believed that, as a result of trauma, a person could become stuck in any of the above phases, or could regress to one of the phases when under even minor later stress. This becomes the source of symptom clusters, or of mental illness subsequent to trauma. Thus, a person stuck in the Thwarted

Intention phase may experience a chronic fight/flight response that can lead to digestive problems from GERD to irritable bowel, or to decreased immune response that subjects them to any number of illnesses. Regressing to self-repair may result in trauma-induced obsessive-compulsive disorder (chronic checking). A person who readily regresses to the Startle may be chronically anxious, and so on.

The re-experiencing symptoms of trauma (flashbacks, nightmares, etc.) can be understood as the body and brain's attempts to master the trauma, but instead becoming stuck in one or more phases, returning over and over to it.

> I think of the example of Nathan 19.1 who called to ask if he could see me for a marital problem. When I suggested it would be most helpful to invite his wife to accompany him, Nathan refused, saying the problem was all his doing. I agreed to a consultation.
>
> When Nathan came in, he described the nature of his "marital problem." It seems that his wife went to bed at 10:00 each evening; Nathan did not find his way to bed until 2:00 am or later. Since they both worked full-time, they rarely saw each other and their intimate life was non-existent. The situation had gone on for years, getting gradually worse and worse. The wife had complained repeatedly until, desperate to get his attention, she threatened divorce. That is when Nathan sought therapy.
>
> "What are you doing between 10:00 pm and 2:00 in the morning?" I inquired. Nathan was a high-level government manager, and he and his wife, children grown, lived alone in a large house. Nathan replied that each night, beginning before 10:00, he would check, unlock, and re-lock every window and door in the large house. When he finally completed his rounds, he would start over until, exhausted, he piled into bed.
>
> Nathan had been a helicopter pilot in Vietnam. It was his job, after everyone was settled in camp, to check all the mooring lines on the choppers to be sure they were properly secured. Some 25 years later, he was still performing his job.

As you may have noted in reading through the above phases, dissociation plays a major role in traumas where the individual goes on to experience symptoms from the event. Tinnin used this inclination to dissociation to treat trauma—by means of dissociation. He developed a hypnosis induction wherein the person goes to a small mountain village, where she finds a shop and an item within the shop that intrigues her. While she is exploring the object through the shop window, he helps the client dissociate a part that observes herself, which he called the "Hidden Observer."[5] The Hidden Observer is not affected by anything she might see or hear, but is only a dispassionate observer. To develop this ability, Tinnin has the client practice looking at the person (the self looking in the shop window) from different vantage points: from the back, from the side, then from up above. I often have the Observer look at the person from underneath, as well, seeing the soles of her shoes and her pants cuffs. Finally, the Observer looks at the person from the front. This is the most difficult task, and if a person can do this, she is ready for the next step. Tinnin then uses that dissociated observer to witness the trauma, ensuring that when the observer tells the trauma story, it speaks to each of the instinctual trauma phases. The hypnosis is videotaped, and afterwards the client is shown the tape in the presence of the therapist to further cement the learning.

Dr. Linda Gantt, Tinnin's spouse, collaborator, and an art therapist (later president of the American Art Therapy Association), developed a follow-up method to the Hidden Observer where she has the client draw on separate pages one scene for each of the Instinctual Trauma Phases, plus a before the trauma and after the trauma picture. Although Gantt and Tinnin stay faithful to the original story, making a complete story and crafting an ending are important changes to the story. Gantt, in a very innovative move, then tells the story back to the client. The process is also videotaped, and the retelling of the trauma story is again viewed with the client, making for the fourth telling of the story over several modalities. I have incorporated this telling back, as well as the concept of using art materials to draw the story, in Foundational Storyboarding (see Chapter 16).

For many years Tinnin and Gantt operated a trauma clinic, first called "Trauma Recovery Institute (TRI)," then "Intensive Trauma Therapy (ITT)." Clients would come for either one or two weeks of intensive trauma work using the Hidden Observer and the Graphic Narrative. Ego states uncovered in the trauma work would be incorporated into the work in a manner similar to Schwartz (Schwartz, 1995; see Chapter 12).

If you run a trauma clinic, or if you are known for practicing a trauma therapy (exposure therapy; EMDR), most clients who consult you will already have identified that they have been traumatized, and although they may have some reluctance to approach it ("trauma phobia"), they know that it is needed. Not so for the rest of us. Many or most of our clients will consult us for depression, or anxiety, or substance or relationship issues, or physical pain of unknown origin with no clue about how these problems are seeded and nurtured by trauma. Clinicians need the ability to approach trauma from two directions: when the trauma is presented directly (a person enters therapy complaining of trauma) and indirectly (an instance of depression, or pain, or drinking, or relationship difficulty is related to a traumatic events in a manner unknown and dissociated by the person).

Sometimes the First Incident Foundational Story will be sufficient to reveal a traumatic underpinning to a symptom. Here the client is asked for his first memory of having a symptom, as in the case of Nathan 19.2, who presented for anger issues:

> I remember we had to eat dinner "as a family." I dreaded it. It would start off well enough, but then something would invariably go wrong and my father would absolutely lose it. He'd yell and curse at my mother—"you burned the f—ing meat again, you bitch!"
>
> One time, when I was about six, my father's attention turned toward me. "Did you wash your hands like I told you?"
>
> "Yes, sir."
>
> "Let me see. You did not wash your hands! You lied to me! There's nothing worse than a lousy liar!" With that he picked up the plate of mashed potatoes and threw it at my face. Luckily it missed, but I got potatoes all down my shirt. I was terrified and angry and wanted to cry, but I wouldn't. I thought, "I'll never be like you!"

It does not mean that the symptom was necessarily *caused* by the client's reaction to that incident. But it does mean that the incident and the client's response are emblematic of the symptom. You have located a foundational story.

Sometimes, especially in trauma, a First Occurrence Story is not accessible. When this is the case, the Affect or Perceptual Bridge Technique can be very useful. Foundational memories, including traumatic ones, are linked by affect and sensation. You may remember that the Bridge involves having the client intensify the symptom or the associated affect, then use that intensified reaction to recall the related story. See Chapter 5 for the specifics of the technique.

In sum, trauma therapy involves first establishing a context that contrasts to that of the trauma experience. This includes creating a safe setting in contrast to the unsafe experience of trauma, and providing a concerned witness in contrast to the lone experience of the trauma. It then involves preparing the client for working with the trauma by helping her maintain her anxiety within the window that can pursue the most active learning. Finally, as you recall from the last chapter, the trauma story itself has gaps and no ending, and the negative theme and moral from the stories ricochet throughout the person's life story. Thus, the therapy involves helping the client close the gaps and find an ending to the stories of the traumatic incidents, and change the traumatic moral and theme that has infected the person's life story.

Notes

1. Much of the rest of their sleep difficulties relates to nightmares, including the avoidance of sleep to avoid the nightmares.
2. Traditionally, there are two general approaches to the therapeutic use of sand and small figures. "Sandtray" is the term used by adherents of the World Technique, while "Sandplay" is the Jungian term. I use the terms interchangeably and do not adhere consistently to either school.
3. The idea here is that the client likely identifies with the scene, so having someone dismantle it in front of her may feel symbolically like taking herself apart, even though the logic is, of course, very different.

4. Some exposure and virtual reality therapies do build to having the client re-experience the traumatic incident, which can understandably greatly increase the drop-out rate. Re-living the trauma is painful, and as shown in the literature on memory reconsolidation, unnecessary, as a reminder of the trauma is sufficient to render the trauma memory vulnerable to change.
5. The name selection, while accurate, is unfortunate, as it can be confused with Hilgard's hidden observer. The two hidden observers are opposite in function: Tinnin's dissociates the affect and pain from the trauma, while Hilgard's hidden observer is the part that retains sensation and knowledge of the pain (Laurence & Campbell, 1981).

References

Armstrong, C. (2011). *Transforming Traumatic Grief.* Tijeras, NM: Artemecia Press.

Armstrong, C. (2015). *The Therapeutic "Aha!" Strategies for Getting Your Clients Unstuck.* New York, NY: W. W. Norton.

Felitti, V. J. (2002). The relation between adverse childhood experiences and adult health: Turning gold into lead. *Permanente Journal, 6*(1), pp. 41–47.

Herman, J. L. (1997). *Trauma and Recovery: The Aftermath of Violence-From Domestic Abuse to Political Terror.* New York, NY: Basic Books.

Hoobyar, T., & Dotz, T. (2013). *NLP: The Essential Guide to Neuro-linguistic Programming.* New York, NY: HarperCollins.

Janet, P. (1907/2012). *The Major Symptoms of Hysteria: Fifteen Lectures Given in the Medical School of Harvard University.* London: Forgotten Books.

Laurence, J., & Campbell, P. (1981). The "hidden observer" phenomenon in hypnosis: Some additional findings. *Journal of Abnormal Psychology, 90*(4), pp. 334–344.

Nathanson, D. L. (1992). *Shame and Pride: Affect, Sex, and the Birth of the Self.* New York, NY: W. W. Norton.

Sandhu, P. (2015). Step aside, Freud: Josef Breuer is the true father of modern psychotherapy. Retrieved from: https://blogs.scientificamerican.com/mind-guest-blog/step-aside-freud-josef-breuer-is-the-true-father-of-modern-psychotherapy/.

Schiraldi, G. R. (2016). *The Post-Traumatic Stress Disorder Sourcebook: A Guide to Healing, Recovery, and Growth.* New York, NY: McGraw-Hill.

Schwartz, R. C. (1995). *Internal Family Systems Therapy.* New York, NY: Guilford Press.

Shapiro, R. (2010). *The Trauma Treatment Handbook: Protocols Across the Spectrum.* New York, NY: W. W. Norton.

Tinnin, L., & Gantt, L. (2013). *The Instinctual Trauma Response and Dual Brain Dynamics: A Guide for Trauma Therapy.* Morgantown, WV: Gargoyle Press.

Van der Kolk, B. (2014). *The Body Keeps the Score: Brain, Mind, and Body in the Healing of Trauma.* New York, NY: Penguin Books.

Part 6

Listening to Your Own Story

Chapter 20

Working With Yourself

I am often struck by what a strange profession being a psychotherapist is. Who spends her days listening to tales of dread and woe? Even if some stories eventually turn redemptive, one can only best assist that by listening intently and identifying, at least partly, with the protagonist. The empathy required means that you, too, tap into rage and dread and horror. Like watching the news all day, you are exposed selectively to the cruelty and unfairness of life. People rarely seek therapy to extend their happiness; it is their pain that brings them. If we do therapy well, we resonate with our clients, and we then become vulnerable to becoming possessed by a pervasive and dark view of life. It is the occupational hazard. Just as firefighters face falls and smoke inhalation and burns, therapists risk capture by cynicism and hopelessness. You cannot be a firefighter without running toward the fire, and you cannot be a therapist without encountering hopelessness and fear and your own ineptness in the face of pervasive and timeless tragic stories.

The risk is magnified by the fact that you did not become a psychotherapist randomly, or to further the family business or to seek your fortune. Like shamans and healers from all lands, you were chosen as much as you chose. Like Nathan 4.1 (from Chapter 4), who was chosen by the elders of his little village to be chief, a responsibility he could not elude no matter how far he traveled, you have likely been chosen by your early story. Your early story, more than that of most, likely contained illness, or tragedy, or trauma. And your wound became a window through which you could recognize the pain and suffering of others. But a window is also the most vulnerable place in the wall. So you must tend it and dress it (we have dressings for both windows and for wounds) and keep it clear.

The best dressing is your curiosity. What kind of story, and what kind of takeaway might have a person act in this manner? How would this man's story be different if seen through the eyes of his husband? What might help this woman cope with her burden? What part of my story is tapped by what this family lives? Curiosity is an antidote to anxiety. It helps you see the surrounds in a larger context, and it melds whatever pain and sadness you witness with wonder. It does not avoid the darkness, it marvels that the darkness could be.

Studies show curiosity is more than a pleasant feeling, but can reach something akin to Csikszentmihalyi's state of flow (1990). It may be related to Panksepp's concept of play as one of the primary affective channels (Armstrong, 2015). It can be contagious to your clients, as well.

Cultivate your curiosity. Next time in the consulting room that you feel inept or miffed or bored, instead of bearing with it, ask yourself, "how come?" ("How come" tends to conjure the child's sense of wonder; "why" can carry the baggage of criticism, as in "Why didn't you clean your room?!" The latter is not really a question, but a critical statement.) What was the last thing that was said before I felt this way? Is there some difficult part of my story that was triggered here? How does it relate to what I know of the client's story? Might it suggest a different subplot or character in her life tale of which I was unaware?

Curiosity and its cultivation is a part of Eugene Gendlin's technique of focusing (Gendlin, 1981, 1996). The standard focusing technique involves five brief steps to get in touch with a vague body awareness of an issue. The five steps are:

1. Clear a mental space by asking what is between you and feeling OK. Imagine putting each issue aside
2. Pick one of the issues. What is the vague sense in your body when you focus on the whole of the problem? That vague physical sensation is the "felt sense."
3. Ask yourself what word, phrase, or image captures that sense.
4. Go back and forth between that word or image and the felt sense itself. Does it match? If not quite, is there a better word or image? See if that matches. If so, sit with it for a moment.
5. Ask yourself what it is about the whole problem that makes it fit the chosen word or image. Accept whatever comes. Then ask yourself if this is a good stopping point, or if you need another round.

After a difficult session or one that just feels "off," take ten minutes or so at your next break and modify the standard focusing technique slightly. After clearing a mental space, instead of asking "what is between me and feeling OK," ask "what is the feeling I am left with from my session with Harriet?" Then wait and follow the rest of the focusing technique. See Gendlin's book on *Focusing Psychotherapy* (Gendlin, 1996) for more techniques.

The other technique for maintaining our balance and dressing our wound is the ancient practice of ritual. While ritual as a major source of therapeutic change is introduced in Chapter 10, ritual can also become an ally in containing what you witness to the therapy room so that it does not bleed into the rest of your life. Take time to design a brief ritual that you can follow mindfully each evening when you leave your office or workplace. It should not be elaborate; it needs to be something you can do at the end of each workday for thousands of times. For example, you may choose some tchotchke or some sandtray figure to leave out on your desk or table when working; then, after all the other necessary closing rituals of completing paperwork, straightening the waiting room, re-setting the heat, etc., make putting this item away the last act you perform. Take several deep breaths, then, as you put it away, say "just like I put away this (paperweight, figure, etc.), I put away all that has happened here today. Just like the paperweight, it will be available to me on my return when needed; but tonight, I put it away."

Another possible ritual involves playing and mindfully listening to a brief song that has themes of transition or of goodbye. A lovely short song I like for this purpose is Sam Baker's little tune "Go in Peace." Knowing the story contained within or behind a tune can help make the ritual more meaningful. Sam Baker, the Texas singer/songwriter who penned "Go in Peace," (2013) was one of thousands of young people who travel parts of the world after college before settling and in hopes of finding a life direction. Sam was traveling in South America, and was on a train which was bombed by the Shining Path guerrillas. The German family with whom he was sitting were all killed. Sam's recovery took 17 surgeries and several years, much of which time he was confined in a hospital room. It was there that he taught himself guitar, and began writing songs to wile away the hundreds of hours in rehab. This led to his musical career. It also led to some unusual tunings to better accompany his voice, his left-handed guitar style (he lost part of his left hand in the explosion, so has to play left-handed, using his right hand to press the strings), and his partial deafness and tinnitus (as best as I can tell, "Go in Peace" is written in F#).

In addition to cultivating curiosity and practicing a ritual for compartmentalization of clinical work, two other techniques already discussed can be helpful: the Family of Origin Map (FOOM) and the Foundational Story Interview. I always find it useful to first apply any technique I am learning to myself when possible. That helps me know when and whether it will be useful, and helps me better relate to the client's experience in taking it.

Perhaps a first undertaking is to complete the Family of Origin Map (FOOM). This exercise is one where it is essential to complete your own map before using with clients. Complete instructions are included as Appendix III. Get a large (at least 12"x18") sheet of drawing paper and several Sharpie or other marker pens of several colors. Follow the instructions and sample drawings, or have a friend or colleague read each instruction as you complete it. An insightful and bonding experience can be to complete your map with a colleague as she completes her map. Take turns reading each instruction for both of you to follow.

After you have completed your map, take a few moments to be with the map and reflect on it, seeing what patterns emerge. If doing so with a colleague, share your insights with him; if completing it by yourself, journal your insights (see the next chapter, Chapter 21, on utilizing a therapeutic journal).

Notice what you wrote on your map in response to "Emotional Climate or Atmosphere." This is an important aspect of the exposition of your childhood story. That atmosphere may or may not be pleasant, but it is familiar, and many people will unknowingly seek this atmosphere in settings throughout their lives. You may find it repeated in work settings or in relationships.

Now focus on the roles you wrote for each member of your family of origin (including your own). List them. Where do some or all of them occur in your present life? The roles are the building blocks of stories. You may find that there are settings where you play the same role you played as a child; just as likely, you may play the role of another family member with someone else in your life inhabiting the role you lived as a child. The protagonist's role has shifted, but the building blocks remain the same.

Consider a client with whom you are familiar. Where would he or she be on your map? Which of the roles on your map does he tend to enact in his life? What complementary role might you be seen to play? Notice how you described your relationship with the person in that role on your map. Does this relationship in any way mirror aspects of your relationship with your client who enacts that role? You can use this in your own self-supervision. When you feel stuck in working with a client, bring out *your own* map and see what role that client may enact in relation to you. Is your relationship to him at all similar to the relationship you had with the person in that role on your map? What if any difference in relationship would you want to forge?

There is a hilarious and tragic semi-autobiographical novel called *House of God* by Samuel Shem (1998). When Shem, a young intern, is on call and has to respond to his first cardiac arrest, the senior resident tells him, "When responding to a code, the first thing to do is to take your own pulse!" Good advice for psychotherapists, too. When you encounter a difficult patch with a client, the first thing to do is to pull out your own map. If this client were in your family, where would he fit? Who on your map is he most like? From whom is he most different? Is your relationship with him, or the feeling you get in his presence, similar to anything on your map? If he is not like or even is very different from anyone on your map, how and where would he have fit if he were part of your family? How would your family members respond to him? How would his presence alter the dynamics in your family? Once you have completed and reviewed the FOOM for insights, keep the map accessible.

A final recommendation in working with yourself is to approach a trusted friend, colleague, or consultant and ask her or him to help you do your own Foundational Story Interview (see Appendix I). Although this, too, can be completed solo by journaling or recording, this exercise is especially helpful to complete with a colleague or friend to help structure, record, and witness.

Pick a few of the questions that you think will be especially pertinent for you. Record the interview. Listen to it. Transcribe any of the responses you think most revealing of your life story. Then reflect on the stories using any of the lenses or techniques discussed in earlier chapters. For example, list the roles in the story around the circumference of a circle, as suggested by Karpman (Chapter 8). Do any of these roles and how you fill them apply throughout your life? In your current life? What are the themes in the story? Do they echo in your life? Do the sentence completion: *From this story, I am* _____; *other people are* _____; *and the world is* _____. Or use Luborsky's (1990) formula: *In this story I wish* _____, *so I* _____. *Other people* _____, *and my response is* _____.
Do this and/or complete the story template (Appendix II) for two or three foundational stories.

Are there any metaphors in your stories? If so, experiment with Kopp's (1995) technique for working with metaphor (Chapter 5).

In short, use any of the methods for understanding foundational and life stories, then discuss with the person who helped you record the foundational stories. Write what fits about your life story from your reflection and discussion, perhaps in your therapy journal (see the next chapter, Chapter 21).

The final step is to use a brief ritual to integrate your insight into your work with clients. At the beginning of your work week for at least the next four weeks, read the summary of your insights about your life story before you see your first client of the week. Set the intention of keeping your own life story in the back of your mind to help you more readily sort what part of your reactions relate to your identification with your clients' stories, and what part relates primarily to your own life story. You may find that your first, internal reaction of "Why don't you just (leave the bum, quit the job, stop snacking in the evening, take your medication, don't buy beer, etc.)" becomes more quickly nuanced. You may find you experience both greater clarity and more compassion.

References

Armstrong, C. (2015). *The Therapeutic "Aha!" Strategies for Getting Your Clients Unstuck.* New York, NY: W. W. Norton.
Baker, S. (2013). Go in peace. On album *Say Grace*. Self Release.
Csikszentmihalyi, M. (1990). *Flow: The Psychology of Optimal Experience.* New York, NY: Harper & Row.
Gendlin, E. T. (1981). *Focusing.* New York, NY: Random House.
Gendlin, E. T. (1996). *Focusing Oriented Psychotherapy: A Manual of the Experiential Method.* New York, NY: Guilford Press.
Kopp, R. R. (1995). *Metaphor Therapy: Using Client-Generated Metaphors in Psychotherapy.* New York, NY: Brunner/Mazel.
Shem, S. (1998). *The House of God.* New York, NY: Dell Publishing.

Chapter 21

Growing as a Therapist

In a beautiful and sensitively written book called *Listening with the Third Ear*, Theodor Reik, an early analyst (not to be confused with Wilhelm Reich of body armor and orgone box fame) laments that every time he learned something significant about therapy, it cost him a patient (Reik, 1948/1998). As psychotherapists, we are entrusted with people's stories, and with helping them with what is most important in their lives. Fortunately, the vast majority of us take this trust seriously and as an honor. This means we are honor-bound to develop our understanding and our tools as best we can. Our primary tool is ourselves. If we believe in what we do, there is no better way to improve what we do than to seek our own therapy. I am a firm believer that every psychotherapist should have a course of psychotherapy. Not only will you learn about utilizing your strengths and forgiving your foibles, you will become better able to keep your own struggle from intertwining with the struggles of your clients. Perhaps most importantly, you will come to understand from the inside the vulnerability of struggling to be honest with another, and the awesome experience of being listened to, of being taken seriously, of having your own story validated and witnessed. There is no substitute.

Over the course of your career as a psychotherapist, you will be treated to an amazing range of topics, far more than any reporter. If you maintain a sense of wonder, you will not be disappointed. I now know something about the experience of being a spy in the Middle East, of piloting an aircraft, of shooting up in the bathroom of an exclusive law office, of the disadvantage of hydraulic train brakes, of the desperate search for treatment of a rare illness, of healing the divided congregation of a small church, of repairing an 18th-century telescope, and of thousands more topics, both intriguing and mundane. I remember one of my summer jobs while in college was in a public library. There was a reference librarian there who kept a file of all the unusual questions he had been asked over the years, and of the answers. What a fascinating file! You, too, will be treated to a wondrous array of learnings.

You will also gain knowledge about being a psychotherapist from what you read, from your colleagues and supervisors. You will not only continue to make what I have called, after Yorke, two-dimensional change in what you know (an increase in knowledge) related to therapy; you will continue to make three-dimensional change (a change in your person) in how you understand and live both psychotherapy and your own story. It is extremely helpful to keep a record of learnings, insights, and intriguing facts—a kind of Therapeutic Journal to harness incremental growth and learning as a therapist. This becomes a place, whether a computer file, a note on your phone, a voice recorder, or an old-fashioned written journal, to record your knowledge and insights, both those related to psychotherapy and those that just fascinate you.

The next time a client mentions she has been placed on a new medication for her diabetes, look it up. Jot a few brief phrases about it. The next time you have an insight about the process of therapy, write it down. Insights, like dreams, are ephemeral. You can easily think to yourself after an intriguing dream, "what an interesting dream! I'm going to remember that one." By lunchtime you remember only that you have had a dream. By dinner, you do not even recall the fact that you dreamed. The act of writing facts and insights helps to cement them. You can return in future years to be intrigued yet again by a therapeutic principle, and you can get a sense of what you were struggling with as a therapist in those earlier years—both how far you have come and how you still wrestle with the same questions.

I call my own journal "The Tuesday File," I think because I began it one Tuesday some 30 or so years ago. It remains a resource.

There are two areas of brief further training that I recommend for all therapists. First, if you have not done so, sign up for a weekend training in basic hypnosis. Those sponsored by ASCH (American Society of Clinical Hypnosis) are usually topnotch, and you will earn CEUs. It goes without saying that you will not become a hypnotherapist in a weekend, any more than a weekend training will make you a CBT practitioner or a psychoanalyst. However, it will greatly improve your effectiveness in using and recognizing clients' imagery and your ability to recognize cues to the client's experience in many situations. You will practice techniques of calming clients; you will also experience hypnosis yourself, recognizing from the inside the dichotomy of how it feels both familiar and nothing special, yet how incredibly concrete and childlike the most sophisticated person becomes.

Eugene Gendlin, already mentioned in earlier chapters, was a philosopher who worked with Carl Rogers. He became interested in what makes some clients—and some sessions—especially effective in therapy. After reviewing hundreds of hours of psychotherapy tapes, he noticed that the clients who made the most gains were able to tune inside and notice their felt experience, then put words to it. Gendlin developed a method of becoming aware of one's felt experience (Gendlin, 1981, 1996), even when it was vague and amorphous, then allowing that feeling to inform what is currently important. He called the technique "Focusing," and its popularity spread far beyond psychotherapy. Focusing groups and trainings became a national phenomenon, and continue to be. I delineated the basic method in the last chapter (Chapter 20). Gaining training and experience in Focusing will enable you to recognize and facilitate your clients when they turn inward; it will help you orient and educate those who do not naturally reflect, but who could benefit from the skill. Doing your own focusing will help you to recognize how to proceed when you feel stuck in a session or in your own life; look for a Focusing training or group in your area. There are online, DVD, and telephone trainings available, as well. See the International Focusing Institute's website at www.focusing.org.

Finally, harkening back to my supervisor's advice of many years ago ("if you want to be a psychotherapist, read novels"), read stories, listen to stories. Read fiction, read biographies and autobiographies and plays. Enjoy it. At the same time, notice how each story is a journey; how each contains conflict, the resolution of which makes a dialectic. Notice the setting, the narrator, the protagonist and her desire, the allies, the antagonist, the plot, the theme, and the moral—the elements of all story. Enjoying story is ultimately about gaining empathy, and about understanding the archetypal stories that your clients will live and present in variation.

Although the above methods are not all directly focused upon story, they are likely to enhance your own cumulative skill as a psychotherapist, and your ability to grow your own story.

References

Gendlin, E. T. (1981). *Focusing*. New York, NY: Random House.
Gendlin, E. T. (1996). *Focusing Oriented Psychotherapy: A Manual of the Experiential Method*. New York, NY: Guilford Press.
Reik, T. (1948/1998). *Listening With the Third Ear*. New York, NY: Farrar, Straus, & Giroux.

Part 7

Conclusion
Weaving It Together

Chapter 22

Without and Beyond Story

Mickey Mantle was arguably one of the greatest baseball players of all time. A baseball hall of famer, Mantle was a switch hitter who played mostly center field for the New York Yankees from 1951 to 1968. Mantle retired with a career batting average of .298—which means that for 17 years in the major leagues, he got on base an average of almost every third time at bat. In 1956 he was a baseball triple crown winner—the best major league player of the season in all three offensive categories: number of home runs, number of runs batted in, and batting average. He competed with Roger Maris to surpass the number of home runs ever hit in a season (due to injury, Mantle missed several games and Maris won the title). Mantle was also a defensive threat, with a fielding percentage of .984 (moral: do not hit the ball to center field when Mantle was playing). He appeared in 12 World Series, and has the most home runs, highest RBI (runs batted in), and most bases of any player while playing in the World Series.

Born in 1931, Mickey Mantle grew up in Oklahoma, the son of a miner. His father died of Hodgkins disease at the age of 40 when Mantle was in his second year in the major leagues. Mantle's father was the fourth family member to develop cancer. The theme of Mantle's life story for much of his life seems to be "live hard, because you will die young." Only he did not. After a 17-year career in the Majors, Mantle would live another 27 years—more than one and a half times as long as his major league career. Mantle's heavy drinking and philandering was largely hidden from fans by his teammates and the media, but with the ending of his baseball career and the increased drinking, it could no longer remain under wraps.

In 1993, after an embarrassing charity dinner where a drunk Mantle insulted his host, Mantle entered the Betty Ford Clinic and became sober. He organized a charity to help those impacted by the bombing of the Edward R. Murrow building in Oklahoma City, and lent his name and influence to a number of other charities, as well. He died only two years later of cancer. Not of the Hodgkins he feared, but of metastasized liver cancer, exacerbated by the toll from lifestyle illnesses—cirrhosis and hepatitis.

It is tempting to see Mantle's story as like that of the tragic Greek or Shakespearean hero, whose fatal flaw leads to his demise; only that demise took another almost three decades. Perhaps it is more accurate to see that the theme of "live hard, play (ball) hard and then you die" ended with the end of Mantle's stint with the Yankees. It was not supposed to work out that way, and, I hypothesize, Mantle was left without a story. It took him a quarter century to build a new story, a sober story of supporting good works, and of becoming a role model who could acknowledge his flaws and encourage others not to follow his old path: a second, albeit short-lived, story separated by years from the first.

We see with Mickey Mantle the special circumstance not of persons with a problematic life story, but of persons who have lost their story. A variant of this often occurs with people who peak early: the high school homecoming queen or football star who never quite gets it together in subsequent years. A further example occurs for those who, because of circumstances, live a story more dramatic and meaningful than they can ever recapture: the old soldier or sailor inhabiting the bar at any VFW across the country, living now through tales of faded poignancy told to comrades for whom, like himself, the best has long since passed.

In a sense, I always felt this to be the case with my own father. A college and then business school drop-out who was subsequently fired by his own father (my grandfather), America's entry into World War II came at an auspicious time for my father. Commissioned as a naval second lieutenant, he quickly rose to become a blimp commander. Stationed, like many blimp crews, in Lakehurst, New Jersey, the mission involved patrolling between New Jersey and Brazil, searching for German submarines ("U boats"). Upon finding a U boat, the crew was tasked with bombing them from the air with depth charges.

Although Dad went on to have a successful postwar career as a small-town accountant, he never again achieved the sense of responsibility and felt agency that he had lived in that airship. I suspect that like so many sailors, airmen, and soldiers, the ending of a military career felt not like the closing of a chapter so much as the ending of one's life story. Many do not survive the void between the war story and whatever narrative could be next; for many that do, the best of their story is past.

We see this for those whose retirement plan is to be able to afford to quit working. A story provides meaning and organizes our perceptions. Step out of your life story, and an ensuing sense of meaninglessness and chaos can be anxiety-provoking and painful.

Oftentimes people consult us for help with anxiety or sleeplessness or destructive but time-filling activities. For some of them, these are the unrecognized symptoms of the absence of story. The therapy then becomes helping create a story in the midst of existential void.

> Nathan 21.1 was a bureau chief with the FBI who took retirement as soon as he was eligible. He had loved a career solving crises like bank

heists and kidnappings. Even money laundering schemes provided a challenge that he enjoyed. "I felt I was doing something important," he explained. Then he was promoted. Now the crises were political, and the challenge was the mountains of paperwork. Thinking he would leave all this behind, he retired, not realizing that he also retired his identity. Storyless, he suffered chronic and debilitating anxiety.

The loss of story is a risk in any major life transition. It is a liminal space where the old story no longer applies, but the new, fledgling story has yet to take shape. It can happen after loss: the loss of a career, of a home, or the loss of a loved one. In those instances, it can leave one bereft and aimless amidst a sea of grief. The loss of story must be a focus of therapy every bit as much as the loss of job, home, or loved one. The therapeutic approach involves first helping the client to acknowledge the additional loss of story. That may entail its own set of mourning, followed by helping the client to build a story anew from the remnants of old hopes and dreams that were sidelined long ago to make way for the story that is now lost. Helping the client find and build upon his sustaining values is foundational. Creating a new protagonist with a new story (see Chapter 12 on working with characters) is yet another approach.

The loss of story may appear in the midst of gain as well as loss. Acceptance to a new learning program; obtaining a new job; meeting someone who feels special. Now, too, the old no longer fits, but the new has not yet arrived. Here the liminal is suffused with excitement, with hope, with imaginings of how things might be—all of which propel us far more easily across the void between life stories.

Beyond Story

> Once, while walking in the forest, a Japanese monk heard the roar of a tiger. The roar came ever closer, so the monk began to run. He raced over roots and stones and around boulders to no avail; the roar was coming ever closer. Finally, the monk reached the edge of the forest and raced through the clearing beyond, only to slip as he barely managed to stop. He had reached the edge of a deep chasm that fell many hundreds of feet downward. Hearing the roar grow even louder, the monk turned to glance toward the woods. Out of the forest came the bounding tiger. The monk looked from the tiger to the cliff, then began to gingerly climb down the rock face. Ledges and handholds were few in the near vertical wall. The monk grabbed a small tree that grew from a crack in the wall. Only a few feet above him the tiger began to pace. The monk gripped the little tree tightly, but noticed that it bent further and further downward. One by one, its roots began to pull free of the wall. Above, the tiger growled. It was then that the monk noticed growing out of a still smaller crack next to the little tree was a single lovely flower. As more and more of the little tree roots unfastened from the rock,

the monk managed to swing himself over to where he could reach with his nose and smell the flower.

(Adapted by the author from *Zen Flesh, Zen Bones* [1985] by Reps & Senzaki)

Life stories focus us and bind our anxiety, but they also limit us. The second, more positive, instances of absent story are those enlightened moments where we see the world without our narrative filter. For most of us, these moments are relatively rare and short-lived. We are constantly running DVDs in our heads. If I think, "maybe we'll have soup for dinner tonight," I see myself in the kitchen beginning to slice and prepare the vegetables. Perhaps I skip ahead to the comfort of my wife and I eating our fresh bowls in front of the fire, or perhaps it reminds me that we have neither potatoes nor leeks, and I am driving to the store in my mind. While at the store, I must not forget laundry detergent, and so I see myself in the detergent aisle. This reminds me that the last time I was at the store, I ran into our neighbor, and I see myself talking with her and I remember that her husband is sick. And I see my neighbor's husband in bed with the covers pulled up, doubly unhappy because he is usually so active, and I see us playing tennis together, and I think I should call him. And I see myself punching in the numbers on my cell phone. And so it goes. Vignettes and scenes and partial stories linked and intertwined; the stories are ubiquitous.

So ubiquitous that any interruption in the stream constitutes what we think of as an altered state. For most of us, interludes in the stream of stories are short-lived at best. There can be moments in meditation in between the hundreds of repetitions recognizing a distracting sensation, a planful future story, or a regretful past story and gently setting it aside, turning attention once again to the object of focus, be it a mantra, a candle, or the breath; moments when there is no chatter, no story (see, for example, Jon Kabat-Zinn's *Full Catastrophe Living*, 2013).

Mihaly Csikszentmihalyi (1990) has researched and written about a state that he calls "flow." The flow experience is a state of focus on a single goal with no defensiveness, distraction, or competing goal. It is an altered state where time may seem to slow and the person feel as if she were floating. It is "a joyous, self-forgetful involvement through concentration (p. 105)." Csikszentmihalyi has documented the state in activities as diverse as rock climbing and assembly line work. His initial work involved the experience of artists in creating a painting. In those moments of flow, one is completely absorbed in the current task such that the separation between oneself and the task disappears. It is a moment of no self and of no story.

Because our Western stories tend to flow from the past toward the future, the moments without story are timeless. Our ordinary sense of time is altered such that it slows or does not exist at all. If one is in the midst of flow, the timeless quality is merely a part of the experience; if one is in between stories and in the midst of grief, this expansion of time can make it seem as if the void and the pain are endless.

In the final chapter we will explore further integrating a storied view with our own approach to therapy.

References

Csikszentmihalyi, M. (1990). *Flow: The Psychology of Optimal Experience.* New York, NY: Harper & Row.

Kabat-Zinn, J. (2013). *Full Catastrophe Living: Using the Wisdom of Your Body to Face Stress, Pain, and Illness.* New York, NY: Bantam Books.

Reps, P., & Senzaki, N. (1985). *Zen Flesh, Zen Bones: A Collection of Zen and Pre-Zen Writings.* North Clarendon, VT: Tuttle Publishing.

Chapter 23

Integrating a Storied View With Your Own Theory

All psychotherapies are by necessity narrative therapies. This is because they are designed to assist storied creatures. In the chapters on the various aspects of story—setting, character, plot, etc.—I have attempted to show how many therapies have a primary focus upon a component of story. Even seemingly dissimilar therapies are related by their involvement with the stories of their clients. Becoming informed of a variety of potential avenues to understanding and changing foundational and life story makes a case for becoming a clinical polyglot. Becoming familiar with the techniques and understandings of a number of therapies accordingly gives the clinician the ability to intervene in a number of aspects of the client's life story.

There is yet another storied way that differing approaches to psychotherapy may be related. The narrative theorist John Yorke (2015) contended that change in story is either two-dimensional or three-dimensional. In two-dimensional change, the protagonist does not change his outlook or characteristics as a result of the confrontation with the adversary. Instead, he alters only his knowledge of the particular situation/adversary sufficient to defeat or banish the foe. Thus, the characters Jean-Luc Picard, Hercule Poirot, or Matt Dillon are essentially the same character from one story to the next. I would add that it is not only a change in knowledge, but an extension in behavioral repertoire, that is gained in a two-dimensional story. Faced with the same adversary, Sherlock Holmes would solve the crime much quicker, even though the personhood of Sherlock remains unchanged.

Three-dimensional change involves an alteration in the character's own life story such that his outlook, his values, and his goals are changed. In the 1991 movie *Fried Green Tomatoes* (Avnet et al., 1991), Evelyn Couch becomes a different person through the witnessing of the story told by nursing home resident Ninny Threadgoode. In the captivating recent novel (Quinn, 2017) *The Alice Network*, the protagonist Charlie is not the same woman at the end of the story as at the beginning. In both cases the protagonists' life stories have been profoundly altered.

I noted that many clients enter therapy in hopes of two-dimensional change, such as, "just help me find the knowledge to deal more effectively with my anxiety or with my substance-abusing daughter." For some this is effective and the more efficient route. It may mean that, like Sherlock Holmes and Professor Moriarity, they battle the same adversary numerous times, but with greater armament and resources. An example is the alcoholic whose only goal is to stop drinking. He may achieve this, but as AA counsels, he will forever be on the lookout for "slippery people and slippery places," prepared with new knowledge and additional behaviors to fight the same foe over and over.

In an old, but seminal and still relevant book, John Watzlawick et al. (1974) refer to two types of change: what they call Type I change, and Type II change. A Type I change is a quantitative change. Our alcoholic in the above example has altered the *quantity* of what he drinks. As Gregory Bateson (2000) notes, he may attend five AA meetings a week, providing coffee to three and finding speakers for a fourth. He is sober and healthier, *but his life still revolves around alcohol*. That primary story and its theme has not changed. What has changed is the creation or enhancement of a second story (the counterscript in transactional analysis). I am still an alcoholic, but I choose not to drink today.

A Type II change is a *qualitative* change. Here our ex-alcoholic's life revolves around other things, be they relationships, work, or spirituality. Alcohol is either just not in his life any longer, or it is a very small and unimportant part. And there is not the same driven quality about his new focus; he has not substituted one addiction for another, albeit healthier one. He is no longer, again in AA terms, a "dry drunk."

For some clients this three-dimensional, Type II change is what they seek. For still others, the route to three-dimensional change is necessarily through an initial two-dimensional change. Finally, there are clients for whom the initial hope for two-dimensional change in their problem, once achieved, inspires the desire for three-dimensional change.

Different therapies focus on different types of change. Figure 23.1 shows a continuum of client story change together with some example therapies that focus primarily on particular aspects of the continuum.

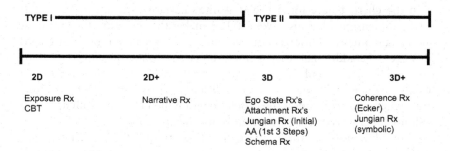

Figure 23.1 Type of Change in Different Therapies

As noted on the diagram, exposure therapy is an example of two-dimensional change. Exposure is based upon extinction. By viewing anxiety as the adversary and facing (i.e., fighting) it directly, either through graded exposure or all at once and repeatedly in a safe context (implosion therapy or virtual reality therapies), the client gains knowledge and behaviors that he *can* cross bridges, fly in an airplane, stand in an elevator, whatever the circumscribed fear may be. Avoidance of bridges was the thesis; the anxiety was the antithesis; confronting the anxiety leads to a synthesis of new knowledge (I can cross bridges) and new behavior. The person is left with two templates, two stories: I must never cross a bridge, or I will die; and I can cross a bridge without dying. The old story has not changed, but an additional story has been developed. Under even unrelated stress, the old story may re-assert itself (my wife is having surgery, or a tree limb fell on my house—now I am afraid of bridges again). But for a long time under normal circumstances the client can choose the story, can choose to cross a bridge.

Many other cognitive behavioral therapies also create a second, logical, competing symptom story. Just because other kids laughed at me when I was a child does not mean people will laugh at me while at a party in my thirties; to think so is an overgeneralization. And the thought that people will laugh at me and it will be horrible, I will be mortified, and they will never have anything to do with me again, is catastrophizing. Thus, by creating a second logical story, many CBT therapies focus on two-dimensional change.

It would be fascinating to see if the dialectical story model I am proposing here could be extended so that two-dimensional approaches could also be used as three-dimensional approaches. I could imagine, for example, using the illustration above, developing with the client a list of the logical "mistakes" in her social anxiety, having her then come up with alternatives which she practices (a standard CBT technique). Then have her, in a visceral and detailed fashion, image the old, illogical and painful party alongside a detailed image of the newer, more logical party. She would try to hold both images in mind at the same time. Thus, we are making the old, problematic story the thesis, and the new, logical story the antithesis, and juxtaposing them for a synthesis (this potentially relies on memory reconsolidation).

In the chart, I have listed David White's narrative therapy as "2D+." It is two-dimensional because, like CBT, it makes the symptom the antithesis and creates a new, additional story co-authored with the protagonist client. However, the additional story is not a direct confrontation with the symptom; rather, it is an enhancement of a found story where the symptom, if it exists, is not problematic. We are still left with two stories: the original story where the symptom is the problem with which to be reckoned, and an additional story where the symptom is not the antagonist.

Three-dimensional stories make for Type II qualitative change, or a change in the story rather than just an increase in knowledge, additional behavior, or the creation of an alternate story. Using ego state therapies as a general example, the symptom usually is seen as the emotional burdens carried by disowned and alienated characters (parts), or the distraction created by other characters (parts) to protect the disowned parts from discovery or from unburdening. Therapy may involve finding and bringing in resource characters to change the creation stories of the disowned parts, or bringing in a resource part to soothe the previously unsoothed and disowned characters, or promoting a dialogue among characters. All these methods change the existing story.

Coherence therapy is labeled here as an example of "3D+" because it promotes a change in the meta-story. The presenting symptom is seen as part of the thesis in a meta-story rather than the antithesis of the client's story. The antagonist/antithesis becomes the deeper necessity for retaining the symptom, even with all its associated pain. That deeper necessity is juxtaposed with the symptom-laden story to form a new synthesis, one which often changes the felt pain of the symptom.

I mentioned in Chapter 19 on trauma that it is helpful to have methods of assisting clients with expressed trauma, where a traumatic event and its associated reaction to it is the presenting symptom, as well as having methods of assisting clients with unexpressed trauma where, for example, the presenting symptom is depression, anxiety, or substance abuse with no comprehension of the link to past trauma. So, too, it is helpful to have the ability to work with clients whatever degree of change they may desire and need. This means learning techniques for assisting clients with both Type I (2D—2D+) change and Type II (3D—3D+) changes.

You may also remember that there are other meta characteristics to stories, as well. Stories are either redemptive or contaminated; virtually all psychotherapies aspire to make the potentially tragic into the redemptive. Of course, different therapies approach this in varying ways. Some attempt to redefine the problem or the antagonist. Family systems therapies, for example, do this by focusing the family on a larger context so that the problem changes to one they are adept at solving. The problem is no longer the identified child's oppositional and rebellious behavior, but the parents' lack of support for each other in setting limits. Narrative therapy redefines the antagonist, as well. Now the problem is no longer the oppositional child, but ADHD against which the family must unite to defeat. Coherence therapy renders the initial antagonist, the symptom, as a misguided helper in coping with a larger, more terrifying, and initially unnamed antagonist.

We discussed that there are four general methods for dealing with a problem or antagonist in a narrative: fight, flee, surrender, or embrace. Many CBT methods help the client fight the illogic of her problems. AA and other 12-step programs famously promote the power of surrender. The first step enjoins the person to acknowledge that she is powerless over alcohol. Acceptance and commitment therapy encourages the client to acknowledge that substantial change in a chronic problem is unlikely; the client needs to accept the problem and focus on orienting his life toward his most important values (surrender). Very few therapies promote avoidance (fleeing) as a long-term strategy, although clients frequently come in complaining of problems that emanate from chronic avoidance (if my ex would just change so I don't have to argue with her about the kids; I hate my job, but it's a hassle to look for another; I'll quit tomorrow).

A recent article in the *Washington Post* (Bahrampour, 2019) describes the case of Tom Misciagna and his wife Peggy. Tom has Alzheimer's, which he has named "Ollie." When he is forgetful ("we adopted two kids from India." "No, Honey, it was the Philippines.") either he or his wife remark "I guess Ollie is here again." Tom is learning to play the violin, and he and his wife are taking dancing lessons. The attitude of embracing encompasses more than the illness of Alzheimer's and its needed care for the Misciagnas; it is an attitude that encompasses their life story.

While some very helpful literature exists on factors promoting resilience (see, for example, Glenn Schiraldi's excellent 2017 book *The Resilience Workbook*), as therapists we have each encountered mysterious clients with a poor attachment history, few positive role models, and non-spiritual, humorless, even outright neglectful or abusive upbringings who nonetheless managed to thrive, even when their siblings succumbed (see Jeannette Walls memoir *The Glass Castle*, 2005, for a poignant example).

While we may be at a loss to explain such stories of resilience, we know what it looks like. It looks like embracing.

I once had a client, a tall, gaunt young man who was pursuing graduate studies in existential literature. Despite the potential that came from such talents as being extremely bright, fluent in four languages, and possessing a love of music, he presented with an almost characterological depression. He dressed in rumpled black, looking goth, and could readily cite a depressing stanza from some little-known existential poet. He seemed destined to live out a minor tragedy until one day his Yoga teacher, undoubtedly sensing the same intractable pessimism as I, challenged him with "so what if this moment in time, this place—2012 in Alexandria, Virginia—is the only Heaven there is? Will you embrace it, or will you miss it altogether?"

It had not occurred to the young man that in focusing solely on the dreariness of life he was actually missing his life. He pondered the insight and discussed it over and over in therapy. He dropped out of graduate school, and with a small inheritance and two friends he moved to Germany, where he opened a combination bar and music venue. Among his more hidden talents was the ability to identify musical acts on the cusp of making it big. The bar became a huge success.

What are our clients' meta-patterns of dealing with adversity? Do they surrender, or avoid and flee? Do they fight the same battle over and over? Or do they embrace their antagonist in a manner that connects with it and with its resonance within, setting up the prospect of a synthesis? How can we promote embracing?

Schafer (1992) suggested that in Freud's theory there was a metaphoric theme, a kind of meta-story. He proposed that for Freud, there were two master narrative themes: "the child as beast," and "the psyche as machine." Ekstrom (2018) extended this to Jung, saying his master narratives were about the divine child, and the building. Take a moment and consider what might be the theme of the meta-story of the theory to which you most ascribe. For some family therapists, for example, the meta-story may be "the family is a mobile—pushing one part moves all the others." For some CBT therapists, it may be "helping the client fight illogic." What might be the meta-story of your theory? How did you first select or become indoctrinated into this theory? What is the foundational story of that selection (take a moment to recall a particular time)? How does that fit for you currently? How well does it describe people? What are the mechanisms of change in this view? Would you add to it, or modify it in any way to fit your current understanding?

If in the course of this book you have come to reflect more on your own approach to psychotherapy and its resonance with your own story, I have no doubt that you will more readily embrace the struggles, the misguided but hopeful attempts, the triumph and the tragedies of those who seek your counsel. You and I could wish for little more.

References

Avnet, J., Lear, N., & Kerner, J. (Avnet, J., dir.). (1991). *Fried Green Tomatoes*. Universal City, CA: Universal Pictures.

Bahrampour, T. (2019). Changing "the tragedy narrative": Why a growing camp is promoting a more joyful approach to Alzheimer's. *Washington Post*, February 21. Retrieved from: www.washingtonpost.com.

Bateson, G. (2000). *Steps to an Ecology of Mind*. Chicago, IL: University of Chicago Press.

Ekstrom, S. (2018). Freud, Jung, and the great chain of being. *Journal of Analytical Psychology*, 63(4), pp. 662–483.

Quinn, K. (2017). *The Alice Network*. New York, NY: Harper-Collins.

Schafer, R. (1992). *Retelling a Life: Narration and Dialogue in Psychoanalysis*. New York, NY: Basic Books.

Schiraldi, G. R. (2017). *The Resilience Workbook: Essential Skills to Recover from Stress, Trauma, and Adversity*. Oakland, CA: New Harbinger Publications.

Walls, J. (2005). *The Glass Castle: A Memoir*. New York, NY: Scribner.

Watzlawick, P., Weakland, J. H., & Fisch, R. (1974). *Change: Principles of Problem Formation and Problem Resolution*. New York, NY: W. W. Norton.

Yorke, J. (2015). *Into the Woods: A Five Act Journey Into Story*. New York, NY: The Overlook Press.

Appendices

Appendices

Appendix I

The Foundational Story Interview Template*

For Helping Determine a Person's Foundational Life Stories

CLIENT'S NAME: _____
Today's date: _____

The major problem or difficulty with which the client would like help is:

_____
_____

In this next part of our work together, I am going to ask you to tell me some of the important stories in your life. This will give us both the bigger picture of what you have lived; and it will help me know better how to help you. So that I remember all of the important details of what you tell me, I would like to (take notes/record) what you have to say. Is that OK? After you have told me about some of the important incidents, we will return to them and I will ask you more about them.

1. Presenting problem story (most recent example of problem occurring):
2. First occurrence/use story (i.e. first time you recall the problem occurring):
3. Context: Where did you grow up? Who lived with you when you were growing up? What was your family's ethnicity? Their religion? How devout were they? What did your parents do for a living? Describe your first house or apartment (if it seems helpful, have the client draw the floor plan).
4. What is your family's story about you? Your name?
5. What is the story of your birth?
6. What is your very first memory (how old were you)?
7. What is your next earliest memory (how old were you)?

236 Appendices

Now imagine that your whole life was a play or novel in five acts. What age would you be at the start of each chapter? Which chapter would you be in now? What would you entitle each chapter? What would be the predominant mood or feeling for each chapter (imagine what it might be for chapters you have not yet encountered)? It can be helpful to display the following chart on a whiteboard:

Chapter	Age (From ? To ?)	Chapter Title	Predominant Mood or Feeling
1	0 --		
2			
3			
4			
5			

8. Tell the story of a particular occurrence in each of the chapters (above) you have lived. For each story, include your age and the predominant feeling. What part stands out in each? What might be the moral or lesson learned?

The next two questions (9 & 10) are additional/optional:

9. Most often, a play or book has a middle turning point, often a crisis or climax. In retrospect all the action seems to lead to this point, and all subsequent action seems to follow from it. Can you identify such a turning point in your own life? Tell the story.
10. Acts in a play or chapters in a book are set off or bracketed by smaller turning points. Each turning point usually has a story. Tell the stories of the turning points between the chapters (above) in your life.
11. **Choose with the client two or three of the following vignettes. Have the person tell the story:**
    a. What's your very first memory of your mother (how old were you)?
    b. What's your very first memory of your father (how old were you)?
    c. As a young child, did you have an imaginary companion or playmate? If so, what was her/his name? Tell any adventures or stories with your companion that you remember.
    d. What is the first memory you have of being punished or disciplined (how old were you)?
    e. What was your favorite childhood story (book, fairy tale, movie, TV episode)—perhaps one that you listened to or watched over and over? Tell the story.
    f. Who was your first childhood hero or heroine? Tell the story of one of his/her exploits.

g. What is the first incident you recall with your sister(s)? How old were you?
h. What is the first incident you recall with your brother(s)? How old were you?
i. What is the first dream you recall?
j. What is your first memory of an incident that occurred in school (how old were you)?
k. Tell the story of a childhood lesson learned.
l. Tell about an episode from your adolescence (how old were you?).
m. What is a memory you recall from your first job?
n. What was the happiest time in your life? Tell the story. How old were you?
o. What was the worst time in your life? Tell the story. How old were you?
p. What was the most poignant, touching, or moving time in your life? Tell the story. How old were you?
q. Tell the story of an important transition in your life (how old were you?).
r. What lyrics do you recall from your favorite song? What mood does it bring out when you hear it?
s. Have you ever had a recurring dream? What was it?
t. Tell about a recent dream.
u. Have you ever had a spiritual or religious experience? Tell the story.
v. (Made Up Story) Make up and tell a story. It can be about any subject. What is the setting for the story? Who are the characters? What is the major problem or desire around which the story revolves? What happens first? What happens next? What is the climax? How does the story end?
w. The Necessary Story (i.e., the story that makes the symptom/problem make sense, provides the context of the symptom, and be necessary to have) Imagine for the moment that your problem (X), while painful, is necessary. Make up a story in which your problem was necessary to have. Perhaps it will be as a solution to some greater problem, or lead to some important outcome, or be required by circumstances, etc.

12. Foundational stories—do an affect bridge[1] from the symptom to an early or important story. Continue the bridging until one of the stories is a story from the pre-operational period (age three to six) if possible.

* It's helpful, after eliciting all the stories, to read each story to the client, then ask: What was the feeling in that story? What part of the story stands out, i.e., if there was a snapshot of the most vivid part, what would it be?

What is the feeling in that part? Why? If this story appeared in a newspaper, what would the headline or title be? What is the moral or conclusion that you might draw from this story? These questions might be helpful to ask of each story after all stories are elicited. By asking the questions of the stories after all have been elicited, it helps the client see recurring patterns in feeling, theme, and conclusion; and is less likely to be overwhelming, allowing for a greater number and more complete stories.

Note

1. See Chapter 5.

Appendix II

Foundational Story Diagram Form

CONTEXT: _____ TITLE: _____

SETTING/ATMOSPHERE

SCENE #1

CLIMAX:
SCENE #2

ENDING:
SCENE #3

MORAL OR LIFE LESSON:

STORY ARC

PROBLEM/GOAL:

RESULTING FEELING:

CHARACTERS:
1. _____ (HERO)
2. _____ (ANTAG.)
3. _____
4. _____
5. _____
6. _____

SUPPORTING SCENE A

SUPPORTING SCENE B

THEME: _____

Appendix III

Family of Origin Mapping (FOOM) Procedure

Instructions for Creating a Family of Origin Map (FOOM)

Ensure the client has a large piece of paper (at least 17"x24"), at least several marking pens of different colors, and an easel or table top on which to work comfortably. It is helpful to demonstrate step by step on an accompanying easel.

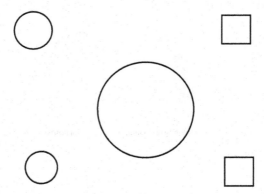

1. Begin by drawing a circle in the center of your page.
2. Add a small circle and small square in the upper part of the diagram.
3. Add small circle and square in the lower part of the diagram.

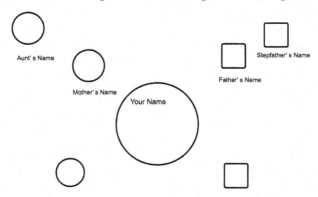

4. Under the small upper circle and square, put your mother's name and your father's name as shown. Put your name inside the large central circle.
5. If you have a step-parent, add them: stepfathers in small squares on the upper right, stepmothers in small circles on the left.
6. If there were any other adults with whom you lived or who lived with you when you were young (third grade or earlier), add them. Use a circle for women, and a square for men. It's better to include too many people than too few.

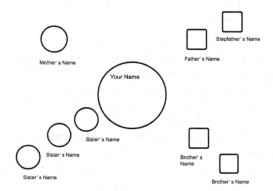

7. Below the small circle in the lower left, put the name of your sister. If you had multiple sisters, put the name of the sister that most stood out for you when you were young. She might stand out for a number of reasons: perhaps she was closest in age and your playmate; perhaps she was older and took care of you; perhaps she was younger and you felt she was always a bother; etc.
8. Add any additional sisters in age order from oldest to youngest.
9. If you had no sister, make a concentric circle, and put the name of the girl who was closest to you in your early years, even if she was not all that close. It might have been a neighborhood friend, a school chum, a cousin, etc. Include stepsisters if they lived with you before age eight.
10. Be sure to add any sisters who died, even stillborn or abortions. Put an X through the circle.
11. Do the same thing with the brothers on the right side of your map (the brother who stood out first, followed in age order by other brothers; concentric circles for closest boy if you had no brothers).

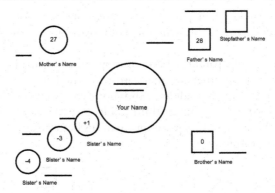

12. In the square or circle for each brother or sister place a number representing how much older or younger than you that sibling was, using a "+" in front of the age difference in years if the sibling was older, a "-" if younger, and a "0" if a twin. For example, a sister who was three years older would have a +3 inside the circle.
13. In the circle and square for your mother and father, put their ages when you were born.
14. On a line beside or near each square and circle write a brief description of what that person was like when you were growing up (just a few words). Include a description of yourself as a child inside the big circle. This task often requires a few minutes, and leads to recalling childhood stories. If you are doing this with a group, be aware of any signs that a group member is becoming unduly spacey or dissociative. Pause after this task and de-brief.

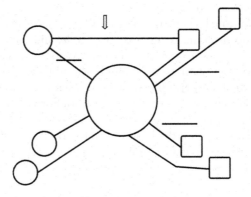

15. Connect each circle and square with the central circle via a line.
16. On or near each line write a brief (one to three words) description of your relationship with that person when you were growing up. Try to avoid overgeneralizations like "good" or "bad."

Family of Origin Mapping (FOOM) Procedure

17. Now connect the circle and square representing your parents with a line.
18. Above that line write a brief description of their relationship when you were a child.

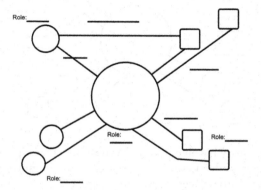

19. In addition to each person's formal (identity) role in a family (mother, father, oldest sister, etc.) each person in a family has an emotional role. Underneath each square and circle place their emotional role in the family. Some examples of emotional roles follow.

Table III.1 Example Family Roles

Adult	Failure	Parentified Child	Scholar
Abuser	Father	Partner	Seducer
Artist	Flunky	Patient	Seeker
Athlete	Follower	Patsy	Servant
Baby	Foreigner	Performer	Sinner
Black sheep	Gambler	Persecutor	Slave
Captain	Gigolo	Playboy	Sorcerer
Caregiver	Girl	Playgirl	Star
Complainer	Guru	Prince	Student
Destroyer	Healer	Princess	Superego
Deviant	Hurt child	Protector	Trickster
Doctor	Hub	Protégé	Victim
Don Juan	Id	Queen	Warrior
Drifter	Innocent	Rescuer	Wanderer
Drinker	Joker	Rival	Whore
Ego	King	Robot	Winner
Examiner	Lover	Roller	Wise Man/Woman
Exception	Lost child	Sadist	Witch
Executioner	Magician	Sage	Worker
Expert	Mentor	Savant	Wrongdoer
Exploiter	Orphan	Savior	
Explorer	Parent	Scapegoat	

244 Appendices

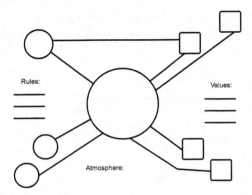

20. Just as every story has an emotional atmosphere that is part of the setting, every family—indeed every organization—has an emotional climate or atmosphere. Some places are frenetic, some places are welcoming, some are indifferent, etc. Place the atmosphere most common in your family growing up under the large circle (one to three words).
21. All families have certain values that are important to them. List yours. A partial list of common family values follows.

Table III.2 Example Family Values

Being first	Honesty
Being the boss	Hospitality
Bettering oneself	Independence of thought and action
Children come first	Loyalty to family
Children come last	Manners
Cleanliness	Not complaining
Competence	Not drawing attention to oneself
Competition	Not showing weakness
Control	Not taking things seriously
Cooperation	Obedience
Deference to adults, teachers, betters	Order
Disengagement	Perfectionist
Distrust of outsiders	Perseverance
Doing one's duty	Propriety
Doing your best	Religious observance
Education	Service to others
Everyone for him/herself	Stoicism
Fair play	Thrift
Hard work	Trusting to luck

22. There are two kinds of rules in families—and in all organizations: spoken (explicit) and unspoken (implicit). List the major rules in your family growing up, both spoken and unspoken. The unspoken rules, because they involve a translation into words, are often more difficult to list. A spoken rule might be "everyone will be here for Sunday dinner

no matter what." An unspoken rule example might be "when Uncle Buck is in a bad mood, leave him alone."

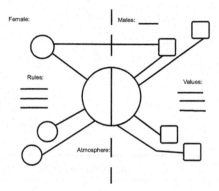

23. Divide the paper in two with a dashed vertical line.
24. On the right side of the line are all the males in the family. Read through how you described them. If this was your only experience of males, what would you say males are like? Do the same for the female side, using just a few words.

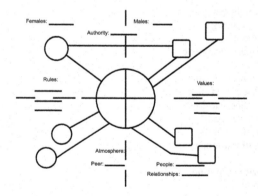

25. Now divide the paper in two with a dashed horizontal line.
26. Above the dashed line are all the people in authority. If this was your only experience of authority, what are people in authority like? How do they wield authority?
27. Below the line are peers. Read through your description of peers. If this was your only experience of age mates, what are they like? What can you expect?
28. Now read through your descriptions of all the people on your map. What was your early experience of what people in general are like (one to three words)? Do the same for relationships by looking through all the descriptions of relationships. What was your early experience of relationships? Now take a few moments to look over your map. Notice any connections and themes.

Appendix IV

Trauma List

Event	Event Occurred (Y/N)	At What Age Did It Occur?

1. Property loss
2. Serious motor vehicle accident
3. Natural disaster (hurricane, flood, etc.)
4. Fire
5. Industrial accident
6. Accidental physical injury
7. Surgery
8. Serious physical illness
9. Humiliation or bullying
10. Sexual harassment
11. As child, witnessing domestic abuse*
12. Growing up with emotional or physical neglect (e.g., not enough to eat, dirty clothes, no adult to protect you)*
13. Growing up with alcohol or drug abuse in immediate family*
14. Growing up with someone who was chronically depressed, suicidal, institutionalized, or mentally ill*
15. As a child, your parents separated or divorced*
16. Growing up with one or no biological parents*
17. While growing up, having a household member incarcerated*
18. Threat of physical violence
19. Emotional abuse (e.g., often sworn at, insulted, humiliated)*
20. Drowning or suffocating

Event	Event Occurred (Y/N)	At What Age Did It Occur?
21. Death of loved one		
22. Life-threatening illness		
23. Domestic violence		
24. Date rape		
25. Witnessing serious injury or death of stranger		
26. Mugging		
27. Victim of other violent crime		
28. Combat trauma		
29. Childhood physical abuse (e.g., often pushed, grabbed, slapped; or *ever* hit so hard had mark left or injury)*		
30. Childhood sexual abuse*		
31. Witnessing traumatic event (specify)		
32. Adult physical assault		
33. Imprisonment		
34. Rape		
35. Other adult sexual assault/abuse		
36. Captivity		
37. Loss of child		
38. Torture		
39. Other		

* Starred items represent items similar to those used for the ACE study. Adding these items gives an approximate ACE score.

Index

Note: Page numbers in *italics* refer to figures, those in bold refer to **tables**, and those with n refer to notes.

3-D Roadmap of Change 46
12-step programs 229
1984 (Orwell) 44

AA program 227, *227*, 229
abandonment 44, 156, **158**, 195
ACE study 183–186
action roles 98, 169
active imagination 137, 139–140, 146
activity and initiative, degree of 75
activity/passivity 161–162
adaptive unconscious 122
adjustment disorders 186
Adler, Alfred 15, 16–17, 24n1, 39, 44, 73–83, 134
adolescence 57–58
Adson, Pat 101
Adult Attachment Interview (AAI) 51
adult offenders 151
agency 56
agentic archetypes 24n4
agentic imagoes 23
ages of three to six (magic years) 52–57, 87
Alexander, I. E. 72
alexithymia 151, 200
Alice Network, The (Quinn) 226
altered state 204
American Society of Clinical Hypnosis (ASCH) 217
amygdala 118
Andrews, T. 76–77
Animal-Speak: The Spiritual and Magical Powers of Animals Great and Small (Andrews) 76–77

anorexia 151
approval seeking **158**
archetypal roles, Pearson's 100–101
archetypes 15, 24n4, 100–101
Archive for Research in Archetypal Symbolism (ARAS) 76
Aristotle 19, 45
Armstrong, Courtney 195–196
aspects of story 29–40
attachment 50–51
attachment therapy 5, 50–51, 53, 156, 161, 162, *227*
author 37
autobiographical identity 23
autobiographical reasoning 58
autobiographical storying ability 57
autonomy 22, 23, 156–157, **158**

background theorists 9–24; Adler, Alfred 16–17; Berne, Eric 17–20; Freud, Sigmund 9–13; Jung, Carl Gustav 13–16; McAdams, Dan 21–24; White, Michael 20–21
Baker, Sam 213
Ballad #281 32–33
Baruth, L. 74, 75
Bateson, Gregory 29, 227
beats 45
Berg, Insoo Kim 164
Berger, David 65
Berne, Eric 17–20, 24n2, 134, 170
Binet, Alfred 13
Bion, Wilfred 96
birth 61n3
blending 107

Bleuler, Eugene 15
blocking character 138–139
Bluck, S. 58
bodily sensation 204
Bondanza, Julie 54
Book of Symbols, The: Reflections on Archetypal Images (ARAS) 76
borderline personality disorder 151
Bowen, Murray 87
Bowlby, John 161
Bradford Hill Framework 186n1
brainspotting 193
Breuer, Josef 10
bridge 66, 67–68
brief psychotic episode 186
Briggs, Katherine 75
Brill, A. A. 13
Brownie's Book, The 40
Bruhn, Arnold 85

calm place 69, 158–159, 173, 197, 198
calm place sandtray 173, 197, 198
Campbell, Joseph 3, 15, 29, 33–34, 45, 100, 122, 123
cancer 65, 101–102, 184, 185, 221
Catastrophe 32, 33, 123
Center for Healing and Imagery (CHI) 152
chain of associations 76
Chandler, Len 3
Chandler, R. F 185
change: in context 126–132; stages of 34, 65; types of, in different therapies 226–228, *227*
change, sources of 115–124; dialectical change 123–124; memory reconsolidation 117–121; positive trauma and ritual 122–123; relationship 115–117, *116*; resourcing 121–122
character emotion, working with 142
characters 38, 133–146; accessing 137–139; changing story character perspective 143; creating 143–145; resourcing 142; self and, brief treatise 145–146; working with character emotion 142; working with, general 139–141; working with, interactive 141–142; working with problematic introjects 143–145
Charcot, Jean-Martin 10
childbirth 60
Child, Francis 30, 32–33

childhood abuse and childhood neglect 183–186
childhood amnesia 42
childhood trauma 151, 185, 186, 191
child molesters 151
Chomsky, Noam 61n1
chronic fatigue 151
circles in FOOM 87, *88*
client resources 200–201
client-therapist relationship 151
Climax 32, 33, 123
cognitive analytic therapy 166
cognitive behavior therapy (CBT) 5, 53, 54, 73, 148, 156, 160, 217, *227*, 228, 229, 231
cognitive revolution 2
coherence therapy 115, *227*, 229
Collected Works (Jung) 14
coming of age 60
communal imagoes 23
complete story, elements of 37–40; author 37; character and roles 38; context 38; moral or lesson 39; overall (meta) characteristics of the story 39–40; plot 38; theme 39; voice/narrator 37–38
complexes 14–15, 133, 134
complication 32, 33, 123
concrete operational stage 56, 57
conditional themes 157–158
connected life stories, concept of 170–171
connectedness 156, **158**
conscious propositional narrative 51, 53
consolidation 117
constructs 144
content 75
context 74, 126–132
Core Conflictual Relationship Theme (CCRT) 148–151, **150**
counter-dependency 159–160
counter-transference 151
Csikszentmihalyi, Mihaly 212, 224
culture 58–61

daydreams 140
defectiveness 156, **158**
degree of dissociation 200
dependence 42, 156, **158**, 161, 162
depression 20, 124, 189
Developmental Counseling and Therapy (Ivey) 51
diagramming 103–107
dialectical change 123–124

DiClemente, C. C. 34, 46, 65
dismissive attachment 51
disorganized attachment 51
dissociation 189–190, 195, 200, 202, 205
divided psyche 134, 137
double bind of roles 97
double blind studies 186n1
drama triangle 98–100
dreams 13–14, 15, 22, 40n1, 66–67, 140
drug-related memory in heroin addicts 120
DuBois, W. E. B. 40

Early Memories Procedure, The (Bruhn) 85
early recollections 17, 73–83
early separation experiences 161–162
Ecker, Bruce 115, 121–122, 163–167, **171**, 173
Eckstein, D. 74, 75
effectiveness/ineffectiveness 75
ego 134
ego states 17–18, 20, 109, 124, 133–135, 137, 138, 146, 160, 206
ego state therapies 124, 134–135, 139, 143, 146, 148, 152, *227*, 228–229
Ekstrom, S. 231
embrace 39, 46, 55, 65, 99, 229, 230, 231
EMDR 82, 193, 206, *227*, 228
Emmerson, Gordon 143
emotional deprivation 156, **158**
emotional freedom technique (EFT) 193
emotional inhibition 158, **158**
emotional memories 120
emotive imagery 145
enmeshment **158**
entitlement 157, **158**
episodic memories 120
Epston, David 20
Erikson, Erik 17, 152, 156–157, 196
Erikson, Milton 97
evaluation 75
exaggerated startle 189
Exiles 124
Experimental Researches (Jung) 14
exposition 32, 33, 35, 38, 118, 123, 126, 214
exposure therapy 82, 193, 206, *227*, 228
external dialogue 146n1
externalizing the problem 160

failure 20, 30, 56, 156, 157, **158**, 160, 165, 183, **243**
fainting couches 10

Falling Action 32, 33, 123
Family of Origin Mapping (FOOM) 87–94; example *88*; overview of 87; procedure 240–245
faulty logic 57, 73
feeling tones 4
Feinstein, David 15
Felitti, Vince 183
fictional finalisms 73
fight, flee, or surrender 39, 46, 229
First Occurrence Foundational Story 65–66
flashbacks 189, 190, 205
flow 212, 224
Flückiger, C. 115–116
focusing 212, 217–218
Focusing Psychotherapy (Gendlin) 212
folk songs 3, 119
fortified place 158
foundational stories 43, 49–61; culture 58–61; life stages 49–61; re-storying foundational trauma stories 202–207; understanding 72–83
Foundational Storyboarding 173–178; example *175–177*; explained 173; steps of 178
Foundational Story Diagram 79–83; example *81*; Form 239
Foundational Story Interview 85–87; template 235–238
Foundational Story Model 42–47
fractal 42–43, 45
Fraiberg, Selma 53, 87
Frederick, Claire 134, 146
freeze 203–204
Freud, Sigmund 9–13, 14–15, 16, 17, 18, 20, 24n1, 42, 76, 83, 98, 127, 134, 162, 200, 231
Freytag, Gustav 32, 33, 38, 123
Freytag's Pyramid 32, 33
Fried Green Tomatoes (movie) 226
Full Catastrophe Living (Kabat-Zinn) 224
functional means-end template 72

Games Alcoholics Play (Steiner) 1, 18
Games People Play (Berne) 18
Gantt, Linda 173, 201, 203, 206
Gates, H. L., Jr. 40
gathering stories 65–70
gender 75
Gendlin, Eugene 212, 217
Genogram 87
Gestalt therapy 152

Giampaolo, S. 50, 51, 52, 58
Glass Castle, The (Walls) 230
"Go in Peace" (Baker) 213
Golden Vanity (ship) 32–33, 40n3
Graphic Narrative 173, 203, 206
"Green Rocky Road" (folk song) 3
grief, unresolved or delayed 162
Griffith, J. 74–76, 77–78, 80, 82, 170
Groundhog Day (movie) 127
guiding lines 16

Habermas, T. 58
Hall, G. Stanley 13
Headline Method 73
Herman, Judith 10, 24, 191, 196
Hero with a Thousand Faces, The (Campbell) 33
hidden observer 202, 204, 205–206, 208n5
Hilgard, Ernest 204, 208n5
holding environment/sacred space 129
homo erectus 1
homo sapiens 1
horizontal views 75, 83n2
Horney, Karen 39
House of God (Shem) 214
Hupbach, A. 120
hypercriticalness **158**
hypnosis 10, 67, 152, 171, 189, 205–206, 217
hypochondriasis 10
hysteria 10, 12

id 134
identity roles 98, 169
imagery sessions 158–159
imagery techniques 158
imagery theory 148
imagoes 22–23
implicit life story 4–6
implosion therapy 228
independence 22, 132, 149, 159–160, 161, 162
Individual Psychology 16
Industry *vs.* Inferiority 157
infancy 50–51
inferiority complex 83
inner dialogue 140, 146n1
Inner Work (Johnson) 140
insecure attachment 51
Instigation Story 65
instinctual trauma phases 206
insufficient self-control/self-discipline **158**

Integral Intake, The (Marquis) 85
Intensive Trauma Therapy (ITT) 206
internal character mapping 107–110, *108*
interpretation, categories for 74–75
In the Mind's Eye (Lazarus) 145
Into the Woods (Yorke) 44
Introduction to Archetypes (Pearson and Marr) 101
Introduction to the Internal Family Systems Model, An (Schwartz) 137
intuition 75
Invented Story 66, 69–70
Ivey, A. E. 51

James, William 13, 146
Janet, Pierre 133–134, 200
Johnson, Robert 133, 138, 140
Jones, Ernest 13
Jones, T. M. 185–186
Jung, Carl Gustav 12, 13–16, 33, 44, 75, 87, 100, 130, 134, 137, 139, 146, 231
Jungian therapy 5, 15, 54, 76, 124, 133, 146, *227*

Kabat-Zinn, Jon 224
Kaiser Permanente 183
Kalff, Doris 110n1
Kaplan, H. B. 73–74
Karpman, Stephen 97, 98, 169, 215
Kaufman, Robert 3
Keen, Sam 15
Kelly, George 144–145
Klein, Melanie 161
Klosko, Janet 156
Kopp, Richard 66, 67, 68, 74, 83, 215
Krippner, Stanley 15
Kuhn, Thomas 117

language acquisition 61n1
Lawrence, Mark 66, 67, 140, 146
Lazarus, Arnold 145
LeDoux, Joseph 117
Levi-Strauss, Claude 15
life stages: adolescence 57–58; ages of three to six (magic years) 52–57; culture 58–61; infancy 50–51; middle childhood 57; toddlerhood 52
life story identity 22
lifestyle 16
life transitions 60
Lifetraps (Young) 157
limits and standards 156, **158**
linear relationship 184, 186n1

Listening with the Third Ear (Reik) 216
Llewyn Davis (movie) 3
loaded for bear 160
Lowenfeld, Margaret 110n1
Luborsky, Lester 148–152
Luria, A. R. 47n1
lying and deception 52

"Maddie Groves" 98
Magic Remote 202
magic years (ages of three to six) 52–57, 87
Mahler, Margaret 161
Malan's triangle of transference 128
Mann, James 148, 160–162
Marquis, Andre 85
marriage 35, 55, 58, 60, 101–102, 107, 123, 166
marriage and roles 101–102
marriage therapy 87, 93
McAdams, Dan 21–24, 57, 58, 85, 146
Melges, Frederick 192n2
Memories, Dreams, and Reflections (Jung) 13
memory reconsolidation 117–121
metaphor 66, 68–69
Metaphor Therapy (Kopp) 68
middle childhood 57
Miller, W. R. 34
Mind of a Mnemonist, The (Luria) 47n1
miracle question 164
Misciagna, Tom and Peggy 230
mistaken beliefs 73
mistrust and abuse 156, **158**, 196
modes 160
Monnat, S. M. 185
moral or lesson 39
Mosak, H. H. 83
motivational interviewing 34–35
Mourning and Melancholia (Freud) 162
multi-mind 135
multi-mind concept 135
multimodal behavior therapy 145
music structure 31, 40n2
Myers, Isabel 75

Nader, Karim 117–118, 119
narrative family therapy 123–124
narrative theory 44
narrative therapy 20, 21, 124, *227*, 228
negativity 142, 158, **158**
neurolinguistic programming 127, 202
Nicolopoulou, A. 56, 61n2
nightmares 189, 202, 205, 207n1
non-sexual child maltreatment 185

Noricks, Jay 138–139, 142, 143
normal science 117
Norman, R. E. 185
notecards 121–122, 166
nuclear episodes 22
nursery rhymes 3, 119

Oedipal victor 24n1
Oedipus Rex 12, 14
Omer, H. 160
opposition 19, 24n3, 229
other 46, 47n1
overall (meta) characteristics of the story 39–40
Ozarks (Netflix series) 42

pampered 24n1
participation and cooperation, extent of 75
parts *see* ego states
Pascal, E. 139
Pearson, Carol 100–101
Pearson-Marr Archetype Indicator (PMAI) 101
Pedreira, M. E. 165
Pennebaker, James 167
Perls, Frederick (Fritz) 134, 137, 139, 146n1
personality, McAdams' approach to 23–24
personification 140, 141
pessimism 50, 158, **158**, 230
Phillips, Maggie 134, 146
Piaget, Jean 12–13, 53, 54, 56, 57
plot 38, 148–154
plot diagramming 103–107
plot map 103–107, *105*
Poetics (Aristotle) 32
positive trauma and ritual 122–123
Powers, R. L. 74–76, 77–78, 80, 82, 170
Practice of Ally Work, The (Raff) 146
pre-narrative level 50
pre-occupied attachment 51
pre-operational period 12–13, 53, 54, 56–57, 237
pre-story level 50, 51
private logic 17
problematic introjects, working with 143–145
problematic memory 120
procedural memories 120
Prochaska, J. O. 34, 46, 65
projection 170
projective identification 170
propanalol 125n1

protagonist 74–75
psychotherapy, defined 43
PTSD 120, 186
PTSD Sourcebook, The (Schiraldi) 194
punitiveness **158**

qualitative change 227, *227*
quantitative change 227, *227*
Quinn, K. 226

Raff, Jeffrey 146
rage 142, 195
readiness for trauma work 201–202
redemptive story 167
Reik, Theodor 216
relational themes 4
relationship 115–117, *116*
relationship episodes 149
relative position 75
reminiscence bump 42
repetition compulsion 11, 20, 127
Rep Grid 144
Reps, P. 224
Resilience Workbook, The (Schiraldi) 230
resourcing 121–122, 142
re-storying foundational trauma stories 202–207
Reversal of the Situation 45
Richner, E. S. 56, 61n2
Rogers, Carl 217
roles 38; drama triangle 98–100; marriage and 101–102; Pearson's archetypal roles 100–101; seminal purpose of 38, 96–102

safe place 158–159, 196, 197
safety 196–198
sample wishes 149
sandplay 110n1
sandtray 110, 110n1, 123, 173, 178, 196, 197, 198, 207n2, 213
Schafer, R. 231
schema therapy 148, 156–162, **158**
Schiraldi, Glenn 194, 230
schizophrenia 15, 20, 97, 159, 186
Schneiderman, Kim 97, 167–170, **171**
Schwartz, Richard 107, 124, 134, 135, 137, 138, 139, 140, 142, 145–146, 201, 206
script 18, 134, 170–171
secure attachment 51
Self 46, 47n1, 145–146
self-control 149, **158**

self-esteem, adequate *vs.* diminished 162
Selfleadership.org 145
self-repair 204
self-report surveys 185
self-sacrifice **158**
sensing 75
sensorimotor level 51
sensory aspects 75
Senzaki, N. 224
separation-individuation dynamic 161–162
sequence 76, 82
Shadow 124
Shakespeare, William 45, 188, 221
Shapiro, R. 200
Shem, Samuel 214
short-term dynamic therapy 160–162
sickness and death 60
silent abreaction 142
similarity 76, 82
Sin Eater 142, 146–147n2
Skinner, B. F. 61n1
sleep difficulties 189, 207n1
smoking cessation 34
social exclusion 157, 158, **158**
Solnit, Rebecca 59
Sophocles 12
spitting in the soup 39
squares in FOOM 87, *88*
stabilization 193–196
Stanford prison experiment 96–97, 127, 191
startle 203
Steiner, Claude 18, 19, 170, **171**
Stone, Hal and Sidra 134
storied view, integrating with your own theory 226–231
story 1–6; aspects of 29–40; connected, concept of 170–171; foundational 43, 49–61; gathering 65–70; telling 131–132
story arc 32, 38, 65, 123
story character perspective, changing 143
story coherence, forms of 58
story exception 121
story grammar 31, 35
story receiving 127–131; thematic witnessing 129–131; time 127–128
subjugation **158**
sub-personalities 133–135
superego 134
supportive treatments 202
surrender 39, 46, 65, 86, 136, 159, 229–230

Sword, Rosemary and Richard 127, 191
symmetry 76, 82
synthesizing 92, 151

tapping 193
Tatar, M. 40
Tavistock 96
telling stories 131–132
temporal relationship 186n1
thematic change 156–162
thematic witnessing 129–131
theme 39
therapist, growing as 216–218
three-dimensional change 197, 217, 226–229
thwarted intention 203
Tichener, Edward 13
time 127–128
Time Cure, The (Zimbardo, Sword, and Sword) 191
time perspective 191
Tinnin, Louis 201, 202, 203–206, 208n5, 298n5
toddlerhood 52
tones 40n2
Top Dog 134
training group (T Group) 96
transactional analysis theory 170
transference 118
transforming the moral and the whole story 163–171, 173–178
trauma: childhood abuse and childhood neglect 183–186; impact of 188–191; list 246–247; re-living 190, 207n4; stages 203–204
Trauma and Recovery (Herman) 10
trauma assessment 198
trauma history assessment 199
trauma phobia 201, 206
Trauma Recovery Institute (TRI) 206
trauma story 188–191
trauma treatment 193–207; client resources 200–201; degree of dissociation 200; readiness for trauma work 201–202; re-storying foundational trauma stories 202–207; safety 196–198; stabilization 193–196; trauma assessment 198; trauma history assessment 199
Trauma Treatment Handbook, The (Shapiro) 200
True North (Adson) 101

truth, historical and narrative 191
"Tuesday File, The" 217
two-chair technique 146n1
two-dimensional change 217, 226–228
Type I and Type II change 227, *227*

Under Dog 134, 137
undeveloped Self **158**
unrelenting standards 157, **158**

Valley-Fox, A. 15
Van der Kolk, B. 204
Van Ronk, Dave 3
Verne, Jules 110n1
vertical views 75, 83n2
Viennese Psychoanalytic Society 16
virtual reality therapies 207n4, 228
voice dialogue 134
voice/narrator 37–38
vulnerability 156, **158**, 186, 216

Wallen, D. J. 51
Walls, Jeannette 230
Washington Post 230
Watkins, John and Helen 66, 67, 134, 139, 142, 195
Watson, John 13
Watts, Alan 15
Watzlawick, John 227
What Do You Say After You Say Hello? (Berne) 18–19
What Story Are You Living? (Pearson and Marr) 101
White, Michael 20–21, 121, 123–124, 160
without and beyond story 221–225
Wizard of Oz, The (movie) 167
Word Association Test 14
working horizontally 51
working with yourself 211–215
World Technique 110n1
worthiness 156, 157, **158**, 160
Wundt, Wilhelm 13

Yorke, John 34, 44, 45–46, 217, 226
Young, Jeffrey 148, 156–162, **158**

Zen Flesh, Zen Bones (Reps and Senzaki) 224
Zhao, L. 120
Zimbardo, Philip G. 96–97, 127, 191